CW00675726

EFFING THE INEFFABLE

EFFING the INEFFABLE

Existential Mumblings at the Limits of Language

WESLEY J. WILDMAN

Published by State University of New York Press, Albany

© 2018 State University of New York

All rights reserved

Printed in the United States of America

No part of this book may be used or reproduced in any manner whatsoever without written permission. No part of this book may be stored in a retrieval system or transmitted in any form or by any means including electronic, electrostatic, magnetic tape, mechanical, photocopying, recording, or otherwise without the prior permission in writing of the publisher.

For information, contact State University of New York Press, Albany, NY
www.sunypress.edu

Library of Congress Cataloging-in-Publication Data

Names: Wildman, Wesley J. author
Title: Effing the ineffable : existential mumblings at the limits of language /
    Wesley J. Wildman, author.
Description: Albany : State University of New York Press, [2018] | Includes bibli-
    ographical references and index.
Identifiers: ISBN 9781438471235 (hardcover : alk. paper) | ISBN
    9781438471259 (e-book) | ISBN 9781438471242 (paperback : alk. paper)
Further information is available at the Library of Congress.

10 9 8 7 6 5 4 3 2 1

For my colleagues in Boston University's
Graduate Division of Religious Studies
A fond farewell

Contents

PREFACE

OUR SPECIES IS OBSESSED WITH TRYING TO EFF THE INEFFABLE—TO LIMN
the liminal, to conceive the inconceivable, to speak the unspeakable, to say the
unsayable. This obsession shoots colorful threads through the tapestry of human
language, and especially religious language. The primary aim of this book is to
trace some of those threads. It's one of the ways religious philosophers (philosophers of religion, philosophical theologians) eff the ineffable: they follow those
linguistic threads, seeing where they lead and how they work their aesthetic and
conceptual magic. I hope to do this in suitably colorful ways, with some emotion
and fun. Serious religious philosophy need not be tedious!

Each chapter of the book traces a thread, or a cluster of related threads,
seeking insight into the act of effing the ineffable, and into the ineffable itself.
Each thread wraps around an existentially potent aspect of life, one loaded with
spiritual significance for most human beings, regardless of their specific religious
contexts. Dreaming, suffering, creating, slipping, balancing, eclipsing, loneliness,
intensity, bliss: these are the life situations that drive religious questioning and
inspire commitment to a spiritual outlook on life—sometimes even to a particular
religious community.

When these situations are liminal and extreme, as they often are, they drive
us to the very limits of language in search of ways to say what ultimately matters
to us and to surface the ultimate reality submerged within those experientially
rooted linguistic exertions. When those situations are mundane, language seems
less stressed but entire language systems can invisibly work a kind of transformative magic in us, and in the groups navigating those systems with us. The language games of religion are astonishing! They are a lot more complex than most
people—and even many religious philosophers—realize. This book will uncover
that complexity, manifesting some of the hidden dynamics of religious language
and revealing how symbol systems do some of what they do.

Identifying the genre of these closely connected essays is a complicated challenge at the present time given the flurry of recent publications about the nature

and future of philosophy of religion. Because this is a volume in my Religious Philosophy series, I first think of the genre in terms of that phrase, the meaning of which I described in *Religious Philosophy as Multidisciplinary Comparative Inquiry: Envisioning a Future for the* Philosophy *of Religion* (Wildman 2010). But these essays might equally be thought of as belonging to philosophy of religion or to philosophical theology. I'll use the phrase "philosophical theology" most often in this book in deference to the fact that my goal is theological in some fundamental sense: I'm tracing the ways we eff the ineffable partly in order to conjure and engage the ineffable itself, the God beyond the Gods of human imagination and social construction, the ultimate reality that transcends the complete emotional, cognitive, and moral grasp of any possible being. This ultimate reality is the topic of *In Our Own Image: Anthropomorphism, Apophaticism, and Ultimacy* (Wildman 2017); the topic of this book is the way we talk at, about, and around ultimacy.

Religious philosophy as I understand it takes shape across vast traditions of literate debate about first-order religious questions and so is fundamentally comparative in character. Its institutional home is not any particular religious tradition but the secular academy. The value investments of the contemporary, secular academy subordinate the institutional interests of any and all concrete religious traditions to the quest for understanding, wherever that takes us. If my colleagues in the secular academy are surprised to learn that any kind of philosophical theology has a place within it, then I would urge them to become empirically more realistic and complete in regard to their interpretation of the world we inhabit. It has valuational dimensions whose depth structures and dynamics demand interpretation in philosophical-theological terms. In other words, if philosophical theology did not already exist, we'd have to invent it to interpret the existential and axiological depths of our own experience rigorously and responsibly.

Of course, philosophical theology does already exist, and that presents us with another problem: we must strive to overcome its parochialism, particularly its biases toward theism and, often enough, the institutional interests of Christianity. Philosophical inquiries into theistic beliefs and Christian doctrines and practices can be valuable, even when the motivation is to support communities of faith and to nurture a complex religious tradition. But religious philosophy demands the embrace of the secular university's morality of inquiry, and that calls for reform and critique of traditional philosophy of religion. Such a critique, and the direction of reform I deem most promising, is implicit in the pages of this book.

Religious philosophy is not stylistically monochrome. Indeed, styles of inquiry in religious philosophy include the phenomenological, the comparative, the historical, the analytical, the theoretical, the literary, and the evaluative (see

Wildman 2010). These styles are illustrated in the chapters of this book, often blended together in ways called forth by the particular type of effing-the-ineffable under discussion. In fact, religious philosophy *needs* to work in different styles and from different interpretative angles to develop a satisfying philosophical portrayal of the religious potency of the mostly hidden depths of the human condition and of the natural environment within which we emerge and whose mysteries we try to utter. It's these hidden depths that make religious language so *fascinating*.

In scientific study of the world of nature, the *relative* simplicity of the subject matter (it is far from simple!) ordinarily allows a strong case to be made for a "best" interpretation at any given stage of scientific progress. Famously, this is not true in the *relatively* more complex philosophical study of the human condition and the way we conceptualize and speak about our ultimate concerns. Human life is dense with meanings to the point of bursting apart at the seams. This superfluity of significance calls for creative and interactive engagement from numerous angles to appreciate and trace out the tangle of meanings. A unified philosophical account of the single best meaning in human life would be a disappointing empirical disaster in a way that the one best scientific account of protein expression from DNA would not be. Thus, we have good reason to embrace the varied styles of religious philosophy, even as we continue to expect that philosophical argumentation will sometimes eliminate certain interpretations as deficient and draw our attention to superior alternatives.

⌇

What will you find in this book? Lots of threes. There is no special significance to this number; it is simply a matter of convenience. There are three clusters of three essays, each with three sections. Each essay is a meditation on some aspect of religious language under stress as its wielders strain to eff the ineffable. Each cluster of three essays has a unifying theme. Here are the details.

The first three chapters (part 1, "Ultimacy Talk") focus on the linguistic techniques that arise when philosophical theologians try to speak as directly as possible about ultimate reality. This way of effing the ineffable is magnificently bold, intellectually questionable, and extraordinarily creative. I think it's at its best when operating comparatively, which is how all three chapters proceed.

Chapter 1 on "Dreaming" is religious philosophy in a decidedly comparative and evaluative mode. This chapter argues that it is exceptionally difficult for human beings to feel attracted to, and properly to appreciate the theoretical virtues of, theories of ultimacy that keep anthropomorphic modeling impulses in check. Such theoretical discipline interferes with human dreaming. Nevertheless, there is a kind of disciplined inquiry that keeps anthropomorphic dreaming at bay and opens up mystical-theological vistas that I argue are truer to the nature of ultimate reality.

Chapter 2 on "Suffering" shows how comparative and theoretical styles of religious philosophy can be bent to an evaluative end. The essay uses the reality of suffering in nature as a source of selective pressure on ideas of ultimate reality. This approach is quite contrary to those theological strategies that defend or elaborate an existing idea of ultimacy, and it rather seeks to determine which of a wide range of ultimacy theories can best handle the selective pressure. I explain why I think that ground-of-being models of ultimate reality survive the ordeal in better shape than personalist models of ultimate reality, and also why I think there are no decisive knock-down arguments to be made here. The competitors in this comparative argument are all logically consistent and conceptually coherent; they differ only in the relative plausibility of their accounts of suffering.

Chapter 3 on "Creating" is an analysis of two idealized interpretations of the ultimate ontological basis of nature that traditional metaphysical analyses have not emphasized. The symmetric view pictures ultimate reality as morally neutral while replete with valuational possibilities, fundamentally indeterminate while abysmally fecund, and in balance with created reality. The asymmetric view is opposed on each of these characteristics. The contrast between symmetry and asymmetry is modeled on the meaning of symmetry-breaking in the mathematical analysis of the early universe within fundamental physics. This analogy is surprisingly useful for conceiving a dynamic process of symmetry-breaking in ontology. It's a minimalist kind of theogony, in fact, and it indicates how symmetric and asymmetric perspectives on nature's ontological ground can be causally and historically related to one another.

⁓≈⁓

The second cluster of three chapters (part 2, "Ultimacy Systems") meditates on systems of religious symbols. Here the thought is less on directly effing the ineffable and more on analyzing the way ordinary religious and theological symbol systems indirectly engage people with their ultimate concerns. All three essays in this cluster express wonder at the reflexive genius of religious symbol systems and document the techniques and strategies that spontaneously arise within them, as well as the seemingly magical social functions that those techniques and strategies facilitate.

Chapter 4 on "Slipping" exhibits religious philosophy in the analytical and comparative modes, using an informal kind of literary criticism as the main tool. The essay shows how the narrative device of a vanishingly small slip recurs in mythic narratives of several traditions and is used to deal with the problem of evil without attributing undue responsibility to any of the involved parties. I trace out the main existential and social functions of this way of effing the ineffable.

Chapter 5 on "Balancing" discusses techniques that spontaneously emerge within religious discourse systems for managing consonance and dissonance among religious symbols, and for trying to express what seems inexpressible. The focus is on systemic mechanisms for balancing personal and impersonal metaphors for ultimate reality. Here again, I describe the existential and social functions of such balancing techniques. This work is primarily religious philosophy in the analytical style with nods in the direction of the comparative and theoretical styles.

Chapter 6 on "Eclipsing" considers an entire symbol system rather than strategic mechanisms within a symbol system. The system in question is that associated with liberal theology and religion. Analyzing this system draws attention to a distinction between the brightly lit topsides of religious traditions that nurture and reform civilizational projects and their shady undersides that power the deconstruction of the human manufacture of social reality. I draw out the way liberal theology hints at the dark and fecund undersides of religion but perpetually fails to follow through in its articulation of this place of shady silence because of its implacable and commendable commitment to institutional maintenance. The irony here is familiar in other chapters of this book: speech about ineffable ultimacy often interferes with fully engaging ultimacy.

⁓≈⁓

The three essays in the final cluster (part 3, "Ultimacy Manifestations") are phenomenological in character. Each picks out a slice of life—loneliness, intensity, bliss—and describes how these liminal situations conjure ultimate reality in our experience and thereby engage us with it. The shared claim is that such liminal experiences manifest the character of ultimacy, so these are yet other ways to eff the ineffable.

Chapter 7 on "Loneliness" is a literary and philosophical exploration of the Epic of Gilgamesh. It explores the theme of loneliness as it bears on religious perceptions of ultimacy, arguing that the ability to experience unmediated and undeflected loneliness is a kind of virtue that we can both cultivate and encounter in the depth structures of reality. This is an authentic alternative to more "pleasant" depictions of reality as such, and it is readily available for spiritual exploration.

Chapter 8 on "Intensity" is a description of key qualities of intense experiences, and it illustrates religious philosophy in the phenomenological and analytical modes. The capacity for intensity is very likely an evolutionarily basic dimension of human experience and thus a primal aspect of religious behavior and belief. For understandable reasons, the presence and roles of intensity are often masked by the proprietary ritual and doctrinal organization of religious life, and thus intensity receives less attention than it should. Yet intensity marks the life experiences that we value most highly, that we describe with most difficulty, and that exercise the largest impact on our decisions and character. The spiritual potency of intensity is the axiological birthright of our species and no religious tradition, not even all religious traditions combined, corrals or controls it.

Chapter 9 on "Bliss" illustrates religious philosophy at the junction of the phenomenological and analytical modes. It depicts the emotionally multivalent, comprehension-defying, morality-transcending, language-stressing character of bliss when we encounter it unfiltered by buffering social conventions and handy psychological defenses. This has implications in two directions. On the one hand, it generates insights into the character of ultimacy itself, which is framed throughout the book as the apophatic mystical philosopher's God beyond God. On the other hand, it unmasks the anthropomorphic, linguistically structured, existential and social coping strategies we deploy to protect ourselves from the full glory of ultimate reality as such.

⁓≋⁓

Another way of thinking about these three clusters of essays is in terms of traditions of philosophical theology. The first cluster ("Ultimacy Talk") expresses the style and commitments of the American pragmatist tradition of philosophical theology, especially in its epistemic post-foundationalism, its thoroughgoing fallibilism, and its post-Kantian embrace of hypothetical comparative metaphysics. The second cluster ("Ultimacy Systems") resonates most strongly with the analytical tradition of philosophical theology, with the focus on linguistic analysis and conceptual micro-moves. The third cluster ("Ultimacy Manifestations") is truest to the continental tradition of philosophical theology, with the emphasis on phenomenology and indirect manifestation of ultimacy in liminal life situations.

I feel at home in all three traditions of philosophical theology. I have been trained in all three and never felt the need to choose one over the others. Holding them together in this way is my indirect testimony to the special virtues, as well as the peculiar limitations, typical of each tradition.

⁓≋⁓

The intellectual point of these essays is fundamentally conceptual and illuminative, rather than historical or analytical. Thus, I have tried to keep the scholarly apparatus to a minimum. For example, if I mention a figure and intend to refer to a body of work by that figure, I do not cite a sampling of works. There are no notes. I employ inline references to keep the entire argument in the flow of the text. The essays draw on large blocks of interpretative tradition stabilized within existing literature on the themes I discuss, but the themes themselves are easy to grasp in a preliminary way. Minimizing a laborious apparatus hopefully will remove an obstacle in the way of my goal to stay true to the essay form.

With the same concerns in mind, I have tried to make the prose style as transparent as the subject matter allows. To that end, I have made a concerted effort to focus on larger-scale inferences, in keeping with the overall focus of the volume on religious language and ultimate reality, rather than getting entangled in deliciously detailed arguments.

Acknowledgments

MOST OF THESE CHAPTERS DERIVE FROM ESSAYS PREVIOUSLY PUBLISHED, AS I have worked my way across some of the varied terrain of religious language when it is under profound stress in liminal life situations. All have been rewritten, in places dramatically, and synthesized for this book. I am pleased to acknowledge the original publishers of earlier versions of some of the chapters of this book, as follows.

Chapter 1 on "Dreaming" derives from a keynote lecture presented to a mini-conference on "Models of God" at the 2007 San Francisco meeting of the American Philosophical Association, subsequently published as "Behind, Between, and Beyond Anthropomorphic Models of Ultimate Reality," *Philosophia* 35/3–4 (2007): 407–25.

Chapter 2 on "Suffering" is based on "Incongruous Goodness, Perilous Beauty, Disconcerting Truth: Ultimate Reality and Suffering In Nature," which appeared in Robert J. Russell, Nancey Murphy, and William R. Stoeger, editors, *Suffering and Cosmology: Scientific Perspectives on Suffering in Nature* (Vatican City State: Vatican Observatory and Berkeley: Center for Theology and the Natural Sciences, 2006): 267–94, which itself derived from work presented at a 2005 research conference in Castel Gandolfo, Italy, sponsored by the Vatican Observatory and the Center for Theology and the Natural Sciences.

Chapter 4 on "Slipping" was published as "Slipping into Horror," in *Soundings: An Interdisciplinary Journal* 84/1–2 (Spring/Summer, 2001): 143–55, and derives from a 1996 lecture on the same topic at the American Academy of Religion annual meeting in New Orleans.

Chapter 5 on "Balancing" derives from work first presented as "Strategic Mechanisms within Religious Symbol Systems" at a 1997 LAUD Symposium conference in the University of Duisburg, Germany, and subsequently published in Lieven Boeve and Kurt Feyaerts, editors, *Metaphor and God-talk* (Bern: Peter Lang, 1999), *Religions and Discourse* series, James Francis, general editor, volume 2: 273–91.

Chapter 6 on "Eclipsing" derives from "The Ambiguous Heritage and Perpetual Promise of Liberal Theology," *American Journal of Theology and Philosophy* 32/1 (2011): 43–61, and before that from a lecture delivered to the annual conference of the Institute for American Religious and Philosophical Thought.

Chapter 7 on "Loneliness" derives from "In Praise of Loneliness," in Leroy Rouner, editor, *Loneliness*, Institute for Philosophy and Religion Series (Notre Dame, IN: University of Notre Dame Press, 1998): 15–39, and before that from a 1996 lecture in the Institute series.

Finally, chapter 8 on "Intensity" is based on an essay written in the mid-1990s and presented to the Boston Theological Society. A related version has been published in *Religious and Spiritual Experiences* (Cambridge: Cambridge University Press, 2010).

∽∾

The phrase "effing the ineffable" and variants are in wide and diverse usage. I'm told that the philosophers Wilfred Sellars (1912–1989) and Robert Brandom (1950–) have used the phrase in conversation, and it has since found its way into the titles of novels, blog sites, and academic publications in a host of fields, from philosophy to health sciences to engineering. I have no idea who coined the phrase but I'm happily borrowing it for this book.

I am grateful to John Balch for his excellent work on the index for this volume.

∽∾

I take the opportunity here to express my gratitude to an unnamed host of conversation partners—colleagues, students, and authors ancient and contemporary—who have helped form my thinking on the intellectually and spiritually precarious activity of speaking about ultimacy.

This book is dedicated to my colleagues in Boston University's Graduate Division of Religious Studies. The dedication mentions a fond farewell, as this adventure comes to an end. Despite our different visions of what matters in graduate education in religious studies, over many years these folk have been first-rate partners in graduate education of the talented young people who trust us with their academic formation. We don't read each other's works as often as we should, but I'm pretty sure that some of them don't know quite what to make of my affirmation of an ultimate reality beyond the socially constructed supernatural agents and divinities of religion and culture. I suspect that some appreciate the critique of religion and culture implied in this view, and that some like what strikes them as a religiously sophisticated form of atheism. But some might also be skeptical about embracing the spiritually lively aspects of this God-beyond-God viewpoint, or about what I claim are its profound continuities with the apophatic mystical and philosophical sub-worlds within the large literate religious traditions. My hope is that this book will help explain why I take my mystical philosophical-theological outlook beyond critique to affirmation—albeit an affirmation that must always vainly attempt to eff the ineffable.

Part 1

ULTIMACY TALK

PART 1 *focuses on the linguistic techniques that arise when philosophical theologians try to speak as directly as possible about ultimate reality. This way of effing the ineffable is magnificently bold, intellectually questionable, and extraordinarily creative. I think it's at its best when operating comparatively, which is how all three chapters proceed. The American tradition of philosophy is most prominent here, especially that tradition's epistemic post-foundationalism, its thoroughgoing fallibilism, and its post-Kantian embrace of hypothetical comparative metaphysics. Chapter 1 on "Dreaming" is religious philosophy in a comparative and evaluative mode. Chapter 2 on "Suffering" shows how comparative and theoretical styles of religious philosophy can be bent to an evaluative end. Chapter 3 on "Creating" illustrates religious philosophy in its comparative, historical, and theoretical modes.*

Chapter 1

DREAMING

INTRODUCTION

HUMAN BEINGS ARE NOTHING IF NOT IMAGINATIVE. WE DREAM INTO REALITY cultures and technologies, languages to activate them, moral worlds to regulate them, and theories to understand them. Some of our most socially potent dreams concern ultimacy, the creative root of life, and the end of all our striving. These dreams yield conceptual models of ultimate reality, animating religious traditions and offering existential orientation to individuals. Our dreams of ultimacy make meaning by effing the ineffable. But are such dreams, and the conceptual models of such dreaming, to be taken seriously? Or are models of ultimate reality more akin to the confusion of the dreamer upon waking in the living world? At those half-awake moments, the artificial clarity of dreams evaporates leaving us with the muddle of collapsed pretensions to profound insight. It is the Cheshire Cat vanishing, leaving visible merely a wry smile hovering in the air.

The main reason for thinking that we should approach the conceptual fruit of our ultimacy dreams with a wry grin, and certainly with humble suspicion, is that there are so many models of ultimate reality, producing the impression of intractable conflict. This is why the plurality of models of ultimate reality is a central problem for religious philosophy. I think the key to evaluating our ultimacy dreams is comparative inquiries across the plurality of ultimacy models. Here I present a comparative argument to show that highly anthropomorphic models of ultimate reality are inferior to a number of competitors. Our ultimacy dreams are conceptually more robust, in this view, when they are less in thrall to our reflexively anthropomorphic cognitive habits of mind and more responsive to reality on many scales, within and beyond ordinary human experience.

There is no pretension to one perfect dream implied here, corresponding to a conceptually unassailable and unquestionably superior model of ultimate reality. But there is reason for confidence that we do not dream of ultimacy in vain, and that our dreams can truly engage us with the spiritual depths of the waking world.

The phrase "models of ultimate reality" (or "ultimacy models") is not common usage. I wish it were. I prefer to speak of "ultimacy models" rather than "God models" because I am most interested in ultimate reality and think that God is a valuable but potentially parochial name for it. Of course, sometimes God is treated merely as a component of ultimate reality, as in Alfred North Whitehead's thought, rather than synonymous with it. Those are instances of God language being used to talk about something other than ultimate reality, and further reasons to prefer the phrase "ultimacy models." In some traditions, of course, reflection on ultimate reality is regarded as secondary, a distraction from pursuing the ultimate paths that lead to liberation; this is true of some forms of Buddhism, for example. "Ultimacy" would be a serviceable comparative category in such cases, but here I am focused on conceptual and linguistically expressible models of ultimate reality. (These preferences for comparative categories reflect the conclusions of the Comparative Religious Ideas Project; see Neville 2000a, 2000b, 2000c).

Speaking of ultimacy *models* immediately suggests the plural, constructed, and approximate character of all thinking about ultimate realities. That such thinking produces manifold theories and portrayals of ultimate reality is the first fact of comparative religious ideas and a central problem for religious philosophy. The people who make these models are dreamers, to be sure, but they are also curious and creative, gripped by fascinating instincts and motivations, and typically immersed in great traditions of religious philosophy through their specialized discourse communities.

These imaginative constructions are also conditioned by the prodigiously diverse contexts in which they are first created and then received and transformed. Their social embodiment leaves models of ultimate reality vulnerable to exploitation for the sake of the social control for which religion is justly famous. I reckon that, if a model of God as a black person had been widespread in the early American colonies, African slavery in America would have been impossible to rationalize the way it was by some sincere Christian theologians. Yet the embodiment of religious ideas also allows models to illuminate and liberate questing souls in generation after generation. Witness the frequency with which artists portray Jesus with the facial features of local cultures.

Because of social embodiment, models of ultimate reality are subject to correction in a disorganized process of practical and conceptual testing against the ultimate reality that is actually engaged and registered in human life (such as it is, and in principle it may be nothing more than the totality of everything in reality as a whole, or the engageable parts of it). Some models fail under the stress of what amounts to a process of natural selection of ideas. For example, the shadowy yet potent idea of God as a white man shattered under the weight of experience. That is slightly encouraging for empirically minded philosophical theologians who prize referential adequacy in their models. Some models survive the tests of time and experience. They are not always popular. Indeed, all of my favorites—mystical theologies of ultimacy as blinding darkness, God beyond God, reality beyond comprehension (see Wildman 2017)—are especially unpopular. But these survivors (both my favorites and their competitors) are imaginatively stimulating, conceptually robust, flexible, plausible, and practical to a superior degree. They can be theoretically elaborated into comprehensive and consistent systems of thought. They are repeatedly rediscovered within a single tradition, and their core instincts almost always appear, reconfigured and re-weighted, in every tradition of religious philosophy. These are the Great Models, the ultimacy models with which every student of religious philosophy must come to terms. This essay addresses how to manage the plural and constructed character of the Great Models.

Some religious philosophers explain the persistence and recurrence of the Great Models by allowing that they are all more or less true—theoretically true as well as found to be true-in-practice within many hearts and minds. They then seek ways to manage the problem of plural conflicting models, usually relying on concepts of perspective-taking or inclusion, superiority or sublation, to explain how Truth Might Be One even though Models Are Many.

Other religious philosophers reject inquiry into ultimate reality as fatuous and futile. They argue that inquiry exchanges existentially vibrant engagement with ultimate reality for an absurdly arrogant evaluation process in which philosophers decide on matters that necessarily lie beyond the powers of human reason. Either pick a tradition and invest in it and its internal intellectual debates, they urge, or else make a Museum of Models that, like an art gallery, permits the capacious soul to appreciate each one as a unique testimony to the depth and wonder of life. I prefer to think of this museum in more dynamic terms, as an array of excellent dancers, representing both living spiritual insights and ideas preserved in philosophic traditions whose members are devoted to commentary and debate in the terms of their finely honed linguistic habits. Investing in a single tradition and appreciating many traditions can be practical and honorable ways to manage the problem of plural models. In either case, however, the comparing inquirer's theoretical and existential problem of *reconciling* conflicting models remains unresolved.

Still other religious philosophers feel dismayed by the moral priorities of the comparing inquirers, the mono-traditional investors, and the multi-traditional appreciators. These responsible worriers see the aftereffects and side effects of religious ideas as they are embodied in institutions and activated in social contexts. They decry all impractical philosophy, and impractical religious philosophy above all, as wrongly putting the philosopher's pleasurable pastime before the world's pain, or as blindly supporting the vested interests of religious institutions when trenchant critique would be more appropriate. And they particularly hate having their viewpoint labeled, framed, and hung in the Museum of Models where steely critical edge yields to the infinite nausea of perpetual legitimate contrasts.

Finally, some religious philosophers take a maximally modest road. They avoid inquiry and morality, and they scrupulously confine themselves to analysis. These analytical ascetics try not to construct anything. They aim instead to police the constructions of others, looking for signs of structural weakness and making design refinements. They are often mono-traditional investors engaged in intricate logical analysis and defense of their local tradition's beliefs. Some are comparativists moving around the Museum of Models like art critics. However they operate, they remain faithful to their modest creed and deny themselves the dangerous thrills of imaginative construction and inquiry.

Most religious philosophers can't help themselves. Each just tends to be a comparing inquirer, a mono-traditional investor, a multi-traditional appreciator, a responsible worrier, or an analytical ascetic. The best of them can see virtues in every way. But most *have a way*, emerging from the exquisite tangle of nature and nurture that defines preference in human beings, even philosophers. Such philosophic preferences run deep and rarely change more than once in a lifetime, if at all. For better or worse, I am drawn most strongly to the way of the comparing inquirer. I recognize the viability of other ways and appreciate their virtues. But I experience the plural, constructed, and approximate character of all models of ultimate reality intellectually as a puzzle to be solved, and existentially as an invitation to engage ultimate realty through thinking and feeling and acting toward a solution.

I consider this preliminary *confessio* essential for avoiding wasteful conflicts about God talk within religious philosophy that arise due to stylistic variations. Openly acknowledging our preferences as such honors the wisdom of other ways and prompts us to take seriously their criticisms of us. In my case, I need to deal with criticisms of comparing inquiry as a futile and fatuous effort to control the uncontrollable, a tiresome and ugly attempt to comprehend the incomprehensible, and a morally confused evasion of philosophic responsibility. Here I merely acknowledge the plurality of approaches and associated criticisms and proceed.

I divide my thoughts on this theme into three sections in what follows. Looking *behind* anthropomorphic models of ultimate reality refers to evaluating them through understanding their origins as imaginative constructions. This will involve assessing the prodigious capabilities and subtle liabilities of human cognition, and taking account of evolutionary psychology, social psychology, and social-historical context. Poking around *between* anthropomorphic models of ultimate reality refers to gaining traction for inquiry by means of critical comparison of the relative strengths and weaknesses of various models. This will involve thinking through the logical requirements of comparative inquiry and illustrating it in relation to highly anthropomorphic models of ultimate reality. Moving *beyond* anthropomorphic models of ultimate reality refers to a comprehensive coordination of the Great Models in some wider intellectual scheme. This calls for a mystical theology that relativizes and relates models while explaining the senses in which they truly express ultimate reality—both through describing it more or less accurately and through enabling people to engage it more or less authentically.

My approach here is two-leveled. On one level, I describe a method to support comparative inquiry into the plurality of models of ultimate reality. On another level, I articulate a particular ultimacy model, one whose special virtue is to make sense of the diversity of the Great Models, and whose corresponding liability is its lack of concrete intelligibility. Given the space available, in some places I gesture toward arguments that cannot be presented (see Wildman 2017 for further details). But there is sufficient space to show how the practices of looking behind, between, and beyond our model-like dreaming about ultimate reality are philosophically feasible and fruitful.

BEHIND ANTHROPOMORPHIC
MODELS OF ULTIMATE REALITY

God does not speak and think in Arabic or Hebrew, in Sanskrit or King James English. Claims to the contrary are incoherent in an amusingly self-canceling way. Thus, if there is supernatural revelation at all, upon reception it must be pressed into temporally bound, culturally conditioned, and linguistically limited forms of thought. In fact, my working hypothesis is that there is no supernatural revelation, because there is no supernatural being to convey it, and no supernatural realm to house it. Rather, revelation is best understood as present in every moment of human insight, in the depths of nature, and in the emergence of intense value that nature supports. But whether or not I am correct about this, ultimacy models do not just drop from another realm into this one, packaged and polished. We *make* our ultimacy models, under the impact of many influences and experiences.

One of those influences is the all-too-familiar fact of finitude. Whether it is fights with loved ones, failures of imagination, the frustrations of sickness, or the finality of death, finitude pervades the human condition. Even if religious traditions are right that there are ways to overcome the bizarre and bad ways we deal with our finite existence, there is no escape from finitude as such. This piece of practical knowledge is directly relevant to how religious philosophers should assess ultimacy models: they must embrace a thoroughgoing fallibilism. While we may be able to minimize imperfections through disciplined effort and technical expertise cultivated in specialized discourse communities, all models of ultimate reality bear the marks of their finite makers, like DNA within organisms.

The marks of the human condition on ultimacy models include the conceptual defects that we associate with anthropomorphism. But strictly speaking all models of ultimate reality are anthropomorphic to some degree, because they are human constructions and limited by the human imagination. So our concern is really with *excessive* or *careless* anthropomorphism rather than with anthropomorphism *as such*. Like other forms of theoretical excess, excessive anthropomorphism is not always easy to detect. Much religious symbolism is self-consciously anthropomorphic, as when Michelangelo portrays God as a bearded man reaching out to enliven Adam, or when Hindus portray Śiva as a many-armed man dancing in a ring of fire. The world of religious symbolism is replete with obviously anthropomorphic imagery that promotes spiritual engagement, and there is nothing naïve about a lot of it. Moreover, some philosophic models ascribe to God characteristics that are obviously derived from human experience, such as feelings, intentions, plans, and powers to act. But the philosophers who do this argue that this level of anthropomorphism is appropriate and indeed necessary to make sense of the claims made about God in the religious traditions whose narrative structures they attempt to elaborate in formal philosophic terms.

We can minimize anthropomorphic defects by paying careful attention to the way we make ultimacy models and the purposes served in the making of them. Historians and sociologists have traditionally played the leading roles in helping philosophers become aware of how contextual factors and group interests influence ultimacy models. The theological rationalizations for American enslavement of Africans I mentioned above reflect this type of awareness. The so-called masters of suspicion, among whom I would count Ludwig Feuerbach (1804–1872), Karl Marx (1818–1883), Friedrich Nietzsche (1844–1900), and Sigmund Freud (1956–1939), speculated about hidden psychic motivations and social reflexes at work in the origins of ultimacy models prevalent within religion (see Feuerbach 1854, 1873; Marx 2002; Nietzsche 1933; Freud 1928, 1930, 1939). In recent decades, the sciences bearing on human cognition have come to the fore with evolutionary insights into the cognitive factors playing a role in the imaginative construction of ultimacy models (see the surveys in McNamara 2006; Wildman and McNamara 2010).

∞

All explanations for the origins of religious ideas are inevitably speculative to some degree. Consider a few examples. First, the historian's smoking-gun evidence for origins would be a document in which a philosopher states his or her reasons for introducing a particular ultimacy model. But that is not decisive. Saint Augustine's autobiographical account in *Confessions* of the motivations and reasoning surrounding his shifting conception of God is subject both to what could be made conscious and to what he was prepared to make public (Augustine 1991).

Second, the human sciences can explain how the idea of God as a personal being attentive to every detail of our lives and purposefully active in the world serves the interests of strengthening corporate identity of certain religious groups—those groups that prize the spiritual ideal of a personal relationship with God and the moral ideal of a holy life lived transparently before a divine judge. But the fact that there is a fit between a particular model of God and the identity needs of a particular group probably bears more on the survival value of that model than on the motivations for creating it in the first place.

Third, the cognitive sciences can take us behind the scenes of human conscious awareness into the realm of unconscious motivations rooted in cognitive structures that were originally selected for their fitness-conferring benefits or that are side effects of other characteristics that were evolutionarily advantageous. But we are left guessing about the evolutionary scenarios that make sense of these claims about human cognition. This is a version of the widespread critique of unverifiable "just-so" stories to explain selection of traits in evolutionary biology. The most famous example is probably Charles Darwin's fanciful narrative of how a species of bears hunting insects while swimming could evolve through natural selection into a whale-like mammal (Darwin 1859, 184).

Fourth, cognitive psychology can devise experiments that disclose the presence of cognitive tendencies but it, too, can only speculate as to how they figure in the construction of models of ultimate reality. People routinely exercise their freedom and their rational capacities to resist their basic reflexes in every domain of life, including the cognitive and religious domains, so the sheer existence of cognitive tendencies is not decisive for an interpretation of the origins of ultimacy models.

These examples show that the philosopher seeking an understanding of models of ultimate reality by analyzing the processes relevant to their creation has a peculiar evidence problem. We have circumstantial and hearsay evidence everywhere we turn, and neither a single eyewitness nor any forensic data that can place a particular motivation or cognitive reflex at the scene of the creative crime. Yet we do have a *vast pile* of circumstantial evidence, and it can be interpreted as pointing in roughly the same direction.

The recent excitement surrounding the study of religion using cognitive science and evolutionary psychology derives from the sheer weight of this corroborating evidence (classic works are Atran 2002, Boyer 2001, but the literature extends back a full decade before those works). Religious philosophers now know vastly more about influences on the creation of ultimacy models than at any point in the past. Philosophers analyzing, comparing, or constructing models of ultimate reality should keep in mind the following three considerations, each of which looks behind the scenes at the way we think and express our thoughts.

⁓≈⌇

First, human reason is a powerful tool for interpretation, but it does have limitations that are relevant to assessing models of ultimate reality. Psychologists have documented these sources of cognitive error, complete with examples of the resulting mistakes in ordinary life. Psychologist Thomas Gilovich (1991) divides the sources of cognitive error into cognitive determinants and motivational and social determinants. Under cognitive determinants, he explains how misperceiving and misinterpreting random data can produce "something out of nothing," as when people see the Virgin Mary in a toasted cheese sandwich. He describes how misinterpreting incomplete and unrepresentative data can yield "too much from too little," as when people believe that horoscope predictions are accurate. And he points out how the biased evaluation of ambiguous and inconsistent data can leave us "seeing what we expect to see," as when we remember unjust treatment more strongly when it confirms our expectations of the person in question.

Under motivational and social determinants, Gilovich explains how motivational factors leave us "seeing what we want to see," as when gamblers firmly believe in special systems that actually do not work. He shows how the biasing effects of secondhand information lead us into "believing what we are told," as when people believe gossip more when they have no hard evidence one way or the other. And he demonstrates how exaggerated impressions of social support render us vulnerable to "the imagined agreement of others," as when drinkers believe that many more people enjoy consuming alcohol than non-drinkers believe.

These cognitive vulnerabilities are well understood by charlatans and magicians, who exploit them for personal gain and entertainment, respectively (a fabulous magician's exposé is Randi 1982). The field of behavioral law and economics studies human cognition and behavior in relation to the legal and economic systems, and it tries to determine how a full understanding of the strengths and liabilities of human cognition should affect regulation of these systems (a good survey of some of the issues in behavioral law and economics surrounding cognitive error is Rachlinksi 2006 and other essays in the same symposium; Rachlinksi focuses on whether and how the legal system should make paternalistic allowance for cognitive error). Research on marketing effectiveness recognizes that one of the factors in buying decisions is cognitive bias, and that advertisers can exploit it to maximize the impact of advertising dollars (on the psychology of buying see Nicosia 1966; also see Plous 1993). Cross-cultural research suggests that these cognitive, motivational, and social determinants of cognitive error appear across cultures, as do certain logical fallacies that derive from them, even though they are expressed quite differently according to the well-attested result that cultures support markedly different styles of cognition. There is a host of evidence on different cultural styles of cognition (see Nisbett, Choi, and Norenzayan 2001). Work on the cross-cultural recurrence of basic forms of cognitive error is less common, but there are good theoretical accounts of the possible evolutionary advantages of certain forms of cognitive error, building on empirical cross-cultural evidence for cognitive bias (see Tobena, Marks, and Dar 1999). In fact, education and experience appear to be more important factors than cultural differences in explaining variations in vulnerability to cognitive error, even though cultural factors remain important. This suggests both that that many forms of cognitive error are genetically rooted (perhaps because they were adaptive in certain circumstances) and also that these vulnerabilities can often be regulated and controlled under the right conditions (for an integrated evolutionary perspective on cognitive error, see Haselton and Nettle 2006).

It takes decades of education to train human minds to recognize and allow for these cognitive liabilities. Many people remain vulnerable to many of the determinants of cognitive error and routinely fall prey to logical fallacies. This fact, allowing for variations in personality and cognitive style, underlies the prevalence of superstition in all cultures (see Vyse 1997). Even rigorously educated people sometimes have difficulty extending to their ordinary lives the carefully honed critical-thinking skills that they habitually apply in the area of their special expertise. This is probably because the signals that alert us to cognitive error are plentiful in an area of expertise (such as engineering) but are weak or missing in some domains of life (such as religion).

This rapid survey does little more than open the book of lessons that intellectuals must draw from cognitive science. But it is enough for religious philosophers to conclude that they must scrutinize all models of ultimate reality for the effects of human vulnerability to cognitive error.

∽⊙⊙∽

Second, beneath the manifestations of cognitive error lies a causal story about how we got this way through the evolutionary process. This portrayal of emergent reasoning and interpreting abilities in the human species is currently far from complete (a classic introduction to evolutionary psychology is Barkow, Cosmides, and Tooby 1992; one of the best discussions on evolutionary psychology and religion is Atran 2004). But already numerous thinkers have sensed that it promises leverage on the various evaluative questions that philosophers like to ask about human beliefs and behaviors (see Dawkins 2006; Dennett 2006).

It turns out that the path from an evolutionary account of human cognition to a philosophical assessment of the reliability of religious beliefs is extremely complicated. Everyone agrees that a predisposition to religious beliefs and behaviors is widespread among human beings. Some say it is exclusively cultural with no genetic component; this view is implicitly present among the many religious thinkers who ignore evolutionary psychology. Some have interpreted this predisposition to religion as evidence for the adaptive value of religious beliefs and behaviors, and they then go on to fight about what this means for the truth of religious beliefs: does their adapted quality make them productive illusions or reliable hypotheses? (For an example of the view that true religious beliefs are adaptive, see Ramsey 2002; for an example of the view that false religious beliefs are adaptive, see Bulbulia 2006.)

I judge the expert consensus on this question currently to be somewhere between these relatively extreme views. Many of the cognitive operations involved in producing religion are evolved traits, but most or all of those traits evolved for reasons other than religion. That is, religious beliefs and behaviors are *side effects* of those traits. Religious side effects can be secondarily adaptive and maladaptive, and have proved to be both in various selective contexts. They can also be valuable or dangerous, and true or false, and usually are all of these things in various respects all at once.

For example, the adapted cognitive skill of pattern recognition probably evolved largely because facial recognition was highly adaptive for early homonids. Once in place, that cognitive skill was co-opted for many other pattern-recognition tasks. The resulting side effects contribute to activities we value such as art and mathematics, and they also produce some of the cognitive liabilities described above, which are due to overactive pattern recognition. Similarly, cause-detection and intention-attribution systems probably evolved because they helped us get a head start on stalking predators that cause rustling in bushes. But the side effects of these adapted systems include overactive imaginations that cause us to run away from bushes when wind rather than anything dangerous is doing the rustling. "Better safe than sorry," we say. When conditions allow, we can poke around in the bushes and see that there is nothing there after all, much as a child sensibly and courageously looks under the bed to rule out the presence of feared monsters. When resources to correct beliefs resulting from our cause-detection and inten-tion-attribution systems are *not* readily available, however, we can quickly fall prey to superstition, to beliefs in intentions behind historical events, or to beliefs in causes behind coincidences.

Other evolved traits that play a role in the production of religious beliefs and behaviors include cognitive universals (underlying folk psychology and folk biology and what can be called "folk religion"; see Atran 1998), the mem-orable character of minimally counterintuitive beliefs (aiding the perseverance of religious beliefs; see Barrett and Nyhof 2001; Boyer and Ramble 2001), and hypnotizability and dissociation (the bases for colorful religious experiences and psychosomatic placebo healing effects; see McClenon 2002). Evolutionary psychologists debate the circumstances surrounding the evolutionary origins of each of these factors. But the consensus is that religious beliefs and behaviors are combinatorial side effects of all of these cognitive traits, rather than the primary cause of their adaptation (see the summary in Kirkpatrick 2006). This consensus is persuasive chiefly because religion is far too complex to be reduced to just one of the relevant cognitive factors.

If this consensus is correct, those arguing for religious beliefs either as false illusions or as true adaptations invariably depend on a dramatic reductionism to close the gap between the multi-trait complexity of religion and the single-trait explanation they typically need in order to clinch their philosophical case. To assess the reliability of religious beliefs, we must negotiate an intricately con-toured landscape joining the evolutionary depths of the oceans of biology to the heady peaks of theoretically expressed models of ultimate reality. The details of the landscape matter; they prevent a simple settlement of the truth and value questions surrounding models of ultimate reality. The challenge for theoretically elaborated ultimacy models is to account for those details. As we shall see, that is an important criterion for adequacy in a process of comparative inquiry.

⁓≈⌣

Third and finally, regardless of available cognitive resources, religious beliefs and behaviors emerge in culturally conditioned and socially charged ways. This fact of life is extremely obvious when one is on the wrong side of someone else's religious orthodoxy or encountering religion in a foreign culture. Yet the same fact can be almost indiscernible when one is at home in a local religious environment. No matter how invisible they may seem, religious ideas can be socially explosive. Attempting to take responsibility for this fact of life introduces moral complexities into the task of religious philosophy.

Consider an analogy. The Union of Concerned Scientists urges scientists to take moral responsibility for their research. Some scientists resist these urgings, arguing that the social effects of their research are someone else's problem—say, corporations that develop technological applications. But this smacks of laziness and blame-shifting, comes the reply. In the same way, religious philosophers must do their part to take responsibility for their work with ultimacy models, and not award themselves a free pass and blame retail religion for the consequences of the religious ideas they discuss. How can religious philosophers take responsibility for the social and psychological potency of ultimacy models?

If we abstract religious ideas from their social contexts for the purposes of analysis, then we should pay attention at some point to the effects of the abstracting move, so as to acknowledge that those ideas are embodied social realities and not mere theoretical abstractions. If we take up a God idea for discussion, we should pay attention at some point to the ways that the selected idea has been present in morally dubious exercises of political power, and to the psychological effects, both positive and negative, of that God model. These kinds of responsibility-taking have become the primary task of a rather large group of theologians and philosophers concerned with the psychological and social effects of ultimacy models. They point out that the model of God as King of a Kingdom can silently but improperly legitimate certain forms of political organization, or that the model of God as Father can reinforce stereotypes about men and women. Even if this kind of analysis is not the primary obligation of every religious philosopher, it should at least figure somewhere in the mix of tasks undertaken; that is part of the meaning of professional competence in our context.

I welcome the growing sensitivity to the social power of religious ideas among religious philosophers. But another kind of sensitivity—to the plurality of models of ultimate reality—continues to be underdeveloped. Few philosophers know their way around the world's religious ideas. Most intellectuals who do feel at home in multiple religious traditions are anthropologists focusing on religious practices, sociologists focusing on social change, or historians focusing on cross-cultural interactions, rather than philosophers focusing on the truth and value of the ideas themselves. The effect of this lack of familiarity with the conceptual and religious Other is often a parochialism that makes philosophical work seem quaintly irrelevant to the outsider. Not all religious philosophy must concern itself with the plurality of ultimacy ideas, to be sure. But what is the rationale for excluding alternative ideas of ultimate reality when they are directly relevant to the philosophical point under debate? Unfamiliarity does not count as a rationale for neglect; nor does lack of expertise. These are merely signs of the need to do more homework.

～≈～

I am designating these three considerations as *lessons* from cognitive psychology, from evolutionary psychology, and from religious studies, respectively. I have argued that anyone wanting to construct or analyze models of ultimate reality in rigorous and responsible fashion cannot afford to ignore these lessons. When absorbed, like nutrients in soil, they add a flowering self-awareness to disciplined philosophic effort. This awareness exquisitely complicates the model-construction process by triggering self-doubt and causing us constantly to inspect our best thoughts for unacknowledged influences. But it also makes thinking clearer and more realistic. It heightens the ability to understand alternative models, eliminates many wasteful theological disputes, and creates space for reasoning to play an honorable role in authentic philosophical debate rather than functioning merely as a tool for blindly legitimating socially potent dreams about ultimate reality.

BETWEEN ANTHROPOMORPHIC MODELS OF ULTIMATE REALITY

So much for looking behind ultimacy models. Can we say anything about what goes on between them? What I am calling the Great Models of ultimate reality are like tectonic plates. They cover the indirectly experienceable surface of ultimate reality, which serves as much to hide what is going on below as to define an interesting landscape for intellectual and spiritual exploration. It is at the edges of the plates, where they grind with inconsistency against one another, that we learn most about the dynamism below the surface.

Comparing ideas of ultimate reality is partly a matter of paying close attention to areas of conceptual friction. The purposes of comparing religious ideas vary greatly. Sometimes the aim is simply to create a database of information for others to use, for which purpose the ideal of neutrality serves as inspiration to be approximated through constant vigilance. At other times the aim is one of social control and the accuracy of the comparison secondary to the power it confers on people who make use of it, as when the comparative category of "religions of the book" allows Muslims to rationalize their extending of courtesies to adherents of certain other religions. The proper philosophic purpose of comparing religious ideas is to adduce a penetrating hypothesis about a religious topic, to stabilize that hypothesis by connecting it to the available data that articulate it, and to test the hypothesis against that data so as to refine it or else discard it for a superior hypothesis (see Strenski 2006). This sort of comparative inquiry is particularly important in relation to models of ultimate reality because there is so little logical and conceptual leverage for dealing with their intricate pluralism outside of comparison.

Wielding comparison of religious ideas and practices to formulate and test anthropological and sociological hypotheses has a long and lustrous history. Theories both justly famous and rightly infamous have sprung from the fevered minds of Western scholars infected by knowledge of multiple cultures and religions, from Frazer (1900) to Tambiah (1990), from Tyler (1873–1874) to Wierzbica (1992), from Durkheim (1954) to Berger (1967), and from Weber (1930) to Huntington (1996). Comparative inquiry exists in all of the major philosophic traditions. In the West, it arcs from the comparative argument at the beginning of Aristotle's *Metaphysics*, through Aquinas's *Summa Contra Gentiles* and Hegel's lectures on world history and world religions, to the comparative religious philosophies of John Hick and Robert Neville (Aristotle 1982; Aquinas 1955; Hegel 1984; Hick 2004; Neville 1991). In South Asia, it is sparked by ancient formal debates between Buddhist and Hindu philosophers and produces competing philosophic schemes such as those of Vedānta, which are both inspired by the Upanishads and aim to register the truth of every other perspective on ultimate reality. (Śaṅkara in the mid-eighth century CE set an example of expounding the Upanishads while taking account of opposing schools, including Buddhism, Jainism, Samkhya, and Vaisheshika; see especially his commentaries on the Upanishads and the Bhagavad-Gita, which were formative for much subsequent Indian philosophy, including in its comparative aspects.) In the East Asian context, comparative religious philosophy is rooted in the internal diversity of Chinese religion, in the migration of Buddhism from India, and in the modern encounter with the West. Its modern high points include the writings of Kyoto School thinkers such as Nishida (1960), Nishitani (1982), and Tanabe (1986).

A key question for the comparing inquirer is whether comparison, inspired by these longstanding traditions, can confer leverage on philosophical questions about the value and truth of models of ultimate reality. Some say no. The case against the viability of comparative inquiry is obvious: comparison is good for organizing and understanding religious ideas, at best, but it has no power to control philosophical interpretation that aims to detect what is true and valuable among religious ideas. This case is compelling, as far as it goes. But it does not penetrate deeply into the potential importance of comparison for philosophical inquiry.

~&~

We can spend our lives listing models of ultimate reality, with their intricate theistic and non-theistic variations, noting cross-cases and exceptions, recording contextual and historical conditioning factors, and still get nowhere in a philosophical inquiry. It is only when we introduce criteria for evaluation that our comparative database becomes an asset for inquiry. Comparative inquiry refers not to sheer description under a rubric of comparative categories, therefore, but to the artful use of comparison both to make criteria for evaluation count for inquiry and to expose those criteria to rational scrutiny (see Neville 2000a, 2000b, 2000c; Wildman 2006c, 2017).

We can think of philosophically elaborated models of ultimate reality as large-scale hypotheses. For example, we might posit a theory of ultimate reality built around a model of a personal divine being with intentions, conscious states, and powers to act in the world. Such hypotheses can be tested against the considerations we have discussed—cognitive psychology, evolutionary psychology, comparative religions—among others. But it is difficult to decide how good our hypothesis is in such tests until we put it alongside an alternative hypothesis and compare how well the two handle the various considerations available to guide testing. For example, we could put the personal theism hypothesis alongside the quite different ground-of-being hypothesis and compare how they handle the data, piece by piece. At the simplest level, this is what is meant by comparative inquiry.

How do we know when one hypothesis fares better than another? The superior hypothesis in respect of the data from evolutionary psychology is the one that best explains why we should expect that data to emerge. The standards for good explanations then have to be sorted out, but typically they include applicability, adequacy, coherence, consistency, and sometimes pragmatic considerations such as ethical consequences, aesthetic quality, or spiritual appeal. Then there is the question about which data sets to prize most highly; answering this question produces comparative criteria for the inquiry. For example, proponents of the ground-of-being hypothesis would probably want to emphasize the importance of the data from evolutionary psychology because ground-of-being theism is effortlessly compatible with it. Meanwhile, they would probably want to de-emphasize data from religious popularity contests, because the ground-of-being view feels spiritually disappointing to more people than find it spiritually compelling. I suspect that proponents of the personal-theism hypothesis would want to rank these two criteria oppositely to match its own weaknesses and strengths. The two sides may not be able to agree on the importance of such comparative criteria, but the argument is there to be had in a process of comparative inquiry, whereas it is often utterly obscured in other forms of argumentation about ultimacy models.

Here is another example. Suppose we place the hypothesis of God as omnipotent creator alongside that of the cosmic moral dualisms of Manichaeism and Zoroastrianism. We could compare them relative to the two criteria of offering a solution to the problem of evil and solving the problem of the one and the many. We can quickly see that absolute moral dualisms handle the problem of evil spectacularly well but stumble on the problem of the one and the many, whereas the advantages and disadvantages are reversed in the case of omnipotent creator theism. Then the question becomes whether it is more important to have an intelligible solution to the reality of evil or a compelling resolution of the problem of the one and the many. That can be debated in the same way that models are.

The various comparative criteria serve initially to emphasize some patches of the relevant data over other patches. But after the hypotheses have offered their explanations of a patch of data and the explanations have been compared for quality, the comparative criteria actually serve to rank hypotheses as better and worse. Consider the following comparative criterion: "an adequate theory of ultimate reality makes sympathetic sense of the most refined philosophical thinking about ultimacy within the world's religious traditions." This criterion would initially select out a patch of data from comparative religions for the various competing hypotheses to explain. But when the explanations are in, the same criterion tends to prefer hypotheses that are compatible with a broader array of ultimacy models. Personal theism stumbles on this criterion but several competitors, including the ground-of-being hypothesis, leap over it naturally. This would narrow the field of excellent contenders in the competition for the best explanation of all relevant data, to the detriment of the personal-theism hypothesis, unless its advocates could argue that this particular criterion should be revised or demoted to an unimportant position. This is why proponents of hypotheses fight over comparative criteria. Unfortunately, much of this fighting over comparative criteria usually goes on under the radar, whereas comparative inquiry helpfully forces it out into the open.

I am describing a comparative framework for a process of inference to the best explanation of all relevant evidence. In reality, there ought to be many competing hypotheses, not just two, though pair-wise consideration of hypotheses is a way to keep the process manageable. Regardless of how comparative inquiry is organized, however, inference-to-best-explanation arguments in religious philosophy are only as good as the comparative infrastructure that articulates and supports them. I have argued elsewhere that this constitutes an unfamiliar comparative style of natural theology that does not fall prey to the much-trumpeted weaknesses of traditional natural theology (Wildman 2006a, 2006b).

Comparison is not neutral, any more than description or interpretation or evaluation are neutral. Rational inquirers are perpetually working in the middle of relatively unexamined premises and heavily scrutinized conclusions. They move their attention about to test what seems problematic in their conceptual environment and to detect bias and distortion, but they are always in the middle. In particular, they always *begin* in the middle of descriptions of religious beliefs and practices that reflect existing traditions of interpretation and translation, constantly refined and corrected by experts. Comparisons make use of categories that are vulnerable to ideological distortions and empirical failures. The attentive inquirer cannot delay beginning until the relevant data is perfectly well organized and impartially interpreted; there never would be a beginning.

It follows that centralizing comparison offers no clean shortcuts for philosophical inquiry; it is the scratchy way through the densest thickets of the forest. But comparative inquiry is the only realistic way to overcome philosophical parochialism. It is also the only way to mount inference-to-best-explanation arguments in religious philosophy that register the relevant data, include the relevant competitor hypotheses, and expose the relevant argumentative criteria to examination. In short, comparison forces the philosophical construction of ultimate realities to do justice to the data of religious ideas and practices, rather than artfully dodging the data for the many reasons we might be inclined to do that.

❧

My ventures into the forest of comparative inquiry have involved confronting an array of theoretically robust models of ultimate reality. These are the Great Models. They include the most sophisticated versions of personal theism, such as those of Rāmānuja and Augustine, which are the most obviously anthropomorphic offerings among the Great Models. Śaṅkara's Advaita Vedānta is there, along with Nagarjuna's Madhyamaka portrayal of the ultimate way for human beings, and the ground-of-being theory already mentioned. Trinitarian theism is present, with its striking postulate of internal relational structure within the divine (Augustine represents that, too), along with the still more differentiated moral dualisms of Manichaeism and Zoroastrianism, and perhaps also the unresolved radical pluralism of ancient polytheism without a High God to keep order. The Chinese vision of the Tao, whose structured spontaneity flows through all of reality, would be there, along with more recent models of ultimacy as a fecund interplay of principles of order and chaos. The Neoplatonic One in eternal self-differentiation would be there, along with Aristotle's Prime Mover, Plato's valuational ultimate, and the highly structured medieval Great Chain of Being. And there would be others besides these, with some models having more in common with models from alien traditions than with other models from their own tradition. For example, within Western philosophical traditions, the ground-of-being viewpoint has more in common with Advaita Vedānta and even Madhyamaka and Philosophical Daoism than with the personal theism with which it has coexisted for millennia.

Demonstrating the possibility or basic intelligibility of these models is not required here; much more than mere possibility is already acknowledged when we grant these views a place among the Great Models. Arguments about the probability of ultimacy models remain relevant, at least in principle. And a large and diverse range of less familiar types of arguments enter this comparative inquiry. For example, whereas we commonly find people arguing over whether personal theism can hold out against scientistic reductionism, we rarely encounter debates over whether the *pratītya-samutpāda* metaphysics of *śūnyatā* or the substantial *jīvan* metaphysics of dvaita *Vedānta* does a better job of accounting for what is known from evolutionary psychology about human nature, and how both compare with personal theism and the ground-of-being theory in that respect. Comparative inquiry opens up worlds of philosophical debate that cross cultures in new ways and place new demands on the religious philosopher. It's a new kind of dreaming about ultimate reality, I guess—one especially suited to philosophical theologians.

It seems that the process of comparative inquiry threatens to become extremely unwieldy, even if it proceeds pair-wise or chunk by manageable chunk. Nevertheless, it is worth asking about its overall prospects. Differentiating better from worse among the Great Models is sometimes feasible, at least in the sense that some models handle entire sets of key comparative criteria significantly better than their competitors. But the chances of identifying a clean winner overall are profoundly uncertain. I conjecture that a few of the Great Models—the Very Great Models, if you like—turn out to be roughly equivalent. What does this mean? Relative to a fairly large set of key comparative criteria, all of the Very Great Models do fairly well, and arguments to promote a favorable subset of those key criteria above others are not decisive, to about the same degree in all cases (see an example of this sort of stalemate sketched in Wildman 2007).

We might complain that, if the results are of this sort, then comparative inquiry yields far too little return on our investment. We might long for the good old days of simple arguments over the sheer possibility of a favored model of ultimate reality, and indeed there is a place for such arguments. But the point here is that this kind of comparative inquiry is precisely as complicated as the subject matter demands. Any other approach inevitably short-circuits the real challenges and produces an artificial triumph, thereby violating the comparing inquirer's fundamental values of open inquiry. This sort of comparative inquiry is not for everyone, but for those who want to pursue it, nothing simpler or more convenient or less demanding can get the job done.

Beyond Anthropomorphic Models of Ultimate Reality

With this we come to the final preposition: *beyond*. Many religious philosophers have no interest in moving beyond highly anthropomorphic models of ultimate reality. I think we need to move beyond them, however, and I'll explain why as an illustration of how comparative inquiry might progress, even if it is only a small step toward making sense of our ultimacy dreams.

In the comparative inquiry I am describing, the more obviously anthropomorphic versions of personal theism are less proficient at explaining many important chunks of data than a lot of other ultimacy models. In fact, I suspect that the highly anthropomorphic models, including most forms of personal theism and polytheism, are not among what I earlier called the Very Great Models, which are the finalists in this drawn-out comparative dance competition. The comparative criteria that most strongly favor anthropomorphic ultimacy models are related to what makes them popular—they are concretely intelligible and inspiring for human life, they promote dramatic and minimally counter-intuitive reconciliation narratives, and they offer a strong basis for hope in the continuation of individual consciousness after death. But these are also the kinds of virtues that any popular model of ultimate reality would have, according to cognitive psychology and evolutionary psychology, because they directly reflect the cognitive biases of the human species.

If you believe our cognitive biases are adaptations that evolved specifically because they promote *accurate* religious beliefs—not just *useful* beliefs but *true* beliefs—then those biases confer likelihood on popular anthropomorphic religious beliefs such as highly anthropomorphic personal theism (see Barrett 2011, 2012). In that case, you can frame the psychological data so as to confirm personal theism and other highly anthropomorphic ultimacy models. But if you are convinced, as I am, that religiousness is not the primary drive for the evolution of human cognitive traits, and that their application to religion is an evolutionary side effect, then the correspondence between human cognitive bias and the popularity of highly anthropomorphic forms of personal theism is more troubling. In this case, the *prima facie* likelihood is that highly anthropomorphic ultimacy models reflect cognitive error more than reliable belief.

Of course, there are less heavily anthropomorphic ultimacy models that are also less popular and more intellectually compelling than highly anthropomorphic forms of personal theism. For example, some models of ultimacy combine personal characteristics such as intentionality, awareness, and activity with nonpersonal characteristics such as non-temporality, impassibility, and immutability. There is a serious problem of coherence in such models because intentionality seems to require temporality, awareness seems to contradict impassibility, and activity seems to entail mutability. This is why these models are so markedly different from the popular forms of personal theism all over the world. Moreover, these models must face daunting theodicy challenges to their coherence. Nevertheless, providing the coherence problems are addressed—and vast traditions are devoted to doing this—I think that this sort of not-highly anthropomorphic personal theism has a place among the Very Great Models.

Long before evolutionary psychology came along, many thinkers had noticed the psychologically suspicious quality of highly anthropomorphic ultimacy models. This is why most ancient philosophers, from Greece to India to China, treated popular mythologies as superstitions. This is also the instinct of the Masters of Suspicion that I mentioned earlier. And the same instinct is now amplified in the contemporary scientific study of religion, with the beginnings of a sturdy empirical database where once there was only speculation. None of these arguments can ever *rule out* personal theism or polytheistic mythologies.

Nevertheless, religious philosophers have more reason than ever to move beyond highly anthropomorphic models of ultimate reality.

Richard Dawkins recently published *The God Delusion*, in which he argues that personal theism is almost certainly false (Dawkins 2006). He thinks that we believe in a personal, attentive, active deity only because we are psychologically predisposed to see signs of intentionality even where there is no intentional agent at work, and because we lack the courage to examine our assumptions about the relevant data. Recall the analogy with the person who runs away from rustling bushes, fearing a stalking tiger. Dawkins thinks we should get a spear for protection and poke around to see what is actually in the bushes instead of talking ourselves into believing in the lurking tiger without hard evidence. When we do investigate the gods in this way, he thinks, we find not a tiger but merely the empty wind, playing tricks on our minds.

This is a blunt and incautious application of evolutionary psychology to belief in a personal God. To stay with the tiger analogy, we know that we are likely to jump to conclusions about the tiger and also that we are likely to be afraid of inspecting the rustling the bushes even with spear in hand and friends in tow, but none of that means there is no tiger. This has been the theistic answer to projection theories of religion for centuries, and it works here too.

Unfortunately, Dawkins's philosophical arguments fail to register even the most elementary philosophical insights into the nature of God as expert philosophical theologians conceive God. He treats God as one cause among many, for example, rather than as the First Cause. For a characteristically lively philosophical review of the book, which does not hesitate to show how thin the argument is at the level of philosophical theology, see Alvin Plantinga's review, neatly titled "The Dawkins Confusion: Naturalism ad absurdum" (Plantinga 2007). Now, the First Cause model of God may or may not be coherent, and it certainly is not a part of the popular understanding of God as an active person, but simply neglecting it in favor of making God essentially an omnipotent creature means that Dawkins is attacking a version of personal theism that few reputable philosophical theologians have espoused. This is the so-called straw-man fallacy grown to massive proportions—the straw T-Rex fallacy, perhaps. The best versions of personal theism effortlessly escape this attack, as do most other ultimacy models.

By now it is clear that I am one of the critics of Dawkins who actually agrees with his negative conclusions about the most popular forms of personal theism. Unfortunately, it is a case of "with friends like this, who needs enemies?" He never takes seriously a view of ultimate reality other than highly anthropomorphic personal theism, and the resulting parochialism is not helpful for moving beyond anything except his book. This illustrates why it is vital to set up the sort of comparative inquiry I have described, with relevant theoretically articulated models of ultimate reality vying with each other relative to explicitly stated comparative criteria.

Of course, the enormous complexity of comparative inquiry is not sexy in the way Dawkins fans would require if they were to invest time reading about it (see Wildman 2017). It is so complex that it makes even the probabilistic natural theology arguments of Alvin Plantinga (2000) or Richard Swinburne (1979) seem drastically oversimplified. Nevertheless, without a comparative framework, crucial alternative hypotheses are routinely neglected. This leads to fatal flaws in arguments assessing the probability of hypotheses about ultimate reality, including flaws present in Dawkins, Plantinga, Swinburne, and others. For example, showing that personal theism is significantly more probable than a flattened out kind of atheism that stubbornly refuses to explain existence and value might well be possible; in fact, I think it is less difficult than Swinburne and Plantinga make out in their writings on the subject (Swinburne 1979; Plantinga 2000). But this achievement offers precious little support to personal theism when we never bother to calculate the probability of its competitor hypotheses among the Great Models—a painfully obvious mistake that both philosophical theologians make. This can only feel like a significant accomplishment to religious philosophers who do not care about the entire Museum of Models but want to focus only on one model, defending it from attacks. There is a place for that. But such arguments say almost nothing about the adequacy of the model being defended. It is much more difficult to compete with robust competitor views of ultimate reality than with Dawkins's metaphysically innocent atheism. Plantinga and Swinburne should choose tougher opponents.

Highly anthropomorphic models of ultimate reality perform sub-optimally not only in relation to the data from the scientific study of religion and from our experience of suffering; they also prove disappointing in relation to the data from comparative religious ideas. Views that can subsume other models within them—say, as perspectives or as interpretative slices—offer the best explanations of the profusion of ultimacy theories in the Museum of Models. Highly anthropomorphic personal theism is relatively ill-suited to this because its personalist metaphysics operates with highly determinate categories—such as intention, awareness, and agency—and thus tends to bluntly contradict alternatives. But a number of other views can subsume personal theism in a way that explains the data of personal theistic religious experience by rendering the key metaphysical categories of personal theism in symbolic terms compatible with their own. This occurs in advaita Vedānta and ground-of-being theism, for example. Sometimes the subsuming view retains the metaphysics of personal theism and implants it within a larger metaphysics that adds a God beyond God, as in the perennial philosophy.

This leaves strongly anthropomorphic God models such as most forms of personal theism in roughly the same position logically and philosophically that they are in religious practice. These ultimacy models achieve plausibility within communities that engage ultimate reality deeply and authentically through them. Criteria for plausibility are carried along and nurtured both within traditions of religious practice and within philosophical subcultures. When exposed to the wider world of ultimacy models, philosophers and ordinary religious folk alike experience the energizing potential of the wider view and also the corrosive effects on familiar criteria for plausibility. As a result, some religious folk set out on a journey in search of a view of ultimate reality that can make better sense of this wider range of experience. Some philosophers likewise invest energy in the kind of comparative inquiry that I have been describing, trying to move beyond highly anthropomorphic personal theism even while trying to do justice to its capacity to foster authentic engagement with ultimacy. Other religious folk never feel the plausibility problem of their restless kin, or else they will it to one side and nestle into the comfortable and beautiful intricacy of their existing communal beliefs, and once again much the same is true for some religious philosophers.

⁓≈⁓

It is easier to look beyond highly anthropomorphic ultimacy models once we truly realize that there are plenty of compelling alternatives. In fact, the neighborhood of the edifice of personal theism is less like New York harbor hosting the glorious and lonely Statue of Liberty, and more like the hills of Easter Island gracing numerous vast and portentous stone statues with uncertain meaning. It was an Easter-Island vision of plural religious practices and beliefs that probably inspired the Upanishads, with their affirmation that Brahman is One—behind, between, and beyond all, both identical with the human spirit and utterly transcending it, grounding and uniting everything that is. The same vision powers the perennial philosophy's attempt to coordinate all of the models of ultimate reality into a hierarchy perfectly suited to accommodate the vast range of spiritual personalities and inclinations, with each soul tending toward the loftier, transpersonal models as it commutes through the samsaric cycle of lives (see Smith 1992). It is a vision of the wealth of religious imagery for God that inspired many of the apophatic mystics to declare that ultimate reality is beyond all imagery, and also to articulate trajectories of visualization that propel the imagination as far as possible in the direction of wise and true engagement with God before lapsing into inevitable silence.

The yielding of imaginative theoretical and spiritual exertion to ultimate silence is a kind of philosophic failure, obviously. But this silent failure is celebrated by apophatic mystics in all traditions. For them it confirms and comforts. This strikes many other religious folk as an absurd embrace of the irrational. They can no more imagine feeling satisfaction at conceptual fracturing of God ideas than they can appreciate the apophatic mystic's ideal for the afterlife, which is to be a dewdrop slipping silently into the shining sea. But there is nothing irrational about it. For the apophatically minded religious philosopher, there is a great deal to say and much theoretical intricacy to negotiate, prior to lapsing into silence. Just as apophatic mystics such as Pseudo-Dionysius promote spiritual trajectories, so apophatic religious philosophers recognize better and worse in models of ultimate reality. This defines what it means to go beyond highly anthropomorphic views of ultimate reality. Let's ponder this point for a moment. I'll discuss it in more detail later (see Chapter 5), but a brief pass by the key ideas here will be helpful.

The apophatic mystic's positive way of naming, the *via positiva*, organizes ultimacy images from the most noble to the least adequate. The associated spiritual discipline involves meditating on each image, slowly blanketing the conceptual wall with the whiteness of silence by affirming ultimacy in everything, eventually even the least likely and most repulsive thing. In the world of religious philosophy, this is akin to organizing the Museum of Models of ultimate reality to conform to a working hypothesis about relative value, while allowing that even the least valuable model conveys some truth.

The apophatic mystic's negative way of denial, the *via negativa*, organizes literal ultimacy images from least adequate to most adequate. The associated spiritual discipline involves denying those images in that order, so as to remove any hint of exaggerated claims to adequacy of such models, even the most authoritative and sacred among them. Silence arrives through the gradual elimination of cognitive content. In the world of religious philosophy, the sort of comparative inquiry I have been advocating can be construed in much the same way as the *via negativa*, though less linearly.

Apophatically minded religious philosophers recognize the virtues of theoretically articulated ultimacy models as intellectual avenues for potentially authentic engagement with ultimate reality. But they advance arguments for why some should be denied as more inadequate than others, corresponding to the mystic's organization of denied images from least adequate to most adequate. The arguments take the comparative form that I have described. While never decisive, those arguments do permit the philosopher to envision the complicated inquiry in the form of a dynamic conceptual field of comparative play—perhaps in much the same way that a coach imagines a football play unfolding, or a choreographer pictures a dance. This vision includes provisional diagnosis of better from worse models, all relative to arguments over comparative criteria—a diagnosis always subject to correction.

If indeed there is a "last group standing," these models are, for the apophatic religious philosopher, not so much the decisive victors as the last words before death—artful words, memorable, and filled with solemn significance as befits a lifetime of striving for wisdom. But just as we would select our final words with great care, circumstances permitting, so well-supported judgments about relative superiority among the world's Great Models of ultimate reality is a weighty matter. The last models standing cast long shadows over their fallen companions, framing them and interpreting them in highly particular ways, before they, too, fall before light inexpressible. I have indicated why I think that highly anthropomorphic models of ultimate reality are not among the last group standing—the Very Great Models. But I also think that evolutionary psychology guarantees that nothing in religion happens without those highly anthropomorphic constructions, and thus that their existence is a condition for the possibility of the emergence of more adequate understandings of ultimate reality.

CONCLUSION

In the final analysis, perhaps the multi-traditional appreciators are correct, and the entire vast Museum of Models, unanalyzed and unorganized, is the better way to go. Let the dreams pour forth, unanalyzed, in all of their crazy symbolic richness! It seems to be the humbler way and it certainly is easier than the way of the comparative inquirers. But the erotic lure of curiosity and ultimate longing drives comparing inquirers to seek out the grand encounter of Great Models in a drawn-out competition that serves their truth-seeking impulses. Think of it in football or ballet or gladiatorial or conversational terms; it makes little difference. In all cases, ultimacy dreaming becomes the domain of comparative evaluation.

The complex outcome is not for everyone, but I think it does have the considerable virtues of welcoming every model with a stake in the conversation, including all data that is pertinent to evaluating models, keeping track in an optimal way of the precise logical import of every argument made, and forcing claims for the likelihood of any given model to take honest account of the eager alternatives standing nearby ready to play or dance or attack or talk, depending on the analogy. Provisional decisions involve artful equilibration of numerous competing factors, as always in life. But the comparative inquirer makes those decisions with fair confidence that everything vital to the decision is at least showing up somewhere in the process—a virtue all too rare in the history of religious philosophy.

This is how we learn to trust our ultimacy dreams. Trust is hard-won, requiring critical analysis and comparative evaluation. And our ultimacy dreams may never resolve into conceptual clarity, in the way we might hope when half-awake and still flush with the dreamer's intoxication. But dreaming is not for nothing: we can advance through inquiry, we can discern better from worse, and we can engage the ultimate reality that inspires all our dreaming.

Chapter 2

Suffering

Introduction

NOTHING CONJURES THEOLOGICAL DREAMS MORE THAN THE REALITY OF SUF-
fering in nature. Suffering, in one way, is not a problem for philosophical theologians; it is the very lifeblood of their book-bent bodies. Every theological tradition
draws from the relentless power of suffering to make us seek dreams. Judaism
staggers under the weight of being chosen to suffer, Christianity has a crucifix at
its center, and Islam has the most profound construal of surrender imaginable.
Hinduism's samsaric vision frames suffering in serenity, Buddhism teaches us how
to escape it, and Chinese religion tells us how to organize our lives to manage it.
Occasionally we see philosophical theologians valiantly defending their chosen
faith in face of suffering, but this act of loyalty means something only to needy
believers and nasty detractors; such defenses are essentially a public service. Less
often we see philosophical theologians refusing the question, brushing it aside
with a story or a joke, or aggressively attacking defenders of the faith as somehow
betraying the very thing they seek to honor and protect. Bless us all. In the
ominous light of suffering, all theology is a kind of agonized writhing. But there
is nothing to be done for us. Again and again we return to the streets of suffering,
scouring the sidewalks for the penny we know must be there, the coin that will
make sense of everything.

Cursed to wander in search of secrets, then, let us not waste energy on
defending the universe or its divine heart, at least not when we are praying or
talking to one another. We will do our spirited public service defenses and our
dutiful institutional rationalizations when we must, of course. And there really
is no problem with any of that; obviously humanly recognizable divine goodness
can be defended in the face of suffering if we are determined enough. We have all
the standard tools ready to hand, from best-of-all-possible-worlds arguments to

unavoidable-side-effect-of-overriding-good arguments. If we get desperate, we can fall back on "God can't stop it," "God has a bigger plan," "God suffers with us," "It is not really real," or "Just wait until it is all put right." And if the arguments are not quite as compelling as we would like them to be, neither are the assaults on the overall goodness and meaning of life, the universe, and everything, so there is no need to panic. Our acts of institutional maintenance and defense are certainly successful enough to keep the hostile hordes at bay and to prevent ourselves from feeling that we are somehow sacrificing our intellectual dignity when we trust the goodness of the universe.

So let's take a deep breath, set all that aside, and return to our first obsession, our calling and our curse: the philosophical-theological task of speaking of ultimate reality in face of the proximate reality of suffering in nature. The varied phenomena of suffering in nature press hard upon all theories of ultimate reality. It is impossible to approach such an interpretative task without appreciation for the creativity displayed in intellectual efforts past and present, within Western cultures and outside them. Likewise, surrounded by the shards of past efforts, it is impossible to step so sure-footedly as to forget that before which we wander and play with our concepts, that greatest of all realities, which drives us to silence when we are most attentive to it and yet suffers our speculations without reproach. Humility is the philosophical theologian's byword, on pain of irrelevance.

A REVERENT COMPETITION AMONG THREE VIEWS OF GOD

It is for these reasons that I set out to bypass theodicies and defenses for now and to speak of ultimate realities instead. Rather than presuming one particular theory of ultimate reality for the sake of a meditation on suffering, however, I'm going to take less for granted and use suffering as a source of selective pressure on ideas of ultimate reality. I am particularly interested in the effects of a full awareness of the reality of suffering in nature on a reverent competition among three theological approaches to God, two of which are also accounts of ultimate reality, and all of which are important in the contemporary theological scene: agential-being theism, process theism, and ground-of-being theism (this reverent comparative competition is worked out in detail in Wildman 2017 and Wildman forthcoming). I'll endeavor not merely to describe these three approaches to speaking of God but also to express each one's beating heart and its fundamental attraction, thereby to discern the theological strategy for making sense of suffering in nature. This reverent competition will allow me to articulate why I think that ground-of-being theism best handles the problem of suffering in nature. This philosophical-theological view is an awkward partner for common human moral expectations but deeply attuned to the ways of nature and resonant with the wisdom about suffering that is encoded in many of the world's religious and philosophical traditions.

The intended audience for this argument is anyone interested in the topic, and it includes broadly theistic theologians, religious naturalists, metaphysicians, and both professional and amateur intellectuals from a variety of religious traditions. I fully realize that I cannot completely satisfy the legitimate intellectual demands of such a complex audience, but I am motivated to try. Some will say that my attempt to produce a general theological interpretation of suffering is intellectually futile and will urge me to pick a smaller audience within which I can realize their favorite theoretical virtue—namely, high confidence in the theological model relative to a religious group that can make use of it. It follows that not everyone is interested in philosophical theology as a kind of general inquiry, as I am. While I do not fault such objectors for their less general and more practical interests, I do think they should not prejudge the possible results of theological inquiry in a broader audience, particularly at the dawn of an unfamiliar era of comparative metaphysics.

I pause to comment on a terminological difficulty. I will treat these three views of God as types of theism. Some would argue that the word "theism" has become so closely associated with the personalist elements of agential-being and process views that it is misleading as a description of ground-of-being theologies. To put my response compactly, I contend that this personalistic focus in the doctrine of God is excessive. Within Christianity, it is a post-Reformation distortion, deeply linked to the "turn to the subject" in modern philosophy and theology. It also tends to reflect the economic and social values of middle-class suburban white Protestants. I am unwilling to allow the general category of theism to be held hostage to what I hope amounts to a passing trend in the history of Western Protestant Christian theology. But I acknowledge the terminological difficulty and do not want it to cloud or mask my view of ultimate reality as ground of being so I'll be clear when it matters.

AGENTIAL-BEING THEISM

The first view in our reverent competition is agential-being theism, which conceives God as an eternal, all-powerful being with a compassionate awareness of every circumstance and moment of suffering, the ability to act in history and nature, and the moral quality of humanly recognizable goodness to a supreme degree. This view can be called "personal theism" because its initial moves are to analogize the divine nature using the intentional and agential capacities of human persons, but I shall continue to refer to it as agential-being theism, which I think is a more accurate term. This is because the best of the agential-being views are not slaves to personal analogies. They make allowance for the ill-fitting aspects of personal analogies for God by introducing balancing symbols (see chapter 5). For example, the common metaphor of blinding light applied to the divine presence suggests that the divine wisdom would necessarily sometimes have to be incomprehensible and the divine will occasionally inscrutable. These balancing mechanisms resist the ever-present danger of anthropomorphism in God-talk. Indeed, the flatly anthropomorphic versions of these views are the object of aggressive attacks both externally from skeptics and internally in the sacred texts of all major theistic religious traditions. From both directions, the critiques regard excessively anthropomorphic views as superstitious, and thus (like all superstition) constantly in need of special pleading in face of the contraindicating evidence of worldly experience. By contrast, subtler anthropomorphic symbolism, balanced with non-anthropomorphic symbols for the sake of empirical adequacy, has played an essential role in all theistic religions.

Our proclivity toward anthropomorphism is due to the particularity of the human imagination. To this extent the projection analyses of religion from Feuerbach to Freud are correct: human beings must picture ultimate reality in terms of the highest and most profound reality they know, which is themselves, or at least their parents, their rulers, their warriors, their shamans, and their priests. And they are also obviously correct that this casts doubt upon all anthropomorphic picturing of ultimate reality. We can allow this and yet insist that nothing about projection strategies for interpreting ultimate reality entails atheism—neither the sheer fact that projections occur nor the reflexivity of their occurrence, neither their pervasiveness nor their moral dangers. This is where some of the projection theorists allowed the enthusiasm of new realization to lead them into theoretical distortion. As grappling with these critiques for more than a century has made clear, the world still demands theological interpretation in terms of ultimate realities even though projection reflexes are an inevitable accompaniment of such interpretations. The theological and practical religious challenge is to manage projection-driven, need-flushed, cognition-framed anthropomorphism, not to eschew it altogether, and by and large the great theistic traditions have done this. Those traditions have been particularly good at robustly critiquing the most obviously superstitious highly anthropomorphic agential-being views; their efforts in regard to the less obviously superstitious highly anthropomorphic agential-being views leave something to be desired.

What kind of agential being is the divine reality? Philosophical theologians giddy with the joy of speech may lose track of the fact that they construct answers to this question. They may attempt to evade responsibility by saying that they merely faithfully and thoughtfully update a tradition that bears forward an answer whose origins lie hidden in untold revelatory transactions, or by self-consciously submitting themselves to a purported revelation whose veracity lies beyond question on pain of banishment from one's beloved community of religious-theological companions. It makes no difference: we construct in our hermeneutical glosses, in our conceptual rearrangements, in our ignorant rediscoveries, in our claims of allegiance, in our self-righteous criticisms, and in our charges of improper novelty. And we incur responsibility as we do so.

Let's skip past the clever subterfuges whereby we pretend at merely receiving and handling sacred ideas. We should embrace the fate of philosophical theologians, which is to speak into life ideas of ultimate realities for each other and on behalf of the great traditions of spiritual practice and social organization that orient the living, including us, as we wander the tangled paths joining living memory to a future unknown. If we are lucky, our ideas of ultimate realities will resonate with the peculiar cosmic harmonies and noisy dissonances that test and constrain our speculations. If we are very lucky, our ideas will bring a measure of contentment and conviction, even though we know we will gladly surrender them as our deaths bring us near to the ultimate reality itself, which always looms before and hovers beneath us. And this is really what we are up to on this view: we are trying to make sense of our lives, of the lives of those we love, even of the lives of those we hate or whose experience we cannot comprehend. To this end, we take to ourselves the power to speak into reality the dreams we dream, to conjure and weave, to construct and argue. We will not shrink from our anthropomorphic instincts and their associated limitations, nor from our simple need to make sense of life in this vale of joy and tears.

With no evasions, then, what will we say is the determinate character of the ultimate reality we call God? We will assert, simply, what we most long to be true: that ultimate reality makes final, beautiful sense of everything; that in God there lies meaningful hope for the downtrodden, and even for our own sorry hearts; that God will make our souls live on in a perfectly purified realm whose proportions we can almost imagine but never realize in this world; that God can be the object of our love and will respond to us personally, knowingly, and graciously. Thus, God will be good in a humanly recognizable way, powerful in a way that is relevant to fulfilling our longings, all-knowing in a way that unmasks those longings, and benevolent in a way that forgives our stupid hatred and fear and self-destructiveness. If God needs to take action in our history and nature to secure the possibility of these unendingly desired outcomes, then God's providential mercy will bend to the task.

In short, God's determinate nature is known in our longings. Everything else we say theologically must serve this overridingly important vision of ultimate reality, and this becomes the *crucial criterion of agential-being theism*. It is anthropomorphic, yes. But our humanly shaped imaginative capacities open this reality up for us, so there should be no shame about constructing a theological vision of an environment for human life that matches our deepest longings. Our great hope is answered in the booming resonances of cosmic space and time, and the answer is yes! This is good news of the stunning, life-changing, shockingly apt sort.

Agential-being theism is fundamentally optimistic, magnificently anthropomorphic, and existentially thrilling. It stays close to the hopes and fears of ordinary human beings. It communicates to most people effectively and inspires sublime art and music and architecture. It requires that sacred texts be submitted to no more than a courteous minimum of demythologization, which really amounts to mere cultural updating. It has relatively few variants, and their battles with one another for credibility do not seriously threaten the big picture. So God may judge and damn the wicked, as our own vengeful hearts demand, or God may run the scythe of judgment through every heart and draw us all into the divine presence with grief-tinged joy and thankfulness; God may send suffering to advance an inscrutable plan or tolerate unwanted suffering for the sake of nurturing souls that can earnestly long for divine fellowship. Such disagreements do not wreck the coherent and attractive flavor of agential-being theism, with its central ideal of perfect personal goodness, so long as we are willing to regard them as subordinate details. Agential-being theism's portrayal of the divine personality mutates over cultures and eras, reflecting different fashions and changing human needs. Yet the same basic idea of God persists through all of these variations.

The crucial criterion associated with this blessed draught is uncompromising. Theologians devoted to a God that miraculously answers human longings are intensely sensitive to intellectual moves that dilute the strength of the brew or import alien elements that confuse its flavor. They find the most perfect recipes for their preferred drink in the sages of the past and are suspicious of new-fangled ideas that always and only seem to wreck perfection in the name of shortsighted, arrogant innovation. Yet they are also unafraid to translate their favorite recipe into the language of the day; there is not a trace of secret gnosis here. Theirs is a welcome and healing draught, after all, and compassionate souls can only commend it to their self-deluded and self-destructive companions on the way. More concretely, they unfailingly diagnose theological compromises with alien cultural wisdom as seductions to be resisted, and they typically see demytholo-gization programs as advancing other agendas that finally cannot be rendered compatible with their own. Yet they have no difficulty understanding that real wisdom may be present in religious traditions other than those they know best, for their vision of ultimate reality is not fatally undermined by the realization that there may be many authentic ways. Narrower theologies claiming exclusive prerogatives face an insoluble problem in the face of religious pluralism, but this agential-being vision of ultimate reality can be made every bit as capacious as it is perfectly fitted to human longings.

Compassionate forms of agential-being theism in our era tend to regard suf-fering in nature as an unfortunate byproduct of otherwise good natural processes. If God wanted to create creatures capable of freely entering into loving fellowship with their creator, then God would have no choice but to allow the natural evils that come with finitude and physicality and the moral evils that freedom brings. In an earlier era, these same theologians may have regarded suffering as divine pun-ishment or testing, or otherwise sent by God to achieve morally unimpeachable divine purposes. For example, the accidental death of a child was (in some con-texts still is) routinely interpreted as God taking the child for special divine com-panionship, and this could and still can bring genuine comfort to grieving parents willing to surrender to this vision of tragedy consistent with perfect divine love, even as it understandably drives others away from the God who selfishly abducted their beloved child.

Theological fashions aside, all of these agential-being views affirm that the world we inhabit is the best of all possible worlds. The crucial criterion absolutely requires this, and without it, the very point of agential-being theism in the form discussed here fails utterly. God must be good in a humanly recognizable way and powerful in a humanly relevant way for human longings to find their perfect answer in ultimate reality, for this creation to be a home rather than a hopeless and hostile environment for futile human writhing. Of course, the ultimate divine purpose for this world of suffering and love may remain rationally obscure, or clear only in the sense that confidence in revelation can make theological claims clear. But even then God's goodness, the creation's wondrous purpose, and the sacred meaning of every human life is assured. At root, this is the best of all possible worlds in the same sense that God is the best possible answer to human longings. The associated interpre-tation of suffering in nature weaves itself around this central axis.

PROCESS THEISM

Our reverent competition's second candidate is process theism. Importantly, this is not a theory of ultimate reality as such. The process God in most of its variations is one actual entity alongside many others that constitute the fluxing process of reality, albeit one with a special role. God's role is to maximize positive value in the cosmic process by making the greatest possible use of every configuration of events, including those involving suffering. God is not creator in this view, so God is certainly not all-powerful. Removing suffering is not a possibility now or at any future time, therefore, but making the most of every welcome occasion and each disastrous event is the perpetual divine responsibility. God does this by constituting the unfolding divine nature with the awareness of all that happens, arranged and related so as to maximize value and goodness. This leads to the first sense in which the process God is good literally by definition: the so-called consequent divine nature is maximally good by construction in and through its prehension or feeling of the world process itself. The other sense in which God is good by definition derives from the process account of causation: God conveys to every moment of the world's process a vision of possibilities that functions as a lure toward beauty, goodness, and truth appropriate to each kind and level of event. The source of this lure is fundamentally the so-called primordial nature of God, which is a wondrous vision of possibilities. God's goodness is postulated at each pole of this dipolar theism, and it is humanly recognizable goodness, at least at our level of complexity.

The goodness of God is assured by definition, therefore, but key questions about ultimate reality remain open, including what it is and whether it is good. Most versions of process theism do not seek a theory of ultimate reality in the form of a God concept. On the contrary, the God concept of process theology—whether in Whitehead's "single actual entity" form or Hartshorne's "society of actual occasions" form (Whitehead 1978; Hartshorne 1948)—is practical for human beings only to the extent that it does not repeat the mistakes of the past, premier among which is to make of God an ultimate reality. This stance does not make a theory of ultimate reality impossible, but it does entail that a process-based theory of ultimate reality, though it includes the process God, must go well beyond God to encompass the various principles to which the cosmos and God alike are subject. Whitehead's philosophical cosmology, as expressed in *Process and Reality,* is pluralistic: there are many fundamental categories. Ultimate reality is not one thing, the ontological solution to the philosopher's problem of "the one and the many" (see part 3); rather, it is the pattern by which creativity perpetually produces one from many. It is that which is closest to experience and thus the least abstract and most pervasive feature of reality. In this sense it is what is ultimate about reality. But it is not God, even though, like all processes within reality, God expresses it.

The basic philosophical-theological instinct of process theism is easy to recognize and deeply moving. It aims to deliver us from an unhealthy obsession with an illusory picture of God. Process theologians are the very few theologians who resist the drug of ultimacy speech in the name of usefulness; they can feel the tug to partake of the brew, but they just say no. If we surrender our attachment to a God of infinite power who creates everything, makes sense of everything, and finally gives meaning to everything, then we can open ourselves to a more modest but more concretely satisfying and prophetically relevant picture of God. The plausibility of traditional agential-being theism is massively strained by our ordinary experience of life. We see around us not a perfectly good world, and certainly not anything that would recommend the idea of a perfectly good omnipotent creator. Rather, our experience suggests that reality is a morally neutral environment for the interplay of a host of processes, within which we witness both beauty and goodness, on the one hand, and disintegration and pointless suffering, on the other.

This shows us that traditional agential-being theism is anthropomorphism run amok; it is a stubborn assertion of human longings against the unrelenting facts of existence. Our attachment to such a picture of God is self-delusory and, in the long run, distorts our view of everything else. Process theism beckons us to move toward a divine light of a different sort, one in which God is explicitly aligned with the parts of the cosmic process that make for beauty and goodness. Stop coercing the cosmos to fit a God-concept driven by over-expansive human longings! Exchange that rapacious God-concept for one actually fitted to human spiritual longings and moral aspirations, and the theodicy problem evaporates. The price for this invaluable benefit is merely surrendering the futile quest for a morally comprehensible ultimate reality.

The deep intuition here is that anthropomorphic instincts in theology work only when they are limited to the patterns and parts of the world process that are scaled to human longings. To project human longings and expectations beyond this limit is, unsurprisingly, intellectually self-defeating and spiritually frustrating. Let the whole of reality be what it is! It is a relief to lower one's eyes and to focus on making concrete sense of our longings and aspirations in relation to the world of our actual experience. In this world many things occur that threaten to destroy us, from accidents to natural disasters, from predators to human stupidity. Instead of calling these things good, as seems to be demanded in some sense when we say they are the creations of a recognizably good deity, just stop trying to make human-friendly meaning out of them. They are threats to the integration of goodness and beauty at human and other levels, even if they are co-conditions of integration and emergence. But nothing stops us from picturing God as unambiguously on the side of maximizing values of goodness and beauty. Taking refuge in this God, we shield ourselves from the harsh light of the entire world process, which is as hostile to life as it is supportive.

For the traditional agential-being view, an asteroid slamming into the Earth and destroying the human species is an unfortunate side effect of a process that God created and sustains for the sake of higher goods, and the (severe) problem is why God did not intervene to prevent the destruction of an entire ecosphere. On the process view this is a disaster, period, and God is left to integrate the horrible consequences of an event beyond divine control into the divine nature. Whereas we may have difficulty relating humanly to the God who creates a world with such possibilities, we have no trouble relating to a God who does not control such events but is left to pick up the pieces afterwards. That's what we do! This shows why anthropomorphism must be limited to the domain within which process theism operates, and also both why it works well within that domain and why it works badly beyond it.

Nothing stops us speculating on ultimate reality within the process framework. Indeed, we might integrate the pluralistic process conception of ultimate reality into a competing idea of God. This gives us two candidates for the use of the word "God"—the process entity, GodP (P for Process), which is scaled to most human spiritual longings and moral intuitions, and creativity itself, GodC (C for Creativity), which is the source of both pain and pleasure, purpose and pointlessness.

Process theologians hold that GodC is religiously useless because it is morally impenetrable, so most resolutely ignore it and advise others to do likewise. Specifically, the process view alleges that traditional agential-being theists deeply mischaracterize GodC when they say it is good in a humanly recognizable way, and wrongly assert that GodC is able to bring meaning to everything that happens in a way that reflects a personal center of consciousness. Whatever GodC is, on the process account, it is exceedingly resistant to anthropomorphic modeling, and certainly nothing like the personal God of so many sacred texts and religious pieties. The human-like activity and moral sense of GodP are what matters to most human beings and to the human species thought of as a civilizational, cultural, and moral project. Process theologians can launch their prophetic critiques of injustice from the secure basis of a God who is unambiguously good, our ally in a wildly morally ambiguous ultimate reality.

If GodC is what matters to some philosophical theologians, it is because they love what can neither be rationally comprehended nor morally assimilated. To the process theologian, this is another unhealthy intellectual obsession with no concrete benefits for the world and only perplexity and despair for the ones so magnificently obsessed. Process theists would gladly liberate their philosophical-theological companions ensnared in the conceptual chaos of trying to conceptualize ultimate reality, whether because of overreaching anthropomorphism that arrogantly forgets its proper limits (as with the agential-being theists) or because of obsession with ultimacy beyond the limits of anthropomorphic aptness (as with the ground-of-being theists). But process theists know from hard experience that not everyone shares their instincts about what is important and useful and valuable. Some philosophical theologians willingly enslave themselves to an impossible master, after which the delusion that the master is good and loving causes only the most exquisite agony, the agony of the slave who cannot afford the luxury of seeing things as they manifestly are, and can survive only in a world woven from illusions.

GROUND-OF-BEING THEISM

The third view in our reverent competition is ground-of-being theism. Ground-of-being theisms deny that God is an agential being. Their theological advocates are deeply wary of anthropomorphism in theology. As the metaphor "ground of being" suggests, they tend to look toward universal features of reality rather than to exceptional features such as human beings for imaginative symbolic material. Though ground-of-being theisms are theory-building efforts rather than apophatic in themselves, they are often aligned with apophatic traditions in philosophical theology because they are stations on the way to refusing theological speech in a kind of mute testimony to that which finally transcends human cognitive abilities. They have a rich heritage in Western and South-Asian philosophical-theological traditions, and in more naturalistic forms within Chinese philosophy. Indeed, they are strikingly similar across these cultural boundaries, particularly in their refusal to tame ultimate realities with humanly recognizable moral categories and in their rejection of an intentional, agential divine consciousness.

Ground-of-being theists share points of agreement with their rivals. On the one hand, they concur with the process critique of the traditional forms of agential-being theism just mentioned. There surely is a place for anthropomorphic modeling in theology, but ground-of-being theism and process theism alike say that agential-being theists slip into a world of illusions when they suppose that the creator GodC is good in a humanly recognizable way. On the other hand, ground-of-being theists share the agential-being theists' instinct to bypass the process deity GodP in favor of the creativity deity GodC. Like traditional agential-being theists, ground-of-being theists are obsessed with the ultimate reality from which the process theist turns away in the name of religious and moral relevance; they willingly enslave themselves to the complexities and perplexities of thinking of ultimate reality as God.

Ultimate-reality-enslaved ground-of-being and agential-being theists do not just docilely accept the process theologians' charge of futile attachment. They retort that process theology is precisely the wrong kind of anthropomorphically woven tapestry of illusion. GodP, they argue, is a condensation of humanly supportive trajectories in the universe that happily skips over the rest in a kind of half-hearted and half-spoken Manichaeism. GodP is a mere invention, with the conceptual level pitched to guarantee divine goodness, to ramify religious hopes and beliefs, and to leverage prophetic transformation. The process refusal to link God with ultimate reality is an arbitrary constricting of the philosophical-theological purview and a betrayal of the philosophical theologian's Promethean calling.

This mutual recrimination over brazen anthropomorphism and futile attachments is one of the exquisite ironies of contemporary theology. The acceptance in our time of a theological viewpoint that eschews a theology of ultimate reality—a rejection formerly unthinkable in orthodox theological circles within all of the theistic religions, yet deeply resonant with some of the portrayals of God in sacred texts—makes this irony possible. Is ultimate reality our bane or our blessing? Should we flee the theologian's self-appointed calling in the name of moral intelligibility or embrace it no matter what the cost? These questions hint at an existentially profound difference in the instincts of contemporary philosophical theologians.

Of course, ground-of-being philosophical theologians participate in these recriminations but also claim unique theoretical virtues and are subject to distinctive criticisms. In offering a theory of ultimate reality, they share the virtues of agential-being theism, while in refusing to say that the creativity deity GodC is good in a humanly recognizable way, they share in the empirically robust realism of process theology. But the endpoint—an ultimate reality not personally good in a humanly recognizable way—can this even be called a worship-worthy God? Agential-being theists argue that the ground-of-being theists' refusal to see ultimate goodness in the heart of reality deals a killing blow to the human aspiration to feel at home in the universe and to believe that human lives have purpose and meaning; that defeats the whole point of theism. Process theists would not put it that way, of course, but they would echo the criticism by saying that the word "God" has to be aligned with goodness at human scales or else it loses its religious relevance. Ground-of-being theism only confirms the process theologian's suspicion that GodC is religiously useless. At least the agential-being theists make an effort to preserve religious relevance by insisting that GodC is good in a humanly recognizable way! Ground-of-being theists basically accept the process theist's analysis of ultimate reality as conceptually incomprehensible and morally impenetrable but then call it "God" anyway. This, say process critics, is more an abuse of terminology than their own alleged misuse of the word "God" for something other than ultimate reality.

Ground-of-being philosophical theologians seek an empirically adequate theory of ultimate reality, and this drives their refusal to allow that this ultimate can be unambiguously morally good. These views tend to regard suffering as ontologically co-primal with creativity in the divine life and in the world. Thus, they do not treat suffering as an unwanted side effect of otherwise good natural processes and good divine purposes; to do this (as agential-being theists do) is an exercise in futility when the unwanted side effects are not minor but rather, on average, of about the same size and importance as the good events. They do not associate God only with human-scaled and human-focused goodness; to do this (as process theists do) would be merely to attribute to God the dubious quality of being convenient for human beings. Ground-of-being philosophical theologians do not affirm that this is the best of all possible worlds; claiming that all of reality is finally good is a mere clutching at straws within the whirlwind of creativity and suffering that spins us around. To what, then, does this interpretation of ultimate reality lead? And why go there?

I return to these questions below. For now I note the fundamental instinctive difference between ground-of-being theism and its competitors in this reverent contest. In a supermarket full of potential theological virtues, and being on a tight budget, ground-of-being theists spend their money on plausibility rather than religious appeal, making the most of the latter, given what the former allows. In the human-longings aisle, they would mistrust some of the prominent items that promise to satiate spiritual hunger, and they would scour the hard-to-reach top and bottom shelves for affordable nutrition. They would stubbornly refuse to be lured by colorful claims of ultimate intelligibility, ultimate meaning, ultimate purpose, and ultimate justice, and instead stalk the realism and deference aisles, looking for simple, everyday items that deliver these wonders in more modest measure. Perhaps this reflects a kind of disappointment, a failure of human longings; it certainly expresses a determined effort to accept ultimate and proximate reality.

If our reverent competition reduces to a mere choice among theological personality styles—and surely such considerations are relevant—then this is where we stand. The agential-being theists are the optimists and fight against disbelief. They prize reality as ultimately good and human life as ultimately meaningful above all. Those who do not, they interpret as stubbornly, self-destructively refusing to accept the wondrous miracle that the character and purposes of ultimate reality are limned in human longings. The process theists are the activists and fight against soporific delusions. They value religious relevance, rational intelligibility, moral clarity, and transformative action above all and so refuse to speculate on ultimate reality while resolutely affirming an alliance between God and human interests. They interpret those who see things differently as in thrall to the illusory mythic sentiment that ultimate reality is a proper object of human religious and intellectual instincts. The ground-of-being theists are the mystics and fight against resentment. They treasure above all the whole of reality as it is without illusions and without limitations to human interests and longings, and they surrender themselves to it, whatever it may be, and without reserve. They interpret those who do not as unable to cope with life as it most truly is and as understandably but mistakenly reserving their love for an idealized, humanized image of God.

The Bane of Anthropomorphism

I naturally resonate with and feel some attraction toward all three of these ways of conceiving God in relation to the challenge of suffering in nature. Yet I argue that the alternatives to ground-of-being theism face significant conceptual problems in mounting their response and that these problems derive chiefly from trying to make of God a moral agent unambiguously good in a humanly recognizable way—an assertion both alternatives to ground-of-being theism hold in common.

The Argument from Neglect

Agential-being theism must face what I call the "argument from neglect." This argument contends that the agential-being theist's conception of God does not rise even to human standards of goodness and so certainly is not humanly recognizable as perfectly morally good in a way that befits deity. The argument turns on an analogy with human parents, as follows.

A human parent, indeed parents in many species, must constantly balance the need to protect and guide offspring with the need to allow the offspring freedom to learn. Loving parents do not hesitate to intervene in a child's life when they discern that ignorance or mischievousness or wickedness is about to cause serious trouble and perhaps irreparable disaster. Parents rescue the child, interjecting education, punishment, or encouragement as needed. As time goes on, children need less guidance but parental interference rightly persists until the child is independent. Wise parental interference does not limit a child's freedom; on the contrary, it enhances it by protecting the child from freedom-destroying injuries and character defects, and by leading them patiently but surely toward freedom-enhancing independence and moral responsibility. We hold parents negligent, and sometimes criminally negligent, when they fail to intervene when necessary for the sake of their child's safety and well-being.

Human beings are like children in respect of moral and social-civilizational matters. God, on the agential-being theist's account, has all of these responsibilities in relation to human beings that human parents have in relation to their children. God should intervene to educate and guide, to punish and redirect. If it is claimed that this does in fact occur, then it certainly does not occur often or effectively enough for God to avoid the same charge of negligence that we would bring upon a human parent acting in similar fashion.

I think creatures besides human beings have a claim on parental protection and nurture from an agential-being God. This becomes an especially important point in relation to natural disasters, where the scale of injury and death in other species is frequently far larger than the human losses we most notice. Animals may not be able to raise their voice in complaint, but human beings can do so on their behalf. Together, we feel neglected, exposed to the elements, and left to comfort ourselves with illusions of ultimate love and perfect nurture that experience finally does not support. We get our love and protection, our education and wisdom, not from God's parental activity but from our own good fortune at living in a cosmic era with few solar-system collisions, from our own determination to build stable and rewarding civilizations, and from our own discoveries about the world that we pass along to our children. The idea of God as protective, solicitous parent may make a difference in our lives in the way that a wondrous story can bring comfort and solace, but that is as far as it goes.

THE ARGUMENT FROM INCOMPETENCE

Ground-of-being theism is immune to the argument from neglect, but process theism is vulnerable to a variant of it. Process theism properly and predictably replies to the argument from neglect that God is always trying the divine hardest to educate and alleviate suffering in ultimate reality, which is partly hospitable and partly hostile to human interests. But then the well-earned counter-reply is that the process GodP may not be negligent but certainly is incompetent. In other words, in what I call the "argument from incompetence," GodP is not powerful enough to merit our worship and allegiance, and we should go in search of GodC—the only deity that finally matters, even if its moral character is indigestible.

Of course, if a philosophical-theological interpretation of suffering in nature requires a theory of ultimate reality, then process theology was never a candidate anyway. If our aim is less systematic—say, intellectual support for a religiously relevant response to suffering in nature—then process theology may be the right sort of proposal, but it is, as I have tried to show here, inadequate. Note that the argument from incompetence does not demonstrate the incoherence of the process idea of God but merely its religious ineffectualness specifically in response to suffering, contrary to claims that its supporters typically make on its behalf. In the case of the argument from neglect, the target is the conceptual coherence of agential-being theism.

THE ALTERNATIVE: RELIGIOUS INDIGESTION OR THE BREATH OF LIFE?

Ground-of-being theism is immune to the argument from neglect and the argument from incompetence. But at what price? Its rejection of a personal center of divine consciousness and activity is religiously indigestible to many people, and knocking out two of its major competitors is the very opposite of a good outcome for such folk. Ground-of-being theism simply does not meet their basic criteria for acceptability as an interpretation of God. So they will understandably continue the struggle on behalf of agential-being and process theisms, loyally representing the interests of their religious constituencies.

Meanwhile, ground-of-being theism is the very breath of spiritual life for some other people. It has a lot to commend it, particularly in relation to the problem of suffering in nature, so long as the ruling theological criteria allow both suffering and blessing to flow from the divine nature itself. This is simply too much for many and yet simply perfect for some. Recognizing this apparently unbridgeable chasm between conflicting philosophical-theological and religious intuitions, I am not eager to persuade others to embrace ground-of-being models of ultimate reality. Rather, I want to argue that ground-of-being theism, so often neglected in contemporary philosophical theology, should be taken with great seriousness as an intellectually compelling account of ultimate reality, even though it is exactly what it seems: a threat to agential-being and process forms of theism. Given the conceptual structure of the problem of God in relation to suffering in nature, moreover, if ground-of-being theism is to be seen as a threat at all, then it should be seen as a major threat rather than a negligible one.

THE BLESSING OF GROUND-OF-BEING THEISM

I am arguing that ground-of-being theism should be taken seriously as a theological interpretation of ultimate reality in relation to the challenge of suffering in nature. The reasons go well beyond its immunity to the argument from neglect and the argument from incompetence. In fact, there are two types of reasons (see Wildman 2017 for a complete analysis).

On the one hand, ground-of-being theism possesses native strengths. Some of these are theoretical and derive from placing ultimate reality close to the world of nature as its ontological ground. Other strengths are practical and draw on the advantages for any authenticity-based spiritual quest of accepting the world as it is without evasion or dreaming.

On the other hand, ground-of-being theologies highlight the weaknesses of alternatives. Moral and theological interpretations of suffering in nature rely on a range of argumentative resources that function as vital strategies in theodicies, defenses, and the like. Agential-being and sometimes process theists use some of these resources to deflect criticisms of their ideas of God based on suffering in nature, including criticisms such as the argument from neglect and the argument from incompetence. In the searing light of ground-of-being theism, many of these strategic resources are not as useful as they may appear at first, and they seem to be little more than shrouded repetitions of the fundamental criteria that determine what counts as an acceptable theological approach.

In what follows, I consider both types of reasons, sometimes together, in a series of brief reflections on traditional strategies within philosophical-theological debates over suffering.

HISTORICAL AND ECONOMIC AWARENESS

Most people in our time living in so-called developed nations typically have high expectations for comfortable and satisfying lives. They expect to avoid many illnesses and to recover from the illnesses they must endure. They expect children to be born healthy, mothers to survive childbirth, and children to grow up and live long lives. They expect that nutritious and tasty food will never be a problem for them and that they can live in comfort with a wide range of pleasurable activities to fill their days in a fundamentally stable society. If they get bored or sad, they expect to be able to make lifestyle decisions to mitigate the problem. They expect to be well educated, spiritually nurtured, legally defended, and militarily protected. They expect that technology will shield them and those they love from the ravages of nature in all its forms.

Such people differ on ideals of distributive justice, with some wanting to share the wealth and others insisting that the poor and afflicted figure out how to solve their own problems, "just like we did." The religious among them tend to believe that life under this description is a divine blessing even if they take it for granted. Their experience of God typically includes involvement in a religious group where most people experience life much the same way they do, ritual rites of passage with cameras flashing and video recorders preserving memories, and moments of spiritual insight involving God's gracious forgiveness and acceptance and support. Untimely death is rare and so God is seen more as comforter in the face of death than as bringer of death. Disasters are uncommon and tend to be far off so God is seen more in the generous and caring responses than in the disasters themselves.

Everyone with any historical sense and any cross-cultural experience understands that this lifestyle and the expectations it creates are exceptional, not typical. It is more difficult to grasp the exceptional nature of the view of God that most people living this way hold. Theistically minded people in other places and eras tended and still tend to see God behind all life events, both the satisfying and the tragic, both the comforting and the discomfiting, both the welcome and the terrifying. They have few expectations that God will make their life circumstances safe and happy, understanding from their own experience even in childhood that they will have to accept unwelcome life events very often in their many fewer than three-score-and-ten-year lifespans. As a result, they tend to see everything that happens as part of the manifestation of divine glory, and they expect that happiness will have to come from an internal spiritual connection to God rather than from cultural and economic conditions.

The case I am making really requires comparative survey data for its synchronic, economic wing and historical analysis of theological opinions among ordinary people for its diachronic wing. I can present neither here, but such data do exist both in the form of international surveys and historical studies of sermons at times of tragedy or popular religious opinions as reflected in the press—see, for example, the extensive literature on the Lisbon Earthquake of 1755. Saying "God sent this disaster for inscrutable reasons" used to work better than it does now as a comforting, realistic response to unexpected tragedy. In many places today, this response causes outrage, tainting the picture of God's perfect "wouldn't hurt a flea" goodness. I am arguing that the ideal of humanly recognizable and humanly relevant goodness is a cultural construction and that it can deeply influence what we are prepared to accept as a plausible theological interpretation of God in relation to suffering.

Perhaps some agential-being theists will say that our comparatively magnificent cultural circumstances have allowed us both to realize that God truly is good in just this way and to throw off the comforting but heavy cloak of God standing behind every event, no matter how painful for human and other sentient beings. Perhaps some process theists will point out that their theological view has become a mainstream option for the first time in an era and within cultures where human control over suffering is such that surrendering the omnipotence of God can seem sensible rather than ridiculous, thus disclosing the way things really are. Seeing this cultural and historical variability in ideas of divine goodness, the ground-of-being theist will continue to praise the divine glory rather than vaunt the divine goodness. They will feel a great sense of solidarity with less comfortable life companions past and present. And they will feel that, in one respect at least, their theological interpretation of God in relation to suffering in nature is not a slave to cultural fashions and economic circumstances.

PHILOSOPHICAL-THEOLOGICAL SIGNIFICANCE OF THE GROUND OF BEING

Speaking of God as the ground of being removes the possibility of proposing a divine character that is profoundly different from the character of the world. This is its chief theological difference from its competitors. Agential-being theism requires a divine goodness that our best scientific vision of the cosmos does not easily support and so positively requires some ontological distance between God and the world and a layer of philosophical-theological machinery to explain why the world is the way it appears to be despite the purported impeccability of God's moral character. Process theism associates God's moral character with some but not all aspects of worldly events, thereby framing God as endorsing and similar to the good aspects of natural events but resisting and unlike the bad. Ground-of-being theism needs neither to explain a discrepancy nor to distinguish among events to articulate the divine nature. The ground of being is the fecund source of all events, regardless of whether human standards in play at a particular time and place would classify them as good, bad, or neutral.

But does this not merely sanctify the world as it is? Indeed, it does, in the particular sense that all structures and possibilities of reality express the divine character. But those expressions include causal patterns and necessities, which also manifest the determinateness of the divine character. Some of these patterns make for life and meaning and some for pointless annihilation; and both possibilities are grounded in the divine nature. The moral conundrum for human beings is not the process theist's bracing Manichaean or Zoroastrian challenge to join the divine side against the chaos of anarchic freedom, but rather the challenge to decide which part of the divine nature we truly wish to engage. Can we choose purposelessness, violence, and cruelty? Yes, and God awaits us along that path as self-destruction and nihility. Should we choose to create meaning, nurture children, and spread justice? If we do, the possibility itself is a divinely grounded one. Does God care which way we choose? God is not in the caring business, on this view. The divine particularity is expressed in the structured possibilities and interconnections of worldly existence; perceiving and judging, wanting and choosing constitute the human role.

Agential-being theists and process theists alike will feel deeply worried about this refusal to align God with a particular moral path. But this merely repeats the quick (but I hope well-earned) caricatures of the former as the optimists and the latter as the activists. By contrast, ground-of-being theists are the mystics who see divine depth in the way things are. This places ground-of-being theism simultaneously close to some forms of religious naturalism, to some forms of apophatic mysticism, to some forms of Hindu and Buddhist philosophy, to some forms of Chinese philosophy, and to some forms of atheism. The distinctions among these views are only crisp when God is an agential being; otherwise they merge in a way that is profoundly satisfying to the ground-of-being theist. In fact, this merging of apparently different views is one of the powerful theoretical virtues of ground-of-being theism.

SPIRITUAL SIGNIFICANCE OF THE GROUND OF BEING

There is a spiritual corollary of the theological decision to place God close to the world as the ground of its being: existentially authentic acceptance of the world's fundamental character is equivalent to love of and submission to God. Despite the mention of God here, the underlying concept is such that there are obvious resonances with the South Asian spiritual instinct that "samsara is nirvana," including in its atheistic Buddhist form. Does this spiritual posture entail that one does nothing about the world as one finds it? No, and here the resonances are more with Friedrich Nietzsche. Nietzsche declared the death of God in much the way that ground-of-being theism rejects agential-being theisms.

What this means morally and spiritually, for individuals and entire civilizations alike, is that human beings must accept not only the world with its structured possibilities but also their capacity to choose; indeed, choice is one of those structured possibilities. On this view, the fulcrum for human moral action lies where it always has, despite all theological obfuscations: with human decision. God does not advocate or resist the decisions we make because God ontologically supports all decisions. Improving the world and making it more just is one of the choices before us. This is an invigorating challenge but also terrifying, as Nietzsche pointed out. He praised the spiritual vivaciousness of the one who can take full responsibility for choosing, without any hint of evasion and without any pretense that God favors one choice or another. This is spiritual maturity in the ground-of-being framework.

IS THIS THE BEST OF ALL POSSIBLE WORLDS?

We can love an optimally good world even if it causes us suffering and even if we feel wide-hearted compassion for other suffering creatures. We may forget our love in a moment of pain, but the habits of trust and acceptance formed in those times when we feel that the world is good to us bring courage and resolve when we need it most, under the burden of suffering. Some may think that cultivating love for a suffering-filled world is a conceptual trick whose essential purpose, regardless of how we rationalize it, is to cope. Indeed, Buddhist phenomenological and psychotherapeutic analyses of responses to suffering disclose a maze of deflections and projections, attachments and distortions that loom over our noble arguments about the world's optimal goodness and press hard the question of sincerity. But in this vale of tears, there are many valuable paths, and some take us into the perpetually uneasy realm of conceptual reasoning and moral judgments about the optimal goodness of the world. We can go there, warily perhaps, but not in total despair.

Is this world optimally good? More precisely, let "suffering landscape" refer to the forms and extent and intensity of suffering relative to the potential for emergent complexity, all within a particular ecosphere. Is the suffering landscape of Earth's natural history and present ecosystem consistent with this being the best of all possible worlds? I think that the possibility of alternative cosmic, geophysical, biological, and nutritional arrangements with varying suffering landscapes is difficult to block from a scientific point of view. In fact, there is significant scientific evidence that these alternatives should be possible, particularly alternative geologies (e.g., fewer tectonic plates) and alternative biologies (e.g., ecologies with different nutrition profiles). We cannot show this decisively because it turns on historical accidents or requires different physical or cosmic contexts.

But we can know with some confidence that we are not entitled to assume that Earth's suffering landscape indicates the best of all possible worlds.

This is an important negative conclusion. It strongly suggests that speaking theologically of "the best of all possible worlds" drives against empirical data for the sake of defending a particular conception of divine goodness. But agential-being theists might attempt to rehabilitate the best-of-all-possible-worlds claim by making it empirically more robust. They can enlarge the scope of this claim to include not only the Earth's suffering landscape, past and present and future, but also the suffering landscapes in every physically (not logically!) possible world. Indeed, if we take the multiverse possibility as a physical reality, then we need to include even suffering landscapes in other universes, relatively few of which would seem hospitable to life and suffering. In that case, the multiverse, of which there is only one, may indeed be the best of all possible worlds. We have rid ourselves of invidious comparisons to other real scenarios because there can only be one multiverse.

Unfortunately, this may not help us to love the world we are in. In the traditional form of the best-of-all-possible-worlds claim, all beings suffer to greater and lesser degrees. We feel sympathy for those who suffer greatly and perhaps begrudge the luck of those who barely taste the bile of misery, but these variations are part of accepting that this is the best of all possible worlds. A principle of plenitude embraces the earth's ecosphere: every kind of suffering and elation will come to light in this strange place, and this necessity for fullness means that there can be no complaint against the Earth and its Great Mother if you happen to dwell in the dark lands of suffering; it is all still worthy of deference and even worship.

There is an analogy here with the rehabilitated best-of-all-possible-worlds claim: there may be one multiverse, but there are many suffering landscapes, and a principle of plenitude governs the whole. Earth may happen to have a middling suffering landscape, a high-suffering one, or a low-suffering one. Regardless of our good fortune or cursed bad luck, this is still the best of all possible multiverses—so we tell ourselves.

Yet, just as the members of a poverty-stricken family suffering from needless disease, brutal government suppression, and raging tsunamis might long to exchange places with a more fortunate family, so we might long to exchange our entire planet's suffering landscape for that of a more fortunate locale, where the lyrical theme of emergence is less flawed by the discordant accompaniment of intense and pervasive suffering. Just as the family finds it hard to love its context, so we might understandably find it difficult to love the inferior world in which we find ourselves. And just as it is no comfort to the family to point out that "this is the way the Earth works; it is all good," so it is no comfort to us when we hear ourselves saying, with tremulous voice, that this is the way the multiverse works—the fact that things are less than optimal here is merely the price paid for the other fact that somewhere (but not here!) there exists a blessedness that makes this the best of all possible multiverses.

I think agential-being theism is in desperate difficulty in relation to this empirically realistic version of the best-of-all-possible-worlds claim. It involves allowing that a compassionate, personally interested, and active divine being tolerates entire worlds with unfortunate suffering landscapes while also beholding worlds with optimal conditions. That's tough to digest. Despite its starkness, however, perhaps this difficulty is not much more severe than that of the traditional form of the best-of-all-possible-worlds claim, in which the hands of broken-hearted God are tied when it comes to individual moments of suffering—restraint for the sake of the greater systemic good—and yet we still affirm humanly recognizable divine goodness.

These considerations show how poor the best-of-all-possible-worlds claim is as a strategy for articulating an interpretation of suffering in nature relative to agential-being theism. In my view, agential-being theists may be wisest to postulate that, despite the suggestions of contemporary science, there is no variability in suffering landscapes, perhaps because there is no other life-supporting place in the multiverse, so that the landscape of this and every world is and would be the same, and that this universal suffering landscape is also the best possible suffering landscape. The anthropocentrism of this view is bitter medicine, but this is what is required to leave the best-of-all-possible-worlds claim in tolerable health.

Of course, neither process theism nor ground-of-being theism needs to resort to such artifices. Both can take the world just as it is in all its variations and disagree only on how to picture God's relation to it all.

IS SUFFERING AN INEVITABLE BYPRODUCT OF GOOD DIVINE INTENTIONS?

A related strategy is to argue that suffering is the necessary byproduct of one or another overridingly valuable state of affairs, such as self-consciousness, moral freedom, spirituality, creativity, relationality, love, the capacity for a relationship with God, the incarnation of Christ, self-cultivation to the point of sagehood, the realization of bodhisattvas, or the ability to attain enlightenment. I think it is incontestable that some degree of suffering is indeed an inevitable byproduct of an ecosystem capable of supporting such virtues. The connection between desired outcome and suffering is indissoluble and rooted in the evolutionary realities of emergent complexity.

Neither process theists nor ground-of-being theists have to worry about the puzzles this fact may pose for a view of God, but agential-being theists have a lot at stake. Agential-being theism needs to establish the best-of-all-possible-worlds claim for the sake of its vision of divine goodness, and the inevitable-byproduct argument is meaningful only if it serves that end. With that in mind, more is required if the suffering-as-inevitable-byproduct strategy is to be useful for agential-being theists. It is not enough that desirable virtues entail *some* degree of suffering. We need to have reason to believe that they entail the *particular* suffering landscape of earth, or of the cosmos, or of the multiverse. Might not the same virtues emerge in a slightly different biological or geophysical setting with less actual suffering than we see here? Thus, this suffering-as-inevitable-byproduct strategy does not appreciably assist the agential-being theist in establishing that this is the best of all possible worlds.

IS SUFFERING FUNDAMENTAL?

Rather than trying to interpret suffering as one component in a complex emergent world, appearing only with the emergence of life, it is possible to broaden the ordinary meaning of the world and make suffering fundamental to the whole of reality. Buddhist philosophical cosmology routinely makes this move, particularly in its South Asian rather than its traditional Chinese forms. The *pratītya samutpāda* (dependent co-arising) account of reality specifically denies that objects and entities have "own being" or essential individuation. Rather, all realities are bundles of relations that emerge from the web of interdependent connectedness. By the traditional standards of Western philosophy, this Buddhist approach to philosophical cosmology seems out of balance, overstressing relationality and failing to register the intrinsic elements of the entities that, admittedly, always stand in relation to one another. But Buddhists take heart from the fact that advancing science, especially in the quantum world of the very small, is making it increasingly difficult to say what a substance is independently of its relations. They regard this as confirming their contention that everything arises in dependent correlation with everything else, and even their particularly intense form of this affirmation that denies independent subsistence to entities of all kinds.

Buddhists are especially interested in human life, as are most religions, but this philosophical cosmology has significance for suffering in nature also. Thinking through the lens of the First Noble Truth, which asserts that all is suffering, Buddhist philosophers came to view *dukkha,* or suffering, as the immediate and inevitable consequence of *pratītya samutpāda.* There is nothing without suffering because suffering is rooted in relationality and change (*viparinā-ma-dukkha*) and simply in being-conditioned (*saṅkhāra-dukkha*). In its particularly complex forms, as in human life, suffering can be analyzed as attachment to the apparently-but-not-actually real, a problem that can be solved through following the Noble Eightfold Path toward *moksha* or liberation. But suffering already arises in nonhuman settings as a correlate of change and being-conditioned. Suffering is universal. Buddhists fight over what liberation means, not least because certain understandings of it, such as suffering-free compassionate presence, suggest a greater distinction between *pratītya samutpāda* and *dukkha* than the philosophical cosmology allows. This is why the doctrine of emptiness, or *śūnyāta*, is so important to Buddhist philosophy. As difficult as it is to speak about the liberated state as *śūnyāta*, this is the deep entailment of any philosophical cosmology that places *pratītya samutpāda* and *dukkha* in such tight connection.

I see no intrinsic problems with this broad and general usage of suffering and the metaphysical visions it sponsors. Importantly, it is easily compatible with a ground-of-being theism, while being more of a stretch for process theology, which has a different account of what is fundamental at much the same level as a *pratītya samutpāda* cosmology. But we need more. A philosophical cosmology boasting an ontologically fundamental concept of suffering needs also to explain suffering in complex emergent forms, such as physical injury, conscious pain, emotional distress, and existential anxiety. So I prefer to use terms such as "change" and "being-conditioned" for the inanimate realm, to reserve the word "suffering" for the biological realm, and to demand a satisfying theory of emergence situated in a philosophical cosmology that links one to the other. This adjustment to suffering-is-fundamental schemes works well with ground-of-being theologies and suits process theology, too.

IS SUFFERING ILLUSORY?

The suffering-is-fundamental strategies, at least in their Buddhist and Hindu forms, paradoxically also affirm that suffering is illusion. This is obvious in the case of human life: suffering is caused by attachment, which is rooted in misperception and misunderstanding of the world, a state of affairs correctable through enlightenment. It is not as evident in the philosophical cosmology of *pratītya samutpāda* and *dukkha*, where suffering seems to be as real as the processes of emergent complexity. But the overall goal of *moksha* reframes *pratītya samutpāda* and *dukkha* alike as a kind of deceptive conjuring that finally is unreal.

The main Western version of the suffering-is-illusory strategy goes by the name of "privation theory" and is famously associated with Saint Augustine. The really bad part of suffering is the evil that causes it, according to Augustine, but evil is merely a privation of good, a distortion with no reality of its own. Privation theory solves a problem in the doctrine of creation *ex nihilo* (from nothing), which was just firming up in Augustine's time, because it appears to place the explanation for evil on some other doorstep than God's. Finally, of course, shifting responsibility for evil cannot avoid tainting the moral character of God, so Augustine, and more elaborately Gregory of Nyssa, were forced to propose a philosophy of history to bring a dynamic temporal dimension to the story of evil (see part 2). Evil may seem real now, according to this story, but it is in fact nonbeing and will be shown to be nonbeing, in the sense of sheer nothing, with the unfolding of God's will in history and nature. Thinking of the ontological-historical destiny of evil as nothingness is the basis for our calling it a privation of good in our presently conflicted and suffering-filled circumstances. Interpreting privation theory in connection with philosophy of history helps to deflect the great weakness of illusionist theories of suffering—namely, their failure to take with due seriousness the practical reality of suffering.

Privation theory is theologically quite useful. It has cross-cultural resonances and an important historical-eschatological dimension, and it is a serious attempt to understand reality as good despite the prevalence and intensity of suffering within it. Yet its implications for the doctrine of God as creator remain as problematic in our time as they were in Augustine's. Relative to an eternal and omnipotent divine entity, the historical texture of the flowering and ontological obliteration of evil does nothing to shield the divine reality from the reality of evil. If evil and suffering ever were experienced, then an eternal and omnipotent God must bear the marks of this possibility within the divine being itself.

This is why the privation view actually suits ground-of-being more than agential-being accounts of ultimate reality (process theism is, of course, not affected by any of this). This is also why the deepest articulation of privation theory within Christian agential-being frameworks has to be fundamentally incarnational as well as eschatological. But the incarnation does not produce a picture of God as a decisively good and powerful entity. Rather it suggests either that God is to be identified with the moral ambiguity of nature and history, surrendering the divine goodness to divine power as in ground-of-being theism; or else it invites the opposite response, the surrender of power to goodness in the manner of contemporary process theology. This is merely to replay the traditional tri-lemma argument of theodicy—God cannot be all-good and all-powerful if evil is real—with the added observation that not even privation theory can effectively secure the non-reality of evil.

It is impossible not to admire Augustine's and Gregory of Nyssa's intricate attempts to preserve the goodness and power of God in the face of the apparent reality of evil, but I suspect theirs is a vain struggle on the terms in which they framed the problem. In the ground-of-being framework, by contrast, the motivation for a privation theory disappears, but its fruit—radical understandings of comprehensive divine incarnation and participation in the world's moral ambiguity—have a welcome place.

IS SUFFERING OUR FATE?

Another strategy for interpreting suffering is to emphasize its inescapability. In one ancient version of this view, it is human fate, and the fate of all plants and animals, to suffer at the whim of the gods. The ancient Near Eastern Epic of Gilgamesh ends when the bizarre hero, having won the secret of everlasting life through a monumental effort of self-assertion against all odds, has the life-giving plant stolen by a serpent while he is momentarily distracted (see chapter 7). The story's point is unmistakable: there is no evading the will of the gods, no matter how strong and creative we are. We will suffer and die because it pleases the gods.

This picture of suffering as the fated lot of human beings has more and less personal versions. In Gilgamesh, things are intensely personal: the gods witness Gilgamesh's agonies, cause some of them and exacerbate others, and deliberately thwart his attempts to escape them. In the course of Stoic philosophy's development, fate gradually became less a matter of the imposition of divine will and more a matter of causal determinism. Fate was a recapitulation in every individual being of the simple fact that everything in nature is rigidly determined, not so much by divine whim as by the very nature of the world, which became more and more the same thing. In twentieth-century existentialism, there were representatives of both views. But on all sides the moral benefits of understanding suffering as the result of determinism or fate are supposed to be courage to face the world as it is, free of self-deceptive illusions and artificial comforts. Bear up! Face misery and death with dignity!

It has long been understood that, despite appearances, doctrines of determinism do not interfere as much as one might think with practical action aimed at improving the circumstances of life. After all, according to determinism, we necessarily do whatever we do, whether it is sitting around paralyzed by despair or actively transforming social conditions and alleviating suffering. Consequently, the charge of determinism is not a genuine practical problem with the "suffering as fate" strategy for interpreting suffering in nature. Moreover, Western philosophical compatibilism offers ways of affirming nature's freedom and human moral responsibility in the presence of divine and physical determinism, just as Chinese philosophy offers ways of understanding human action as spontaneous within the highly structured flow of power within nature.

Process theism cannot support this picture of suffering as fate. In the context of agential-being theism, the most obvious theological difficulty with the suffering-as-fate idea is that it requires us to picture God personally inflicting suffering on creatures. As I suggested earlier, awareness of our historical and economic location will help us see that there have been times and there are still places where such a picture of divine power is reassuring—a God who can afflict us surely has the power to save us from our enemies! But it is an unfashionable view when technology and political economy combine to make life conditions for human beings mostly comfortable and safe, thereby reducing moments of suffering, at least in the sense of injury and pain, to the level of inconvenient interruptions from which we are entitled to expect rapid deliverance through medicine or the justice system. In such blessed cultural havens, to think of God as wielder of weal *and* woe serves merely to insult the socially accepted view of the perfectly good divine character.

Process theology surrenders divine power to guarantee divine goodness, in response, so the process deity (GodP) inflicts no suffering even if ultimate reality (GodC) does. Most agential-being theists affirm the humanly recognizable goodness of God by rejecting divine infliction of suffering while maintaining divine omnipotence. Ground-of-being theism offers more flexibility in relation to the suffering-as-fate interpretation and can take it or leave it depending on other factors. In general, I think the idea of God as source of worldly fate is the most underexplored strategy in our time for theologically articulating the meaning of suffering in nature. There is more potential in this idea, even for the less anthropomorphic versions of agential-being theism, than is usually assumed in comfortable Western cultural contexts. The best example may be Islam, which in most settings continues to emphasize the idea of a personal God of unlimited power, merciful and compassionate yet decisive in action, and beyond human moral judgment absolutely.

KENOSIS STRATEGIES

This takes us directly to kenosis strategies. These explicitly theological proposals are supposed to explain why God does not intervene to deliver us and the rest of nature from needless suffering. God enters into a covenant with nature in which divine power is self-limited to enable complexity to emerge in nature, whereby moral and spiritual life can flower. I think that such kenosis strategies reflect the cultural and economic conditioning I have described; in fact, kenosis can be quite indigestible as an explanation of suffering in other cultural settings because it defangs a deity whose fierce, protective intervention is desperately needed. Moreover, I do not think that the biblical concept of kenosis (Phil. 2:1–11, especially v. 7) has anything to do with this kind of covenantal divine self-limitation; biblical kenosis is explicitly and solely Christological in character, and Paul's aim in introducing it is to inspire humility within arrogant and fighting church factions. Yet we can liberate recent kenosis proposals from their mistaken claim to biblical authorization based on this Philippians passage, and we can also set aside cultural conditioning factors as genuine but not determinative of the truth of the matter. After that, we must consider the philosophical-theological import of the kenosis strategy on its own terms.

The more humanly recognizable we want our model of God's goodness to be, the more we need some explanation of the apparent absence of effective divine intervention to alleviate needless suffering, and thus the more important it is that we make the kenosis strategy work. Theologies that regard humanly recognizable goodness in God as a mistaken or dangerous criterion for theological adequacy, such as ground-of-being theism and some forms of agential-being theism, can take or leave kenosis, at least in some sense. But kenosis is vital to agential-being theisms affirming God as a caring personal being. Thus, it is in relation to such variants of agential-being theism that we must consider the effectiveness of the kenosis strategy. In this context, however, kenotic interpretations of God's personal goodness in relation to suffering face a severe conceptual problem, as follows.

Either the kenotic God retains omnipotence or not. In the first case, kenosis seems artificial and unconvincing because it is merely a reversible divine decision rather than a fundamental and inescapable feature of divine creation. That is, if God deliberately embraces self-limitation for the sake of allowing moral and spiritual life to flower, then there ought to be nothing to prevent God from making exceptions as needed. Kenosis in this sense does nothing to protect the humanly recognizable goodness of God.

The second case requires a reflexive and automatic kind of kenosis. God must be determined in some primordial creative event as already and eternally self-limited, so that no decision to be any other way in any subsequent context is possible for God. Process theology illustrates this, in one sense: a process theogony could have ultimate reality (GodC) creating the world in such a way that God can be present to the world always and only as the process deity GodP. (This is only a fantasy, of course: the process God is an actual entity that plays the hand it is dealt just as every actual entity does, and no theologically relevant theory of ultimate reality is possible. But it is worth noting that such a view is conceptually possible.)

So it appears that kenosis is most convincing as a part-explanation of suffering in nature when it is ontologically forced, but in that case it is not exactly embraced willingly and lovingly, and thus is not truly kenosis as traditionally understood. If kenosis is a matter of deliberate divine self-limitation through which omnipotence perseveres, then it is no longer truly binding and thus is unconvincing as an explanation of divine silence in response to needless suffering in nature. The upshot is that kenosis does much less than its proponents claim to preserve the humanly recognizable goodness of God. It is merely a hidden repetition of the fundamental (and otherwise understandable) criterion of theological adequacy active for agential-being theists—that is, optimism that human longings are indicative of ultimate reality. Despite appearances, therefore, the kenosis strategy offers no materially new conceptual resources.

WILL EVERYTHING BE ALL RIGHT IN THE END?

We saw earlier that privation theory is at its best when it incorporates a historical dimension whereby the essential nonbeing of evil, though not evident now, will become evident at some point in the future. Unsurprisingly, agential-being theists typically deploy an eschatological vision in which the ontological destiny of suffering is *nihil*, nothing. Suffering will fall away when the consummation of all things comes, finally confirming God's personal moral perfection and power. The most interesting aspect of this to me is that eschatological deployments from the camp of agential-being theism display an awareness of the empirical difficulties that this view must manage.

Ground-of-being theists can also deploy eschatological visions of suffering, but in slightly different terms and to a very different end. In one such vision, suffering will plunge back into the abysmal creative surge from which it sprang, along with life and spirit, leaving nothing at all or else only the glorious emergent fruits of the vast cosmic-historic process to that point. This cosmological vision can take or leave the hypothesis of an overall direction to the cosmic process; this is always and only an empirical question about the way the divine character expresses itself determinately in the structured possibilities of reality. Interestingly, one of the best-known ground-of-being theists, Paul Tillich, uses many pages in the third volume of his *Systematic Theology* (1963) to say that there is no overall direction of progress in the universe as a whole, even though there is abundant meaning. At this point he shows his affinity for the view of cosmic history in Schelling rather than Hegel, two other ground-of-being theists. But perhaps the question really ought to be settled empirically rather than speculatively.

The samsaric version of this view is particularly impressive but deeply perplexing. *Karma,* a kind of universal moral law of cause and effect lying beneath the experience of suffering, gives birth to life and spirit, goodness and bliss, and delivers souls through a tortuous path into the arms of Brahman via enlightenment and *moksha.* Though the Vedas do speak of cosmic epochs and Śiva's periodic resetting of all of creation, there appears to be no post-samsaric recreation of reality in this vision but only deliverance from it. This is a one-by-one personal eschatology rather than an eschatology of nature and all of creation; suffering is the means of liberation to something else, but is never defeated in itself. The *samsara*-is-*nirvāna* option in this context is akin to realized eschatology within Christian theology: liberation not in some other world but here and now in the midst of suffering. The samsaric vision is the probably the most positive of all interpretations of suffering in nature because it renders suffering *in itself* as productive and nurturing, the path along which all beings trudge on their way to a blessed goal. This seems quite different from regarding suffering as a necessary but unfortunate side effect of an otherwise valuable process. We can appreciate all this, but we must also note that there is no solution to the raw challenge of suffering in nature here. There is reframing, akin to reframing suffering as privation or illusion, but there is no easing, no overcoming. But perhaps there should not be any overcoming of suffering or of the samsaric reality that structures existence.

It falls to more history-minded religions and philosophies to articulate the possibility of an eschaton that transforms nature itself, not merely individuals within it. Keeping in mind the argumentative stakes—the agential-being theist deploys eschatology to give evidence of God's personal goodness in relation to suffering in nature—let's trace the argument about the possibility of such an eschaton.

Beginning from the scientific point of view, can there be an alternative embodiment of life and spirit that is free of the travails of nature that we know and see about us? I have hinted that it is possible to imagine alternative biological and ecological circumstances that might be freer of suffering than our Earth is. But in all of those biology-based scenarios, we cannot get along without glucose, or some substitute biological fuel, among other things, and thus suffering in nature might be reduced relative to Earth's suffering landscape, but it cannot be eliminated. Thus, even if Isaiah's vision of the lion eating straw like the ox were to come true, we would still have suffering in nature, especially in the form of plant injury and accidents. What about leaving biology behind altogether and imagining a form of life that uses light as the sole energy source? If feasible, this would eliminate predation altogether, but it would still leave accident and injury and disease to worry about. So there is no science-supported basis for picturing a new heaven and a new earth that is free of suffering. Well, perhaps that is to be expected. A new heaven and a new earth without suffering would be so spectacular a transformation that it would have to be supernatural in character, so we should probably assume that our scientific knowledge should be ignored as irrelevant.

But perhaps this is too hasty. Consider the matter from the angle of eschatological lifestyle. In Judaism, Christianity, and Islam, eschatological visions of a new heaven and new earth typically involve moral and spiritual beings living in relation to one another, worshipping God, able to recognize loved ones and to remember life, able to grow and learn and change, and all this without any trace of suffering either in these blessed beings or in their natural environment. But I doubt that we can picture embodiment, change, and growth without the use of natural resources, even if light is our food. Moreover, if the suffering-as-inevitable-byproduct arguments have any credibility, then they apply to these pictures of the new heaven and the new earth just as much as they apply to the world we know. I freely admit to feeling the allure of idealized pictures of a suffering-free afterlife, and I have no difficulty admiring the boldness with which the history-minded religions artfully wield their supernatural eschatological resources to justify their affirmation of God's perfect personal goodness—in fact, within this framework, nothing less would take suffering as seriously as it ought to be taken. Yet I cannot see how the proposals are coherent, no matter how badly they are needed, or how much we long for them.

Furthermore, I suspect that the fruit of theoretical success in articulating a coherent eschatology would only be an intellectual disaster for agential-being theism. It would reinforce skeptical questions about God's humanly recognizable moral goodness by introducing an embodiment scheme that boasts growth and change and relationality yet no suffering. In other words, *that* world and *not this* world would be the best of all possible worlds. Such a God would be flagrantly morally inconsistent.

Conclusion

This has been a typologically driven argument rather than one rooted in specific theological positions, so many complexities and subtleties have been neglected. Yet typologically driven arguments can still produce robust conclusions. My conclusion is that there is no adequate reply to the argument from neglect, as it is directed against the coherence of agential-being theism. Neither is there any satisfying answer to the associated argument from divine incompetence, as it is directed against the much trumpeted efficacy of process theism in supporting a religious response to suffering.

It is good, some say, to be in the middle of theoretical disputes, participating in the virtues of all sides. When the middle proves to be unstable due to underlying incoherence, however, there is real cause to look around for some other place to stand, there to reconfigure alternatives so as to understand oneself, once again, as standing in a new middle, but now upon firmer ground amid more fruitful theoretical disputes. Agential-being theism of many kinds requires God to be a compassionate entity with personal knowledge of suffering, the power to act in history and nature, and all the while to be perfectly good in ways that human beings can grasp. This places agential-being theism in the middle of a host of daunting theoretical difficulties. There has been no shortage of attempts to defend it but the resources for the main defense efforts face serious difficulties, as I have tried to show. The problem, in a nutshell, is that this idea of God is an admirable but finally ineffective attempt to deal with the empirical gap between life as we experience it and the goodness we long to affirm in God as ultimate reality. Nothing shows this more clearly than the problem of suffering in nature, as leveraged by the argument from neglect.

Yet there are other central places to stand, theologically, and other ways to configure the surrounding theoretical landscape. I urge battle-weary agential-being theists to look over at the intellectuals gathered around the ancient idea of God as ground of being, the power and creativity of the structured flows of nature, the ontological spring of matter and value. This God is not good in a humanly recognizable way, nor personal in character, yet when we defer in worship to this God despite its incongruity with our anthropocentric ways of thinking, our minds are led higher to larger patterns and wider virtues in which suffering is no longer merely an unwanted side effect of otherwise wondrous physical processes but a creative source in its own right. This God is beautiful from a distance in the way that a rain forest is beautiful, but just as it is unpleasant for humans to live unprotected in a rain forest, so it is perilous to be in the direct presence of divine glory. We suffer there as well as surrender in bliss (see chapter 9). The truth about this God is deeply disconcerting, not easily assimilated into our humanly configured cultural worlds and religious habits of thinking. Yet this is the truth that sears our souls, that awakens us again and again from our anthropomorphic theological slumbering, and that drives us to love that which destroys even as it creates.

This image of God is a less perplexing concept in many types of Hinduism, or even in most forms of Islam, past and present. It is built into the heart of Chinese religious cosmology and is amply present in most tribal religions that ventured to narrate models of ultimate reality. It was less difficult in ancient and medieval Judaism and Christianity than it has become in modern times and in first-world cultures. The paucity of contemporary Christian imagery and symbolism corresponding to dancing destroyer-creator Śiva shows just how difficult this idea might be in the context of the Christian religious and theological imagination—and this despite unmistakable biblical imagery of this type in Job and in apocalyptic literature, especially the book of Revelation.

The destroyer-creator ground-of-being insight survives most clearly in the Western epic tradition, thanks to Blake and Dante and others, and in medieval art depicting hell as punishment. But the incarnational-sacrificial Christological rubric utterly reframes this insight in the terrifying narratives and imagery of suffering saints and martyrs. Christianity has always had an idiosyncratic approach to suffering because of its Christological lens. For precisely this reason, however, Christian theologians might take a more positive view of suffering in nature than they have typically taken. Despite my appreciation for the Greek metaphysical tradition, at this point the early Christian theologians seem to have underestimated the philosophical resources of their primary narrative, rashly subjecting it to Greek intuitions about suffering as incompatible with fully realized being. The result is an insoluble conundrum in which suffering in nature has to be framed as a foreseen but unintended side effect of a creation that is good because of its other virtues, and this creation is the gift of an omnipotent, wise, compassionate, and agential God who does not intervene as often as moral obligations demand because it would ruin the beauty and moral independence of the creation. This is a theological conundrum, if ever there was one.

Suffering in nature is neither evil nor a byproduct of the good. It is part of the wellspring of divine creativity in nature, flowing up and out of the abysmal divine depths like molten rock from the yawning mouth of a volcano, searing and burning—maybe with ecological benefits, maybe with no discernable redemptive elements whatsoever. Luminescent creativity and abysmal suffering are co-primal in the divine nature as they are in our experience. To acknowledge the ground of our being in these terms is to accept suffering as our fate and the fate of all creatures, and also to do what we will with these circumstances, whether that means sitting idly by or launching into the world with banners waving and guns blazing. All things testify to the divine glory. All things without exception.

CHAPTER 3

CREATING

INTRODUCTION

THE QUESTION, "WHY IS THERE SOMETHING RATHER THAN NOTHING?," IS SAID to send shivers up the spine of the serious metaphysician. The profundity of this shock of being, this miracle of determinateness, is supposed to transport us into feverous raptures of ontological wonder. When the fever breaks, we return to normalcy dazed and in desperate need of some final explanation for everything that is.

This question really is precisely that intoxicating for some people. But others seem immune to its effects. Perhaps some never feel the shock. Or perhaps we can get used to the shock of being by training ourselves to see the demand for a final explanation as an undesirable effect of a conceptual confusion. After thus inoculating ourselves, we eventually achieve immunity and simply move on with our lives, no longer obsessed with being, no longer driven to hunt for a One behind the determinate many. We are content to strive for an understanding of the structures and processes of being, without obsessing over the very existence of determinate things. How else are we to explain Alfred North Whitehead's (1978) refusal of the "Why is there something rather than nothing?" question? It has to be possible either not to feel the shivery mystery of the shock of being, or to train oneself to reinterpret and redirect it.

Western metaphysicians handle the question "Why is there something rather than nothing?" within the so-called problem of the One and the many. This is a far-reaching metaphysical theme that arcs from the shock of being to the very possibility of rational intelligibility, and from the possibility of universal origins to the meaning of common relations among determinate things. It is not difficult to see why such far-flung themes are held together in the problem of the One and the many. When we supply the right kind of ontological One for the many, we also guarantee that everything has enough in common to be interpreted together, that nothing is finally alien from anything else even if particular beings are wildly diverse and the emergent relations among them impossible to predict. The final intelligibility of the many depends on final ontological grounding of the many. For this reason the problem of the One and the many is the problem of metaphysics with the most far-reaching effects on any wider philosophical interpretation of reality.

When metaphysicians such as Whitehead minimize the shock of being, they knowingly confine themselves to local rather than universal answers to the question of the One and the many. They can explain how the process of reality works in a concrete instance, and they can identify shared abstract patterns within that process. But they cannot supply an ontological One behind the concrete particulars of reality and thus they cannot secure the rational intelligibility of reality—not even of the propositions that make up their metaphysical interpretation of reality. Indeed, Whitehead's "category of the ultimate" in his *Process and Reality* is a mere list of elements and very far from a coherent interpretation. It is an interesting situation to be in: holding a view of ontology that undermines, or fails to establish, the rational requirements for stating it. But that is par for the course in philosophical reflection at the limits of language.

Surely we have here the ultimate philosophical reason for taking the problem of the One and the many with complete seriousness, including acknowledging the shock of being as valid and insisting on an answer to the question, "Why is there something rather than nothing?" After all, it appears impossible to take full intellectual responsibility for our metaphysical adventures unless we secure their rational basis.

As is so often the case in metaphysics, appearances are deceiving. It is easy to see how an epistemic foundationalist—someone who thinks rationally demonstrable certainty is the leading mark of truth—might feel compelled to accept that securing a rational basis for metaphysics requires positing a One as ontological ground for the many. Confidence is everything for the epistemic foundationalist. But the epistemic pragmatist is easy going—the metaphysical equivalent of the "hey dude" surfer guy (for a less casual presentation of the epistemology and theory of inquiry implied here, see Wildman 2010). If there is a problem with the rational basis for metaphysics—as there certainly is when we dodge the full force of the problem of the One and the many—the fallibilist metaphysician can manage just fine. We just need to watch how inquiries go. If they always work completely rationally, then there is an empirical reason to think that there may be a One that ontologically and rationally grounds the many. If our inquiries break down, displaying irrational features, then maybe there is no such One after all, or the One is finally and fundamentally irrational.

"What about the criteria for assessing the rationality of inquiries?" screams the anxious epistemic foundationalist. "No problem, dude," comes the laid-back reply. Like everything else, criteria for evaluation float in a sea of trial and error, a mutable network of hypotheses and correction navigated with a host of socially mediated forms of inquiry. The thoroughgoing fallibilist really does not need a rational floor for inquiry. As with the surfer, only the surface action counts, pragmatically; everything else is inference. A bottomless ocean is just as acceptable as one with a floor. Let experiences of inquiry decide the question of whether there is a One behind the determinate many. In this matter, our greatest asset is precisely the correlation between an ontological ground and a rational floor. We look for the rational floor by studying our inquiries, and in particular when and how they break. We do so using whatever cobbled-together practices at any given time serve for us as optimally rational inquiry. No rational floor means no One, or an irrational One, to which we may respond with despair or equanimity or even glee. Find a rational floor and we find a rational One at the same time, and we might reasonably imagine something like the same range of emotional responses.

Suppose the argument to this point seems so compelling to its readers that they are willing to concede. "Fine," I imagine that they allow. "We don't absolutely need a grand solution to the problem of the One and the many in order to do metaphysical inquiry in a manner that counts as rational for the fallibilist pragmatist." It's a lovely fantasy, but scholarly visions of universal concession are always fantasies. Some simply don't concede and, most importantly, sometimes even fallibilist pragmatists are not convinced.

Consider self-identified fallibilist pragmatist Robert Neville. The philosopher responsible for the only significant advance in the theory of *creatio ex nihilo* since medieval philosopher Duns Scotus, Neville reduced the problem of the One and the many to its purest form—the ontological conditions for determinateness. In *God the Creator* (1968), he demonstrates that there is a best account of the One behind the many using this pure form of the problem as the leading criterion. He gets a solution to the rational floor of inquiry for free, having solved the problem of the One and the many.

But there is a trick in the argument. In Neville we have a fallibilist pragmatist who believes a rational floor of inquiry is indispensable for any type of intellectual activity. But he actually invokes as a premise of the argument that there is a rational floor for inquiry. He doesn't make a big deal about it; the premise is not made explicit. But it is a functional premise nonetheless. If the idea of an ontological ground and the concept of a rational floor are as tightly correlated as they seem, Neville's argument begs the question. It presupposes its own answer. His One is fated to be the triumphant solution because the criteria active within the inquiry are freighted in its favor. He might appear to get a rational floor as a result of identifying an ontological ground, but in fact it is the other way around. His uncompromising demand for a rational floor guides his inquiry and yields his *creatio ex nihilo* answer to the problem of the One and the many, eliminating competitor views along the way. Neville's argument is very strong, and possibly logically valid (it is a complicated comparative argument and so validity is difficult to assess). But the rational-floor premise is deeply questionable.

I think this rational-floor premise is worth fighting about. I reckon Neville functions here only partially as the surfer-dude fallibilist pragmatist. It might be the characteristic suit and tie that gives away his incomplete commitment to the surfer lifestyle—though I do admire the way he dresses down when working in the garden or on sabbatical. It seems as though he is ruling on the issue of whether we need an ultimately rational floor for inquiry without considering the relevant evidence. Surfers are always patient and rarely surprised. It is part of the spirituality of waiting for waves and noticing their endlessly varying shapes and potentialities. Neville might have given more patient thought to whether we truly need his One-style rational floor.

I think we can get by without an ultimate rational floor for inquiry. In fact, about half the time I think we *are getting by without it.* The other half of the time I lean toward thinking that Neville is correct, that the rational floor, and the grounding One that goes with it, really are there. And this raises a question I find stunningly interesting: what if the question of whether there is a rational floor can't be decided?

On my own account, this Very Big Question can be answered only by examining the qualities of inquiry to see whether rationality or irrationality dominates—an infuriatingly circular process that provisionally presumes rationality and depends on irrationality appearing as failures of putative rationality in the interstices and at the margins of inquiries. When we do this, what do we find? Well, here comes that generalization than which no more outrageous can be conceived: we see a mixed bag of successful and frustrated inquiries. And we must acknowledge the difficulty of deciding whether inquiries are frustrated because we didn't organize them optimally, because the feedback on which we rely to correct hypotheses is absent or weak, or because there is irrational absurdity at the root of reality. If the latter, we must further acknowledge the distracted genius of irrationality: reality supports the very possibility of constructing inquiries that we are prepared to call rational, but now manifested as teasingly rational surds within an irrational ambit having no boundaries, no intelligible features, and no possibilities of final comprehension. Even judgments of rationality necessarily must be merely functional declarations.

ULTIMACY TALK

The Very Big Question is tricky to talk about and difficult to answer. It's ultimacy talk and a classic philosophical instance of effing the ineffable. In fact, ultimacy talk is the boldest and oddest form of human discourse, save only for editorial cartoons and live chess commentary, which are bolder and odder, respectively. The fundamental excuse for engaging in ultimacy talk is that, given everything we don't know for sure, there really is nothing left to do except have fun playing. And the guiding rule of fun is that it is better to apologize than to ask permission. We just have to hope that nothing so totally embarrassing happens that even belated apologies are out of the question, for that would be excessive fun.

Four main answers to the Very Big Question are possible, each of which has a notable philosophical lineage.

We can say that the question is decidable and then

1. opt with Robert Neville and Immanuel Kant (and many others) for a grounding One and a rational floor, albeit very differently conceived, or
2. choose with Friedrich Nietzsche and Albert Camus (and not so many others) for no One and a gleaming flourish of unspeakably vibrant life in place of a rational floor.

Alternatively we can say that the question is undecidable and then

3. embrace with August Comte and Freddy Ayer an ascetic agnosticism that refuses hypotheses about undecidable questions, or
4. journey with the most profound of the apophatic thinkers of all traditions in a quest to explain how the undecidability of the Very Big Question actually reflects accurately the character of ultimacy.

The Very Big Question is tough enough that it is impossible to fault someone for choosing differently than we do. I myself have hypothetically explored all four answers in search of empirical and rational traction, which is to say for avenues of inquiry that may eventually yield to calculated effort. Indeed, I am emotionally torn among all four, save that I find the asceticism of number 3 to be an odd form of worshipful deference and am temperamentally inclined to want more fun than this view allows. But there is no cause for stress here. The drinks are free and the bartender will mix whatever we want (just water for me, please), so we can yield to our deepest instincts and play with these ideas. There might even be time for more than one drink.

I confess that my heart murmurs sweet nothings most passionately for the last view (4), which I shall dub "abysmal ground" for convenience. Put it down to being dropped on my head as a kid (which I was), to excessive empathy for opponents (which I have), or to distaste for taking a simple stand on anything complex (which torments my students). I am drawn to the idea that the undecidability of the Very Big Question accurately reflects the character of ultimacy, of the One. This, then—hypothetically, as befits the profound surfer-dude epistemology—defines the fundamental experiential touchstone, as well as the conceptual outline, for the One in my answer to the problem of the One and the many.

More exactly, I am claiming—hypothetically and actively seeking correction, and that will be the last reminder of the import of fallibilist pragmatism—that ultimacy somehow presents itself at the margins of rationality and irrationality, that there is a match between our living experiences of reality and this conception of a chasm-like ontological ground, and that alternative conceptions of ultimacy are shard-like perspectives on the unassimilable whole.

I am not taking refuge in mystery here—not at all, and certainly not in order to avoid steely demands for conceptual clarity. After all, anyone serious about deflecting that demand by premature appeals to mystery would have done so long before reaching the type of absurdity that this view embraces. On the contrary, clarity is served when empirical data is not coerced for the sake of supporting ill-fitting hypotheses. I think this theory (4) fits the data ever so slightly better than its two close competitor views (1 and 2)—note again that (3) is not a view of ultimacy so much as a life-rule about how to comport ourselves in relation to supposedly undecidable theological questions about ultimacy.

The empirical case is difficult to make out. At the outset, I need to frame the available evidence in such a way as to allow my interpretation of it to have any chance at all of a fair hearing. To that end, I claim that this view's more obvious practical features—it tends to be psychologically destabilizing, socially disruptive, spiritually indigestible, morally irrelevant, and philosophically obscure—make it no less likely to be true (or what passes for true in the hazy territory I am describing). This is a tough sell, obviously.

In *Science and Religious Anthropology* (2009) and *In Our Own Image* (2017), I tried to explain how philosophical-theological truth could lie in directions very different from those capable of winning religious popularity contests. I also argued there that theologically popular views deserve institutional and intellectual support as the only feasible means of engagement with ultimacy for most people. Without highly anthropomorphic conceptions of ultimacy—especially personalistic and focally attentive and active Gods or Boddhisattvas or Spirits or Ancestors—most people would not be able to worship meaningfully at all, nor would they get even remotely close to a correct interpretation of their religious-existential situation.

It follows that there is truth in any authentic form of engagement with ultimacy even under theologically inadequate conceptions of the logical object of engagement. But there is truth beyond this, also, and this remains so as long as rational resources permit the speaking of it. Even if the quest for deeper truth can never escape the rational limitations of human cognition, expert human inquirers can discern in the fissures of rational argumentation glimpses of the molten chaos that lies beneath.

This imagery expresses the point that the abysmal ground of all that is births both rational inquiry and irrational collapses of inquiry. Both offspring testify to the character of the originating source. Every attempt to name the abysmal ground by means of its offspring fails eventually. But skillful means permit testimony to linger in the roar of the fire. And the philosophical theologian, endlessly falling into the abysmal chasm's glowing depths, can hope for nothing more than to worship by lifting up the voice in the midst of a cacophony of praise and speaking as clearly, as honestly, and as long as possible. It's the meaning of serious play. We all fall into silence, whether we deny it or long for it. The skillful apophatic philosophical theologian makes a graceful fall with a quiet voice that outlasts the others. But it, too, yields to muteness.

Obviously the techniques of apophatic theology need to be pushed to the limit to express this. The unappetizing specter of the irrational collapse of discourse, like rising nausea on an interminable boat trip, must be kept in check—not denied!—until the last second of inquiring power has been expended on the task. Relevant techniques that need to be deployed and refined are:

- *Assertive* techniques, which symbolically name the unnamable and recklessly juxtapose and layer names to testify to that which surpasses and evades naming;
- *Negation* techniques, which assert literally and then negate both the assertion and the illocutionary act of asserting;
- *Balancing* techniques, which testify through deliberate juxtaposition of equally compelling intuitions; and
- *Trajectorial* techniques, which point the imagination in directions governed by the ordering of symbolic names, the ordering of literal negations, and the selection of balancing insights.

A deployment of the apophatic philosophical theologian's balancing technique can help explain the theoretical virtues of the abysmal-ground view of ultimacy (see chapter 5 for another example of the balancing technique at work).

Balancing Creation Symbols

Consider Neville's *One* (as I'll call it), utterly indeterminate apart from an eternal act of creation in which the One attains a determinate character along with the world (1; see Neville 2013–2015, volume 1, and long before that Neville 1968). Creation here is not the act of an *actor*; the divine creator is made determinate and meaningful only in the act of creation that produces all determinations whatsoever. This is a strange situation, and not at all like theistic doctrines of creation, where the creator God is self-sustaining in being and has determinations (that is, a character) independently of the world. We can't figure out the nature of God apart from studying creation in Neville's view. There is no determinate condition for creation; there is just no there there.

In my experience, people don't easily grasp how radical Neville's view is. In fact, I think even Neville himself sometimes forgets how radical his own view is (an appraisal only possible between good friends). For example, now and then we find him making statements about God as such (*a se*), as against God as made determinate in the creative-act-without-an-actor. He also mutes the brilliant extremity of this viewpoint. For instance, this view entails a kind of occasionalism (since causal relations are determinate and thus have to be created *ex nihilo* along with every cause and effect), and thus profoundly obscures the rational conditions for scientific inquiry and human freedom, among many other things. Neville doesn't surface those extreme implications as straightforwardly as I think he should. Anyway, the view itself is conceptually coherent and metaphysically profound, and that's what matters for my current purposes.

Now place alongside Neville's view another: Plotinus's One. On this view, the One becomes determinate initially independently of the world in an eternal process of theogony (god-birthing); the world is a side effect of the theogony process (see Plotinus 2004). This is *creatio ex nihilo* versus *emanatio ex deo* (I prefer *ex deo* to *a deo* in order to emphasize the birthing qualities of emanation). In the *ex deo* view, the divine theogony and the creation of the world alike depend upon diremption, whereby infinity gradually breaks into determinate things, like snapping off pieces from an endless and paradoxically edgeless chocolate bar. By contrast, in Neville's *ex nihilo* view, everything determinate is created new, including the One in its relatedness to the world.

Ex nihilo Neville rightly points out that *ex deo* Plotinus posits a breaking of the indeterminate infinite into finite determinacy that is incoherent; how can you break an infinite, edgeless chocolate bar into finite pieces? *Ex deo* Plotinus would rightly point out that *ex nihilo* Neville evacuates the divine life of any eternal dynamism, so that nothing is gained by speaking of ultimacy at all. The only God Neville can talk about is the one made determinate in creation, and our empirical investigations of the purportedly created world might force us to conclude that there is no such determinate God at all. Indeed, that's precisely my tentative conclusion, which is why it's right to call me an atheist as well as a mystical philosophical theologian who affirms the God Beyond God. Plotinus might say that the timeless-yet-shocking arrival of infinitely many determinate little bits of chocolate—the confectionary translation of the import of Neville's *creatio ex nihilo*—takes away all the fun of breaking off bits of chocolate from an edgeless sheet (that'd be theogony). Plotinus (along with most who come to understand Neville's view) might also say that Neville voids speech about a creative act of any meaningful reference. Instead of creation, Neville might as well speak of "suchness" or ascetically refuse the question of the One and the many altogether.

Traditionally the western philosophical theologian is supposed to choose between the two, between Neville's theogany-free appearance in creation of a determinate divinity and Plotinus's dramatic unfolding of the divine energies, between radical *creatio ex nihilo* and radical *emanatio ex deo*. But I believe that thinking of this as a forced choice is deeply misleading. Saint Augustine, supposedly the premier early representative of the *ex nihilo* view, commits an almighty fudge when he affirms *creatio ex nihilo* but asserts that God has a nature *a se*, independently of the created world (1991). This commits Augustine to an *ex deo* view as well; the created world reflects the divine nature because it flows from the divine nature. Augustine needed to do this in order to be able to guarantee both the goodness of God and the goodness of divine creation, as well as creation's complete dependence on God. This is refusing the disjunction between radical *creatio ex nihilo* and radical *emanatio ex deo*; it's having your cake and eating it, too.

In truth, the Western tradition has never chosen cleanly between *ex nihilo* and *ex deo*, despite rhetoric to the contrary, and precisely for Augustine's (implicit) reasons. I believe Neville is the first philosophical theologian to choose cleanly. And he gives up a lot to do so, including the excitement of a divine nature *a se* and a theogony to explain the dynamism of the internal divine life. He also has to live with a massively unknown determinate deity-in-relation-to-the-created-world—which could be anything from Whitehead's God to the miracle-working God of personal theism, or even nothing at all, but it is definitely something determinate so it can't be all of these at once.

Why choose as Neville does? For one thing, it is fairly impressive to diagnose vagueness in the long *ex nihilo* tradition in such a way as to make a clean choice for the first time a meaningful possibility. After pulling off such a prodigious intellectual feat, you have a right to choose whatever you like. But in the choice itself, we see the aforementioned dependence on the rational-floor criterion for an adequate solution to the problem of the One and the many. Plotinus's idea of diremptive breaking of the infinite, edgeless One into finite determinacies does indeed contradict the rational-floor criterion of fully coherent discourse. So Neville makes a clean break. He walks away from the traditional, instinctively wise Augustinian balance, infuriatingly expressed in perpetual conceptual muddles about ultimacy, and opts decisively for a radical version of *creatio ex nihilo*—which is how he winds up with a One that supplies an ontological ground and a rational floor for reality while having no nature in itself, apart from the creative act-without-an-actor by which it is made determinate.

In so choosing, Neville gives up theogony, he gives up large-scale philosophy of history played out in the ambit of the divine life (à la Hegel and Schelling), and he gives up all traces of absurdity at the root of things. There is chaos, yes, and wild processes unscaled to human interests. It all may add up to nothing but a giant bubble of play. But the absurdity of that view is a human emotional response and does not derive from irrationality at the ontological root of reality—not for Neville. In short, he will accept a piece of chocolate only if he can believe that it appears *ex nihilo* in front of him.

Plotinus didn't have the same choice. But I reckon he would have conceded Neville's argument about the irrationality of diremptive breaking up of the infinite. Then he would have affirmed the absurdity of theogony in the divine life, picked up a piece of chocolate, told himself that it was broken off an infinite, edgeless sheet by a One with dynamic potentialities for its partially determinate character, and savored it all the more for the absurdity that brought it to him.

Abysmal Ground

To juxtapose Neville and Plotinus in this way may convince you that a choice is absolutely required, despite the Augustine-rooted tradition of not cleanly choosing either side. After that you would hypothetically side with *ex nihilo* Neville (1) or *ex deo* Plotinus (2) and spend your time exploring the world from your chosen angle. But my aspiration here is to juxtapose these two views in a balanced way so as to exhibit their equivalent plausibility, their matching strengths and weaknesses, and their usefulness for drawing our attention to an alternative (4). The abysmal-ground alternative (4) is that the God-world relation is vague with respect to the choice between *creatio ex nihilo* and *emanatio ex deo*, that our experience supports both interpretations of ultimacy with more or less equal force, and that we can frame both shard-like interpretations, in a last gasp kind of way, as facets on a richer whole.

The rationality requirements of theorizing demand that I explain the sense in which *creatio ex nihilo* and *emanatio ex deo* can be represented as perspectives on a richer picture of ultimacy—that is, represented as true simultaneously through being applicable in different respects. In the nature of the case, this requires a theogony to situate rational possibilities and irrational absurdity in a wider field of interpretation, and an acceptance that human or any reason may not be able to go further without breaking. The theogonies of Plotinus, Meister Ekhart (1986), or Ray Hart (2016) might prove useful for this purpose. But that is too large an undertaking. So I shall pursue my aspirational task along two other lines.

First, at the root of the abysmal-ground view of ultimacy, we find the perspectival move that frames *creatio ex nihilo* and *emanatio ex deo* as complementary. It can be described abstractly but quickly and without the fabulous speculations of theogony.

How does determinacy proceed from indeterminacy? In figurative terms, how does one break an infinite, edgeless chocolate bar into pieces of finite size? If Neville is partly wrong about the rational floor of reality, as the abysmal-ground view requires, diremption should be salvageable, at least in some respects. Consider the following complementary contrast.

On the one hand, we can view a determinate thing in respect of its haecceity, or determinate thisness, which calls for relations of contrast with that which it is not, as well as qualities that express the togetherness of the contrastive relations in one determinate thing. These are Neville's conditional and essential features, respectively. Continuities, derived natures, and causal processes always threaten to eliminate haecceity (as in *pratītya-samutpāda* cosmology) or dishonor haecceity (as in reductive materialism that is oblivious to value structures). Thus, creation must be a making-determinate-of-everything-all-together in a vastly simple eternal act that admits no deriving of haecceities one from another.

On the other hand, we can view a determinate thing in respect of its power of being, its expression of ch'i energy flows, its aura of axiological possibilities, and its persistence through changing conditions. Continuities, derived natures, and causal processes are the heart and soul of this perspective, and haecceity is the great puzzle. This is why the *pratītya-samutpāda* cosmology stresses dependent co-origination, presumes an everlasting universe in both past and future temporal directions, and rejects own-being (*sabhāva*). With this goes the rejection of the need to defend haecceities from philosophical incursions and the conclusion that talk about an eternal creative act is beside the point.

I claim that these two perspectives are compelling and convincing in their own terms. But *both are abstractions from concrete existence.* One is better at accounting for the haecceity of being because it adopts the lens of the creation of determinate particularity, after which (in Whitehead and Neville alike) there is always a struggle to explain continuities. The other is better at accounting for the continuity of being because it adopts the lens of dependent co-origination, after which (in the Mādhyamaka tradition) it has grave difficulties even caring about, let alone explaining, haecceity.

Look at reality in respect of thisness and you will see haecceity everywhere and posit ultimacy in terms that can explain it—and there is no explanation better than Neville's theory of *creatio ex nihilo.* Look at reality in respect of the power of continuous character, and you will see continuity everywhere, and thereafter posit ultimacy as the fecund source of all that is—and I think Plotinus's *emanatio ex deo* and Nagarjuna's account (1955) of the *pratītya-samutpāda* cosmology are about equally good at conveying what this entails. Reality is concrete; philosophical analysis of the conditions for the reality we experience produces abstractions that reflect the interests of inquiry and the contexts and traditions that inspire and guide it.

Second, we need to touch on theogony just enough to picture how the abysmal-ground theory of ultimacy can sustain the complementary perspectives on reality just sketched and also how it can be compatible with affirming and denying the fundamentally rational character of reality. At the root of any theogony, there is a key logical transition. This is the logical "moment" at which the One "starts" to become determinate.

Pure *ex nihilo* theories (really, and sadly, Neville's is pretty much the only instance) do not have to worry about this because the eternal creative act requires no determinacy of the divine nature until it all suddenly appears solely in relation to the created world. Traditional *ex nihilo* theories are impure in a creative way, as I suggested above, so among them there are many discussions about why God "chose" to create. Was it to express the divine glory, because God was lonely, out of a desire to express the internal divine life on a wider scale, or as a kind of play? Of course, the *emanatio ex deo* theories also have to worry about this. It is quite the puzzle and enough to make one seriously consider becoming a Nevillean *ex nihilo* believer.

For my immediate purposes, the important point in any theogony is to keep in mind that space-time is a creature and that ultimacy is not in it or of it. Thus, Charles Hartshorne's (1948) God is not ultimacy and is not under discussion here. For related reasons, Whitehead's (1978) God is also not under discussion. I'm interested only in a theogony of ultimacy, not of the non-ultimate creature-Gods that may appear and act in the process of reality. To speak of theogony is to imagine the birth of determinacy in the divine nature by referring not to temporal or spatial or causal transitions, but rather to logical moments and contrasts. As such, we are abstracting from the immediate reality we can observe and inter- rogate, and constantly in danger of failing to allow for the spatial, temporal, and causal assumptions that guide our thinking.

Undaunted, let us imagine this key logical transition at which the One "starts" to become determinate. Obviously, it can't be gradual, which is a tem- poral concept. It can't be extended or causally conditioned, either. But a theogony fearlessly posits that it "happens" anyway. Many theogonies, including Plotinus's and Friedrich Schelling's and Georg Hegel's, but also Trinitarian and Kabalistic entries, are enormously elaborate with a host of stages and processes. Some are sparser, such as Paul Tillich's and the Qur'anic theogony, but still express some dynamism in the divine life apart from the world. *All of them have this initial logical moment at which self-determination begins.*

I think that analyzing this first moment of the determinacy of ultimacy clinches the case for the complementarity of the pure *ex nihilo* and *ex deo* perspec- tives, and confirms the reflexive wisdom of the *ex nihilo* tradition in remaining impure. Only an infinitesimally small movement of the One toward determinacy is needed for the floodgates of divine self-expression to open—this follows from the non-temporal framing of such a theogony. Once it starts, it is all over, eternally. How do we explain this infinitesimally small originating movement? (I take up this theme of a vanishingly small "slip" in more detail in part 2.)

From the pure *ex nihilo* standpoint, the infinitesimally small originating movement is all there is, primally. We call it an act though it isn't the act of any- thing, we call it creative though it has no character and so is not creative but a cre- ation, and we allow ourselves to stretch language in this way because the problem of the One and the many demands that we face down this infinitesimally small originating movement and throw explanations at it until we start to feel better. From the *ex deo* perspective, the infinitesimally small originating movement is the most characterful moment in the eternal career of reality. There can be no account of it and yet we must affirm that it expresses more completely than anything the meaning of the divine nature *a se*.

The infinitesimally small originating movement at the root of the determination of ultimacy is an irrational surd, an inexplicable blemish on the smooth rational skin of reality. But it is just the right sort of blemish because it is the power source for all of the fractures that later show up in our experience, from the unintelligibility of suffering to the unachievability of justice, from the necessity of poetic indirection to the inevitability of civilizational failure, from the unpredictability of complex systems to the impossibility of securing a rational basis for mathematics and theoretical physics, and from the irreconcilability of the world's great philosophies to the fissured existential character of every personal life. The blemish is an indispensable resource for making rational sense both of rational processes where they exist and of the failures of rationality that bespeak a kind of dramatic and rootless chaos that far surpasses ordinary divine wildness on the psychological disturbance scale.

Look at the infinitesimally small originating movement in respect of it being the logical condition for all determinacy, and rationality pours forth from it, casting everything in the warm glow of intelligibility. The shadows betray realities unscaled to human interests but it is *creatio ex nihilo*, and we have a reassuring answer to the problem of the One and the many firmly in hand. But *this warm glow of rationality is built atop an irrational surd that bespeaks the divine character* and demands the narration of a theogony in which *emanatio ex deo* is part of the story. Look at the infinitesimally small originating movement in respect of its uncaused spontaneity, therefore, and we see the meaning of the divine nature *a se*—as eternally determinate, at least as far as that infinitesimally small originating movement is concerned. That may not be much determinacy, but it is enough to warn us that there may be irrational absurdity at the root of things.

Symmetry and Asymmetry

A picturesque analogy helps to explain the contrast between my abysmal ground view of ultimacy and either the Nevillian pure *creatio ex nihilo* or the Plotinian pure *emanatio ex deo* views. The analogy is drawn from mathematical group theory, which is a key resource in modeling the emergence of the early universe in big-bang cosmology. The payoff of applying this analogy to metaphysical issues is questionable because the analogy can be deployed in many different ways and at a variety of levels. But I will use it in only one sense.

In mathematics, a group is a mathematical structure governed by certain rules. The rules are simple and serve especially to identify symmetries within the group—structures that allow operations to be performed without regard to order, for example, or structures that allow the interchange of components in such a way as to leave the structure functionally unchanged. There are many different groups with many different symmetry properties. Most do not have applications in physics but a few have proved exceptionally useful for modeling theorized events in the early universe.

The standard model of particle physics posits four forces, each mediated by a boson (force particle). For example, the electromagnetic force that makes chemistry work and civilization hold together is mediated by photons. The weak nuclear force that lies behind radioactivity and allows stars to work as they do is mediated by several bosons, which I will just call "bosons." Normally you would never be confused about whether a particle interaction was of the electromagnetic or weak-force type; you would just look at the force particle to decide. If it is a photon, we have an electromagnetic interaction. If a boson, we have a weak-force interaction. So much for normal life.

Now, run the universe's clock back very early into the big bang. At this point, densities and energies are so high that particles slam into one another and the weird subatomic "chemistry" of nuclear reactions is the rule. Still moving backwards in time, if energies and densities increase past a certain threshold, a confusing kind of reaction becomes possible. Photons being exchanged in an electromagnetic interaction can get slammed and change into bosons before the particle exchange is complete. Thus, it is not possible to classify interactions as electromagnetic or weak. This state is a kind of symmetry because you can exchange force particles and everything stays essentially the same. Classifying an interaction as electromagnetic or weak in character is merely a matter of perspective and says little or nothing about the reality of the situation.

There is a mathematical group that expresses the "era" of big-bang cosmology in which the electromagnetic or weak interactions are indistinguishable. Now, run the big-bang clock forwards again. When the universe cools enough to pass back down through the threshold temperature, the electromagnetic and weak-force interactions untangle themselves because their force particles rarely get hit hard enough to change into one another. And there is a different mathematical group that expresses this (more familiar) era of big-bang cosmology.

The two mathematical groups have different symmetries. In the mathematical model of moving from one cosmic era to the next, the process of switching the group governing the model is called "symmetry breaking." When symmetry breaks, there is more determinateness in the system because previously interchangeable perspectives now appear to be distinct. But this is also confusing because it masks the underlying unity of the forces. That is, the true nature of the electromagnetic and weak-force interactions is expressed not only in our world, where they virtually never interact, but also in the early universe, where they are shown to be two aspects of the same reality, the so-called electro-weak force.

The concepts of symmetry and symmetry-breaking nicely describe metaphysical situations where things are not quite what they seem and two superficially opposed positions turn out to be perspectives on a deeper reality. I think this is probably the case for the paradoxical contrast between the Nevillian pure *creatio ex nihilo* view (1) and the Plotinian pure *emanatio ex deo* view (2): the apparent choice reflects the broken symmetry within a micro-theogony, while seeing both as perspectives on an abysmal-ground points to a more fundamental symmetry (4). The abysmal-ground view is not only vague (and thus specifiable) in respect to the Neville versus Plotinus contrast; it is also vague with respect to the question of whether there is a rational floor for inquiry. And it expresses a fascinating posture on the question of whether God has a character. The answer is yes, in respect of the infinitesimal move toward divine determination in the micro-theogony I have described; this is *divine self-determination*. The answer is also no, in respect of the vanishingly small size of that move; it is as though the infinite potential for divine self-determination is *compressed into nothing*.

Conclusion

I have argued that, despite appearances, the *ex nihilo* and *ex deo* views of ultimacy are two complementary perspectives on a deeper reality. In an appropriate theoretical framework, the two views are manifested as perspectival construals on what I have been calling, for want of a better name, the abysmal-ground theory of ultimacy. In terms of the analogy, the conceptual framework of the abysmal-ground theory exhibits a symmetry that breaks when moving to the conceptual framework in which the *ex nihilo* and *ex deo* views of ultimacy are diametrically opposed to one another.

As in particle physics and big-bang cosmology so in metaphysics and philosophical theology: hunting for symmetries that allow us to frame opposing views as complementary perspectives rewards effort. In this case, the fight between the *ex nihilo* and *ex deo* views of ultimacy is conducted within a conceptual framework that conceals an underlying symmetry. This fight thus makes enemies out of views that, properly understood, represent indispensable insights onto a richer and conceptually more intractable reality.

Note that this underlying symmetry is deeply opposed to the Augustinian have-your-cake-and-eat-it-too approach to the contrast between *ex nihilo* and *ex deo* views of creation. That's not symmetry! If Augustine is correct, then there really is a God with a determinate character *a se*, apart from creation. But I find this less plausible than both the Nevillian and Plotinian alternatives, and all of them less compelling than the symmetric abysmal-ground view I am trying to describe. Honestly, it's a close call because the abysmal-ground view is profoundly paradoxical and the case is difficult to make; it's a 60–40 or 70–30 result at best. Keep in mind that it's tentative, too, because it takes shape within the surfer-dude epistemic framework of pragmatic fallibilism. It probably also owes something to my personal philosophical-theological temperament, which seems to have settled around atheism in respect of anything like intentional divine agents (the Augustinian view is one of these), and apophatic mystical theism in respect of the ultimate referent of theological language about ultimacy.

Symmetry breaking helps me picture how understanding-enabling rationality and conception-defeating absurdity can coexist deeply in the fecund ontological origins of reality. It helps explain why the western debate over the One and the many had to go on for two dozen centuries before someone came up with a pure *ex nihilo* viewpoint—like Augustine, philosophical theologians instinctively resisted giving up the *ex deo* aspects of their views even when they called them *ex nihilo*. And it helps me understand my experience of feeling so compelled by the insights embedded in apparently opposing metaphysical viewpoints.

It is a slender case. And I may not be a wholly impartial evaluator. But the abysmal-ground view of ultimacy looks significantly better to me than the alternatives. Long live symmetry! And long live the playground where we philosophical theologians perpetually attempt to eff the ineffable!

Part 2

ULTIMACY SYSTEMS

PART 2 *meditates on systems of religious symbols. Here the thought is less on directly effing the ineffable and more on analyzing the way ordinary religious and theological symbol systems indirectly engage people with their ultimate concerns. All three essays in this cluster express wonder at the reflexive genius of religious symbol systems, and document the techniques and strategies that spontaneously arise within them, as well as the seemingly magical social functions that those techniques and strategies facilitate. The analytical tradition of philosophy is most prominent here, with the focus on linguistic analysis and conceptual micro-moves. Chapter 4 on "Slipping" exhibits religious philosophy in the analytical and comparative modes, using an informal kind of literary criticism as the main tool. Chapter 5 on "Balancing" is primarily religious philosophy in the analytical style with nods in the direction of the comparative and theoretical styles. Chapter 6 on "Eclipsing" considers an entire symbol system rather than strategic mechanisms within a symbol system, and it expresses religious philosophy in the evaluative and analytical styles.*

CHAPTER 4

SLIPPING

INTRODUCTION

THE UNDERSIDE OF INDIVIDUAL EXPERIENCE AND SOCIAL LIFE IS THE NEXUS of events and behaviors that lead with horrific frequency to tragedy, depravity, oppression and cruelty, from tormented psyches to institutional corruption, from moral degradation to socially sanctioned exploitation. Religious traditions and texts grapple practically and intellectually with this underside in varied ways. It is another way of effing the ineffable, one with potentially serious practical effects.

More precisely, those traditional religious linguistic grapplings with the underside of life have a double effect. On the one hand, they express sensitivity to the evil and chaos of human life, and they cultivate communal empathy toward people who suffer. On the other hand, these ritual, ethical and doctrinal exertions serve to inure religious communities to the harsher realities of life, either through eschatological escapism, habitual distancing, or systematic descriptions of life that sequester its underside away from easy viewing.

There is something socially and psychologically useful about such distractions, of course, because the horror of life is hard to bear. The saints, sages, and prophets of every culture may be able to look the underside of life in the eye and not wither in horror, but most people need to keep it out of sight as much as possible in order to function effectively. Cultural activities that foster insensitivity to the underside of life therefore serve a useful function for the individuals and societies they influence. This is part of the explanation for large-scale, social expressions of denial, including dangerous scapegoating mechanisms. But the insensitivities of denial, displaced rage, and vengeance also retard attempts to transform social conditions.

Such side effects of effing the ineffable leave me utterly fascinated. How do they *work*? How does our socially embedded speech about the pain of life perform its morally ambiguous *magic*? And what kinds of pressures do cognitive-emotional preferences and social obligations impose on speaking of suffering and its ultimate ground?

AMBIGUOUS UNDERCURRENTS IN RELIGIOUS NARRATIVES

Many religious texts sponsor religious thought about the underside of life. Each of the texts to be considered here has the underside of life in the background, while in the foreground a narrative addresses questions about it—questions about its origin, nature, and overcoming. Certain traditional lines of interpretation of each of these narratives lead to theoretical construals of the human condition that, in different respects, both cultivate empathy and inure communities to the horrific underside of human experience and social life.

THE STORY OF ADAM IN THE QUR'AN

First, consider the Qur'anic material concerning Adam (see especially the presentations in 2:27ff., 7:7ff., 15:26ff., and 20:15ff.). Adam is created by Allah to be viceroy on earth and given special knowledge not possessed by the angels. Allah thus enters into a primordial covenant with Adam. Allah demands that the angels prostrate themselves before Adam, and all do so except Iblis, who dissents out of pride. Iblis is cursed by Allah and banished, but permitted—and thus designated by Allah—to fill the role of the enemy of Adam and his offspring, the one who sets snares and tries to turn people away from the worship of Allah. Allah warns Adam and his wife about the enemy he has established for them, and permits them to eat from all but one of the trees in their garden home. Iblis convinces them to eat from the forbidden tree, however, so Adam breaks the primordial divine covenant of obedience to and love of Allah. Nevertheless, Allah relents and forgives the error. As originally intended, Allah establishes Adam and his progeny as viceroy on earth, both promising a pleasant habitation and warning of enmity among them. Allah also promises guidance so that they need not go astray again.

The story presents Allah as establishing human beings, unlike the angels, to be creatures blessed with special knowledge and responsibility for the earth, and to exist in moral tension by virtue of being under the divine command. Human beings have the peculiar perfection of being under the divine imperative to be perfect, even as the rest of creation actually *is* perfect. Humanity is not essentially flawed through being suspended in this moral tension, nor does the almost negligible mistake of Adam and his wife plunge humanity into a disastrous fallen state. Rather, Allah forgives them, and the story of the establishment of the earth's viceroys continues, as does the divine imperative, the primordial covenant, and the promised guidance of Allah, expressed preeminently in the testimony of the blessed prophet and the Qur'an.

This story of failure hovers in the background of the portrayal of humanity in the Qur'an: the primordial covenant is always vulnerable to being broken by human inattention to the law. The misery of human life receives its final answer in the vision of Allah mercifully and justly making decisive judgment at an appointed future time. But the reasons why such misery is even possible find expression in the mysterious story of Adam's mistake. It was a tiny slip—a slip due mostly to the cunning and trickery of Iblis in his divinely appointed role as the opponent of humanity. The smallness and almost accidental character of Adam's mistake seem crucial to the narrative. A huge mistake would portray Adam as a miscreant, the primordial covenant as futile, and Allah's plans as easily derailed. And no mistake at all would make the misery of life seem arbitrary, and Allah's creation an exercise in cruelty. The mistake has to be a tiny slip to keep the narrative in balance.

What of the possibility for Adam to slip in this way at all? The story explains this by means of the divine designation of Adam to be like the rest of his race: suspended in moral tension. There is a principle of plenitude hovering in the narrative here. Allah fills every niche of being in creation. The angels are perfect, but sense no moral tension; other creatures are not capable of sensing this moral tension. But human beings are the ones who enter into a primordial covenant with Allah to strive after perfection. Allah, who "disdaineth not even to coin the similitude of a gnat" (Pickthall 1930, 12:26), out of the divinely transcendent wisdom, fills heaven and earth with every possible kind of creature. When the angels questioned Allah about his intention to make creatures of this kind, creatures that would shed blood and cause a multitude of miseries, Allah simply replied that "Surely I know that which ye know not" (2:30). Even Iblis fulfills a designated role in the divinely ordained economy of beings. Thus, in accordance with this principle of plenitude, every ontological-moral possibility is realized in creation. It follows that the slip of Adam and his wife is explained first with reference to their lack of wisdom in listening to Iblis, second with reference to Iblis's role as the enemy of humanity, third with reference to Adam's constitution as suspended in moral tension through being under the divine command, fourth with reference to the principle of plenitude, and finally with reference to the transcendent divine will that is beyond all human reckoning.

On the one hand, the overwhelming character of divine transcendence potentially fosters insensitivity to the horrors of life through being the explanation for them that ultimately lies deeply beneath every preliminary explanation. Such horrors fade into insignificance, and so out of human concern, in the light of divine glory. Furthermore, what can be done about them when their possibility springs from the transcendent divine will? Yet, on the other hand, the divine command directs our attention to the horrors of life and demands that we overcome them, through not making things worse, and through helping to ease burdens where we can. The Qur'anic context for these narratives stimulates empathy toward those upon whom the dark underside of life casts its dangerous, patient eye through the text's emphatic affirmation of the goodness and mercy of Allah, and its careful stipulations about personal holiness and social propriety.

This narrative has four features that are typical of the others I will mention more briefly in a moment. First, the story encourages recognition of the underside of life and empathy toward victims in some respects, and fosters insensitivity in other respects. Second, the narrative turns on a slip that is momentous in significance yet vanishingly small in magnitude. Third, the smallness of the slip—its almost accidental character—plays a crucial role in the narrative by blocking the assignment of total blame to any of the characters in the story. And fourth, there is a theological rationalization for the slip; in this case, though alternatives in Islamic thought exist, I have mentioned the one that takes the form of a blame-deflecting principle of plenitude.

THE FALL OF ADAM AND EVE IN THE TORAH

As a second example, consider the garden story of Genesis (Genesis 2–3), and especially the interpretation of it offered by the second century CE, anti-Jewish, arch-heretic Marcion (which we can reconstruct through Tertullian's *Against Marcion*; see Roberts and Donaldson 1951). Much like the Qur'anic version, the Genesis version has an apparently arbitrary decree—"You must not eat from the tree of the knowledge of good and evil" (2:17a [NIV 1978])—violated by a curious, innocent pair. In the Genesis version, however, the consequences seem totally out of proportion to their juvenile adventure. It is the command and not the eating that awakens the knowledge of good and evil, which makes the creator-God seem most unjust in the narrative. Yet clearly the creator-God's hands are tied, so to speak, for the human creatures have moved into a metaphysical space of knowing freedom. Accordingly, he spells out the consequences of their action in the form of curses, tries to put a good face on it all by showing them how to make clothes, and tosses them out of the garden.

Consciousness of the underside of life and empathy toward its victims are encouraged in this narrative both by the aura of divine command and concern, and by the picturesque contrast between before and after that is elaborated as the story proceeds. Insensitivity to the underside of life is fostered by the apparently inexplicable arbitrariness of the divine command, and the suggestion of carelessness about the horrific consequences for humanity. And once again, as in the Qur'anic narrative, there is a slip underneath all of this: Adam and Eve err almost trivially—and yet portentously—having been tricked by Satan. It is not really the creator-God's fault, it is not really Satan's fault, and it is not really the fault of the human creatures either, but it happens nonetheless. Trying to cope with this slip forces disproportionateness into the narrative.

Marcion apparently sensed the problem with this story, and put his own spin on it, for his own reasons. Beginning from a dualistic distinction between a creator-God and a savior-God, Marcion seems to have regarded the matter-oriented creator-God's command not to eat as unjust, and made of the serpent a hero, the symbol of a spiritually oriented savior-God who resists the fickle arbitrariness of the creator-God, and who leads the duped human beings into salvation precisely through their knowledge. Marcion resolved the ambiguity surrounding the causal heritage of the slip by bluntly and dualistically blaming the creator-God, whom he understood to be the God of the Old Testament, the God obsessed with laws, and opposed to the God of Christianity, the God of Jesus Christ, the God of grace and love. Tertullian frequently attacks Marcion's two-Gods thesis and his assignment of the good-God role to the savior-God—who is the God of Jesus—in contrast to the creator-God—who is the legalistic God of the Jewish religion (see Roberts and Donaldson 1951 *Against Marcion*, book 1, chapters 2–7).

This is one way to characterize what was taken to be Marcion's heretical impulse. Though it is not much celebrated as a point of doctrinal debate, the gradually emerging mainstream of the Christian tradition seems early on to have been committed to maintaining descriptions of this primordial slip that are neutral as regards the cause of the slip—it is neither wholly God's fault nor wholly the fault of humanity. This is one way to understand the importance within Christianity of the doctrine of original sin: its assertion of human vulnerability to sin serves also to exculpate any one individual from total responsibility.

Once again, therefore, we see the four characteristics of this family of narratives. First, both empathy and insensitivity toward the underside of life are cultivated in different respects. Second, the narrative turns on a minuscule slip. Third, the slip's smallness plays an essential role in the narrative by blocking decisive assignment of blame. And fourth, there is a theological rationalization for the slip that, in the case of most Christian commentators (though not Marcion), took the form of a doctrine of the fall. It is important here to note in passing that Jewish theological rationalizations of the slip are generally quite different from Christian ones, and rather varied among themselves.

THE LAST JUDGMENT IN THE APOCALYPSE

Consider now the account of the Last Judgment and associated events in the New Testament book of Revelation. I will not retell the story, but rather leap all the way to the conclusion that it, too, exhibits the four characteristic features of the narratives I am examining. First, empathy toward the underside of life and its victims is cultivated through the vividness and detail of the divine engagement in human affairs that the story presents, and through the testimony to the deadly seriousness of divine command. Insensitivity is fostered by the seemingly unavoidable, escapist dimensions of apocalyptic expectation and by the apparent futility of all efforts to improve human society. Second, there is a narrative slip in the form of the trigger for final consummation. Third, the vanishingly smallness of this narrative slip, notwithstanding its enormous consequences, is essential for blocking wholesale narrative blaming of the characters for the gruesome horrors of the apocalyptic intervention; the trigger has something to do with worsening conditions of human life, something to do with the timetable of evil beings, and something to do with inscrutable divine will. Fourth, theological rationalizations for the slip and its consequences exist in various forms. One kind focuses on the conjunction of two affirmations: the thoroughness of potential divine control of both the grand sweep and intimate details of history and nature, and the apparently indefinite deferral of final, decisive exercise of that control. A tension is established between power and restraint, which reinforces the cultivation of empathy and activism, on the one hand, and withdrawal and insensitivity, on the other.

THE FATEFUL SWIM IN THE EPIC OF GILGAMESH

Small slips make a difference elsewhere, too. In the Epic of Gilgamesh, after a long series of adventures, the hero of the story, Gilgamesh, is told about a plant that is the secret of everlasting life (see especially Speiser 1969, tablet 11, lines 257–91). Gilgamesh finds the plant and begins the journey home. Along the way, he takes a relaxing swim only to have the plant stolen by a water serpent. No matter what human beings do, it seems, they cannot get out from under the burden imposed upon them by the gods. This wonderful adventure sponsors empathy for the tragedy of life through its detailed accounts of human suffering and struggle and by means of narrative encouragement of our identification with the hero. Yet fate is always darkly hovering, and the futility of resistance saps courage and determination and fosters passive acceptance of, or indifference to, the underside of life. The narrative slip takes the form of the loss of the special plant, and the smallness of the slip emphasizes the untraceable inevitability of fate. The rationalization for the slip is suggested in the story clearly enough: though the power of the gods can be resisted by human ingenuity and determination temporarily, the gods always find a way to interfere in human affairs so as to protect divine interests. Put differently, the rationalization for the slip consists in the way the power of human beings—which itself is unaccountably hard to understand in view of the power of the gods—suddenly and inexplicably gives way to the intrusion of fate. We'll return to Gilgamesh later (chapter 7).

GAUTAMA'S DISCOVERY OF SICKNESS, DECREPITUDE, AND DEATH

Finally, recall that it is a small slip in the form of inexplicable encounters with strangers that allows Gautama to encounter sickness, decrepitude, death, and then the possibility of the monastic life (this story is related in a number of places, but most famously and popularly in the *Buddha-carita* of Ašvaghosha; see Cowell 1884, especially books 1 to 5: 1–61). His father was scrupulous in his efforts to shield Gautama from such knowledge. He wanted his son to be a great ruler but, according to a wise seer who spoke to the King on the occasion of the child's birth, Gautama was to be a great spiritual adventurer (1.54ff.). Because of this, and out of love for his son, Gautama's father spared no expense in surrounding his son with all the pleasures of the ruler's life, thereby hoping to prevent him from learning about that alternative future (2:25, 3:3–6, and so on). Even so, seemingly miraculously—by the intervention of the gods according to Ašvaghosha's version of the story—Gautama had those life-changing encounters (3:26–62), and he was driven to seek enlightenment.

The narrative slip in this case is the invisibly small cracks in the shield built around the young boy's consciousness and the events that somehow managed to penetrate those cracks and trigger a cascading chain of transformations. The slip must be small to express the fact that the causes of the raising of consciousness are finally untraceable, just as we are never able to say just what it is that really causes us to wake from sleeping. In due course this yields among some Buddhists to philosophical descriptions of the nature of consciousness, of the ultimate unreality of the dependently co-arising world. At the most fundamental level, the slip expresses the simple inevitability of enlightenment when it occurs, and the impossibility of waking up without in some sense already having woken up.

The slip from sleep to waking is necessary and momentous in significance, yet it is untraceable and therefore uncontrollable and unavoidable.

This story encourages empathy toward the underside of life through its poignant account of the contrast between Gautama's life of comfort and the suffering strangers, and through the narrative tension surrounding the very possibility of those encounters. It also fosters insensitivity toward the underside of life through its suggestion of the unreality of the world and the need to escape from its delusions. The rationalizations of the slip in subsequent Buddhist thought reinforce this dual effect.

SLIPPING AND THE UNDERSIDE OF LIFE

THE NARRATIVE MECHANISM

The metaphor of a "slip"—a near-accidental mistake, of apparent unimportance in itself, but with tragic or far-reaching consequences—expresses a conceptual pattern that is essential to the integrity of each narrative I have discussed. Of course, this slip is developed differently in each narrative. But the conceptual pattern is recognizably similar, and it is intelligible as a strategy for accounting for the underside of life without taking the religiously perilous paths of over-blaming either the mysterious context for human life, or human beings themselves.

Note *how* small this slip is: it must be infinitesimally small, because it *must not function as a causal explanation*, lest the narrative leave traces of cause that give grounds either for ascribing responsibility for the horrors of life to the ground and horizon of our lives, or for assigning to human beings more blame for their misery than is just. We cannot blame the mysterious ground of our lives without unfaithfulness, nor can we blame ourselves unduly without self-betrayal. The vanishing smallness of the slip thus serves to deflect the possibility of one-sided blame. It is a nonexplanatory explanation.

Narratives are ideally suited to express the nonexplanatory explanations that are slips because the capacities of dynamism and indirection possessed by stories are better than the relatively stable terms of theory for suggesting natural *trajectories* of thought. It is these trajectories that lead the imagination gradually through the series of approximations necessary for expressing vanishingly small things of great significance. By contrast, theories are better than stories at detecting bias and making corrections in the processes of world-making for which stories are vital. Thus, while this essay began with a discussion of slips in stories, it ends by asking more theoretically framed questions about how such stories influence religious attitudes toward the underside of life, which is a big part of world-making for every society.

I have argued that each of these narratives fosters the double attitude of sensitivity toward the underside of life in some respects and insensitivity in others. I have also given examples of the way that the notion of a slip and its attendant rationalizations reinforce this dual process of simultaneously intensifying empathy and decreasing sensitivity. Now, in closing, I wish to argue three further points. First, the dual character of this process is essential for social stability. Second, the importance of narrative slips derives in part from the efficiency with which they foster this dual process; this is the reason that narrative slips appear in stories from many parts and periods of the world, and the reason why stories embodying narrative slips play such an important role in religious world-making. Third, in our time, religion is not only a crucial institution for supporting the dual process of increasing empathy and decreasing sensitivity in society at large, it is also a reasonably efficient means of cultivating the maturity needed to face the underside of life without the aid of denial or transference psychological mechanisms.

THE INTERESTS OF SOCIAL STABILITY

It is difficult to make generalizations about societies because they vary greatly, but plausible generalizations are possible, especially if we limit their scope to modern societies. I think societies cannot afford to let empathy become too pronounced because the underside of life is too painful and the corporate consequences of failing to meet individual psychic needs for self-protection are extremely dangerous. Release mechanisms are necessary when awareness of tragedy and horror is high, as the phenomena of lynching, witch hunts, racial prejudice, and bullying illustrate (though they illustrate other social dynamics as well). The limited cultivation of insensitivity toward the underside of life and its unfortunate victims serves preemptively to reduce the need for social release mechanisms (see Girard 1977).

By the same token, modern societies cannot afford to let insensitivity become too pronounced. The hellish expressions of suffering and exploitation typically have a socio-economic and often also a racial or colonial or class-hierarchy cast, and too much insensitivity amplifies tensions potentially to the point of forcing revolutionary impulses into the open. Social chaos seems to follow whenever empathy and insensitivity become unbalanced.

Now it is one thing to speak pragmatically of the interests of social stability, and it is quite another to speak of what is good and true and beautiful.

Insensitivity to the underside of human life and its hapless victims, while understandable in both its psychological and social expressions, is still morally repugnant. It is a sign of human depravity every bit as much as is the violence we visit upon each other. The resulting paradox is an indication of the inescapably frustrating and corrupt character of human social organization. Before I speak further about the dubious moral status of a balance between empathy and insensitivity, however, it is necessary to clarify the role of narrative slips in the maintenance of social stability.

THE ROLE OF SLIPS AND THEIR RATIONALIZATIONS IN WORLD-MAKING

One of the reasons sensitivity to the underside of life is so difficult is that it is extremely painful and alienating to be a victim. Another reason is that there is so often little to be done to help. Open-ended empathy that leads not to action but to silence is agonizing in its own peculiar way. In view of the intransigent and complex character of suffering in modern societies, therefore, it is no wonder that empathy is difficult to achieve. It follows that sensitivity and empathy are least painful and most widespread when rationales for action, emotional postures, and social policies are self-evident. This is the case precisely when there is a clear object of blame for the myriad forms of suffering that so dominate the underside of life, be it God, the devil, nature, human weakness, a conscienceless villain, a class of powerful people, a race—anything specific enough to allow the determination of a strategy that promises to improve the conditions of life.

All of this means that empathy unchecked by sturdy social analyses very often produces fanatics who find strategies for action shockingly easy to determine. In much of pre-World War II Europe, a nationalistically rooted mutual empathy for each others' struggling lives led a significant portion of Europeans in many nations to believe that the Jews stood in the way of the realization of their national, economic, and personal goals. This in turn permitted the most fanatical of them to formulate and implement a staggeringly simple strategy for dealing with their problem. A man develops a profound empathic connection to the unborn babies aborted by doctors in the United States and determines that the natural strategy is to murder one of the doctors. Any amount of human heartedness or sound social analysis would have voided both strategies, but fanaticism has no time for such abstract virtues; the confidence forged by primary experiences of empathy seems self-confirming, even to the point of delusion.

Similar stories could be told about insensitivity to the underside of life. Here, too, blaming is important, but the emphasis is not on blaming a particular party—that leads to action—but on exculpating oneself from blame, and so from involvement. The audible beating in the next apartment that never gets reported is the fault of a vague "somebody else," and so the problem of everyone or anyone else but me.

Empathy and insensitivity are dangerous reactions to the underside of life because of the ease with which they are transmuted into fanaticism and passive negligence, respectively. When stories with the narrative slips to which I have drawn attention play dominant roles in world-making, however, a natural muting of these extreme possibilities occurs. That is because these narrative slips are non-explanatory explanations that leave no causal traces and so block both the easy assignment of blame and the facile exculpation of oneself from responsibility for the horrors of the underside of life. We slip into horror together, and everyone and everything is involved.

The Dangers and Virtues of Contemporary Religious Institutions

While narrative slips have their virtues, many stories play into the world-making construction of interpretations of the underside of life. Religious narratives engaging this dark underside using the narrative device of a slip might have the potential to check fanaticism and negligence, but they are very often in our own time not influential enough to do so. Here, then, lies a special social virtue of contemporary religious institutions: to the extent that they model their procla-mations after critical reinterpretations of their own ancient wisdom—a crucial caveat—they furnish a nonexplanatory explanation for the underside of life that has a socially beneficial dual effect. They simultaneously increase empathy and decrease sensitivity in different respects, and thus they throw soothing oil on the chaotic waters of social life by inhibiting the dangerously extreme manifestations of empathy and insensitivity. World-making guided by ancient stories about the underside of life turning on slips are some of the traditional ways to secure these virtues, and I think they remain important for that purpose today.

By the same token, the dangers of such world-making stories are plain: nar-ratives about the underside of life that are subtly ambiguous with regard to iden-tifying the final cause of the problem tend also to make people under their sway sympathetic but slow to act, kind hearted but morally lukewarm, all good-natured constancy but no courageous convictions—easy targets, then, for a Kierkegaard or a Nietzsche. Moreover, by becoming so effective at supporting ordinary social processes, religious institutions usually become thoroughly entangled in them to the point that they get in the way of the very transformations for which they stand, and become corrupt—easy targets, it would seem, for a Voltaire or a Marx.

There is more to be said, however, and here we move away from pragmatic social considerations. Lukewarm, passionless goodness marks out both the socially ideal peon and the spiritual weakling; these are the characteristics of souls lacking a maturely developed capacity to face the horror of life without something to blame, without a vent for their frustration and fear, without a way to assure themselves that they are not responsible. But religious institutions at their best have a dynamic character that transforms souls. In fact, religious practice helps people engage more and more of reality in ever richer and more significant ways by means of complex and powerful systems of symbols.

The crafting of the soul that these practices permit has been a common and effective way of cultivating the maturity needed to look the monstrous underside of life in the eye without panicking, to empathize with victims of absurd brutality without becoming fanatical, to transform our own turgid traditions, and courageously to devise and implement the complex strategies needed to address even the most intractable agonies of the human condition. The saints and sages of all traditions are our models for such efforts. In spite of their moral ambiguity as institutions, religious communions continue to produce many such remarkable people. It is with their inspiration, and not hopelessly, that we slip, to suffer and to change, into horror.

CONCLUSION

In the next two chapters I examine other system-level dynamics of the relentless human drive to eff the ineffable. In concluding this meditation on slipping, however, I want to reflect for a moment on symbol systems as such—the unifying theme of this book's second cluster of essays.

Religious symbol systems are stunning accomplishments, but of a very particular kind. They are not cathedral-like accomplishments because no architectural mind designed religious symbol systems. They are more like the organic accomplishments of biological evolution, fruits of a reflexive optimization process in an environment that imposes a host of constraints—challenges that the emergently complex organism has to navigate.

Recurring similarities in biological environments pose similar problems that evolved organisms solve in similar ways. Sometimes the structural similarity of solutions derives from common genetic resources, which is probably the case with the basic body plans of animals. Other times, structurally similar solutions are phylogenetically independent; this seems to be the case with eyes, which evolved multiple times, with fascinating differences—that's convergent evolution at work.

As in biological evolution so in religious symbol systems: sometimes common histories (shared "genetic" heritage) lead to structurally similar solutions while other times similar solutions are rediscovered independently and repeatedly (convergent "evolution"). We see examples of both causes for structural similarities in the examples of sacred texts managing the "slipping" challenge. The Jewish-Christian-Muslim "slipping management strategies" have structural similarities (as well as differences) rooted in a shared historic lineage. By contrast, the Buddhist and Abrahamic "slipping management strategies" display structural similarities of the independent, convergent-evolution kind.

I find the evolutionary analogy extremely illuminating for understanding the dynamics and functions of religious and theological symbol systems. Indeed, the various disciplines related to so-called cultural evolution have become important in the study of religion precisely because this analogy is so useful. The effort to apply those disciplines to religious and theological symbol systems has only just begun in the last couple of decades but the promise of such lines of inquiry seems almost unlimited.

Just as in biological systems, there a lot going on in religious symbol systems that nobody planned. That makes system-level dynamics and functions often difficult to detect and analyze; even becoming aware of them can be challenging. But this very fact tells us a lot about the ways we eff the ineffable, particularly within the language games of corporate religious life worlds. We can get good at playing a game without ever really understanding what the game does, what magic it weaves, what side effects it may have. More than that, the wondrous functions of religious symbol systems may *depend* on our not being aware of how the magic is performed. Once we see the trick, we may still be awestruck at the genius and skill of the magician, but the trick no longer works on us.

CHAPTER 5

BALANCING

INTRODUCTION

ONE OF THE GREAT MYSTERIES SURROUNDING THE FUNCTION OF RELIGIOUS symbols is how, precisely, they facilitate a person's "participation" or "taking part" or "engagement" in that to which they purport to refer. For philosophical theologians, the work of effing the ineffable can be a kind of symbolic engagement with ultimate reality, even when such ultimacy talk takes place within the ambit of a highly specialized community of discourse. For people without access to such specialized linguistic techniques, participatory engagement with ultimacy occurs through religious symbols, often arising within traditions of speech and practice whose historic resonances most people never fully grasp.

Much is known about this process of participation. For example: it is intimately connected with the similar processes of world-making and world-interpreting; it crucially involves the human imagination; it often, and perhaps necessarily when linguistic, involves metaphoric speech; it is multileveled in that it simultaneously involves an explicitly known immediate referent and a (sometimes implicitly suggested) religious referent; and it is not mechanistic but depends on the state of the symbol wielder's "soul." But some aspects of participation or engagement remain poorly understood, including questions surrounding systems of symbols.

Symbols usually function in systems, so participation is typically conditioned by structural and global features of such systems as well as by individual symbols. But what kinds of influences do symbol systems have on participation? How do the global features of symbol systems—their structure and tone, the leading concepts they express, the typical forms of interpretative distortion they sponsor—modify the ways symbols are wielded and participation unfolds? How do systemic relations among symbols allow one symbol to enhance or constrain the participation facilitated by another? How do symbol systems help to make available or to obscure the participatory potency and suggestiveness of individual symbols? How, in other words, do symbol systems encode and express strategic mechanisms? Speaking of strategic mechanisms does not presuppose origins lying in deliberate construction. On the contrary, most strategic mechanisms seem to arise spontaneously, and their effectiveness probably relies on the lack of deliberation involved in their birth.

To focus my efforts, I'll examine the strategic balancing function that certain metaphors play within religious symbol systems, extending the kind of analysis attempted in chapter 3. Naturally, individual metaphors shed little light on the problems surrounding strategic mechanisms within religious symbol systems taken as a whole. So I shall reflect on several interestingly different coordinated presentations of symbolic resources—presentations dense enough to justify speaking of the presence of a symbol system—and isolate the strategic balancing mechanisms at work.

I don't take a stand here on the controversial question of the reference of religious symbols. The main features of participation can be accounted for more or less adequately in theories of religious symbols that offer quite opposed interpretations of the religious realities to which those symbols seem to refer. Functionalist overlaying in the human imagination of ideas whose correspondence to ultimate religious realities is irrelevant, the positivist denial of such religious realities, and the Neoplatonic (or otherwise framed) conception of mystical union all offer serviceable accounts of participation. I want to focus on the strategic balancing mechanisms themselves, which often operate unnoticed. Understanding them deepens our appreciation both of the spontaneous arising of symbol systems and of the process of participation.

Four Strategies for Balancing Personal and Impersonal Metaphors

Strategic balancing mechanisms are immediately evident when one considers the tension between contrasting families of personal and impersonal metaphors for ultimate reality. I present here four examples illustrating distinctive ways of employing strategic metaphors to manage this tension, referring chiefly to the religious symbol systems appearing in the Bhagavad-Gita, and in the writings of early medieval mystical theologian Pseudo-Dionysius, religion scholar Huston Smith (an advocate of the so-called perennial philosophy), and German-American philosophical theologian Paul Tillich. I name the four strategies to be identified as the perspectival, the paradoxical, the subordinationist, and the integrationist, respectively. In each case, in distinctive ways, one family of metaphors serves strategically to control the potentially dangerous elements in the other family.

I am particularly interested in the fact that these spontaneously arising systems of symbolic checks and balances seem only ever to be partially effective. One family seems inevitably to gain ascendancy over the other. This bias in favor of either families of personal metaphors or families of impersonal metaphors is a fascinating indication of the existentially loaded and narratively structured requirements of participation: we *need* our symbol systems to constitute a solid *story*.

PERSPECTIVE: THE BHAGAVAD-GITA

Part of the Mahabharata epic, the Bhagavad-Gita is a religious classic profoundly expressive of Indian culture and tradition. It has been interpreted in numerous ways and remains popular in widely varying parts of Indian life partly because of the Gita's narrative setting and poetic texture and partly because the ideas presented are not easily pressed into a univocal system. This hermeneutical openness is directly relevant to what is said about systems of symbolic material within it. A hermeneutical stand must be taken if I am to proceed, therefore, and it will have to be taken without much argument to avoid a major distraction from the specific goal of this essay.

The key to the interpretation I favor is the Gita's perspectival approach to ultimate reality and to human life and its sensitivity to differences among people's life situations. The Gita synthesizes these perspectives into a larger whole by means of its expositions of the paradoxical relationships that hold among duty, knowledge, devotion, action, desire, and discipline. Yet the whole can be represented only by means of multiple, complementary perspectives upon it. Speaking as an English reader of the Sanskrit classic, I accept that this synthetic-perspectival interpretation is demanded because the Gita seems to move from one perspective on life to another without fully reconciling those different perspectives, and without finally declaring that one perspective is universally superior to the others, except perhaps for a particular kind of person. The attempt at synthesis is made, to be sure, and devotion to Krishna is a key element of it, but the synthesis is not allowed to trample over the validity of perspectival differences.

The interpretations from the scholars who have made English translations of the Gita differ mainly in emphasis. Representatives of the differences are Sarvepalli Radhakrishnan and Barbara Stoler Miller (see the rapid summary of the Gita in Radhakrishnan and Moore 1957, Radhakrishnan 1948, and the introduction to Miller 1986). Radhakrishnan emphasizes the complementary but independent viability of the Gita's various perspectives on life, while Miller stresses devotion to Krishna as the principle by which the various perspectives are unified. Radhakrishnan sees the Gita developing a synthesis of the impersonal Brahman of the Upanishads, the Vedic cult of sacrifice, the Samkhya form of metaphysical dualism, and the personal God for whom overcoming human suffering and delusion is a priority. Miller, by contrast, prefers to see the various orthodox and unorthodox philosophical developments of Brahmanical and Vedic religion only as background sources for the main concepts taken up in the Gita, and he treats the synthesis as more practical than metaphysical in character.

Resolving such differences of emphasis is not necessary, as the perspectival interpretation adopted here is neutral to most of the points of debate. But my interpretation does oppose two extreme readings of the Gita: that it presents a synthesis so complete that perspectives are superfluous for conceiving life and reality, and that it espouses an emphatic perspectivalism that denies to the Gita its own specific, synthetic, historical character. My view is midway between these extremes and general enough to comprehend both Radhakrishnan's and Miller's readings.

The Gita is set against the tense background of imminent battle between two wings of a large family poised to fight over the succession of rule. A visionary narrator recounts the conversation between Arjuna, the mightiest of the warriors, and Krishna, his charioteer. Arjuna, having directed Krishna to move his chariot between the two armies, is paralyzed by grief at the thought of the stupidity and violence of the battle about to begin. He does not know what to do, torn between his sacred duty as a warrior to fight and the thoughtful compassion that leads him to seek a better way. It is to Arjuna's inner turmoil that Krishna addresses his teaching. Krishna shows Arjuna that action in the name of sacred duty derives its importance, its justification, and its necessity not from the ignorant passion of the single-minded warrior—which had in Arjuna's case been disrupted by his compassion and intelligence—but from eternal cosmic truths. When the ongoing processes of cosmic destruction and creation are viewed from beyond the passion of the moment, the battle and everyone involved in it are seen as part of the inexorable flow of events.

The Gita's theophany reveals Krishna as an avatar of a divine creator-destroyer who periodically appears in human affairs to consummate destruction and to restore sacred order amid chaos. The theophany and the vision of the necessity of human affairs contextualize Krishna's teaching about sacred duty. Arjuna's sacred duty is to cultivate the knowledge and the discipline needed to overcome the greatest enemy of all: attachment to the fruits of his actions, attachment driven by desire. Trusting devotion to Krishna facilitates both the relinquishment of attachment to the fruits of one's actions and the embrace of one's sacred duty.

I am impressed by the Gita's perspectival approach to synthesizing various ways of conceiving reality and human life. This perspectival approach applies to the paths by which human beings may exercise their sacred duty, depending on their time in life (the Mahabharata's student, householder, forest-dweller, and wandering-ascetic stages of life) and their social location and responsibilities (expressed by position in the caste system). It also applies to the ways by which human beings may triumph over the scourge of desire and attachment—through knowledge (*jñana*), work (*karma*), or devotion (*bhakti*). But particularly interesting to me is the way this perspectival approach functions in the Gita as a mechanism for balancing personal and impersonal symbolizations of ultimate reality.

This balancing mechanism pitches the Upanishadic conception of an impersonal absolute against personal images of God as a concerned, active, and loving Lord. The Gita is able to develop the personal conception of God with great drama owing to its epic literary context and the charismatic personage of Krishna. The God of creation and destruction, the one who maintains order within a universe replete with chaos, has the humble form of a human being in the Gita. Everything that goes with being finite and human is thereby made a vehicle for conceptualizing this divinity: location in space and time, appearance and personality, will and understanding, and specific concern for human beings and their enlightenment. The Gita cultivates devotion to Krishna precisely because he is a personal representation of divine solicitousness, of personal divine interest in each and every devotee.

One might imagine such a personal divinity in a wider cosmic context in many ways. In the context of the typical self-absorbed pantheon, such a personal God might be a renegade member with an atypical concern for human beings. In the context of a world created as a testing ground for human souls, a personal God would further the very purpose of the universe through being concerned with its human subjects. But the Gita's contextualization of the personal God of whom Krishna is an avatar is, by comparison with these other possibilities, unexpected. The universe is a seamless moral fabric in which each being gets what it wants and wants what it deserves to get. It is a great "block universe" in which everything past, present, and future is determined to occur in its proper way, and every action has its due consequence. In such a universe of moral cause and effect, at least when it is taken to the extreme, even the God of creation and destruction is but an implementer of the grand moral design; this God's personal interests are finally merely emphatic reinforcements of the cosmic, karmic pattern. This is the universe grounded by impersonal Brahman, the Ultimate Reality beyond all attributes from and within the great life of which every being springs and every moment unfolds.

The Gita makes no attempt to reconcile the personal God, whose decisions and concerns matter, with the impersonal Brahman to whom we can attribute no determinate characteristics. Rather, these points of view are artfully juxtaposed with each other in the Gita's portrayal of the ultimate context of human life. The Gita's synthesis of these points of view does not overcome the tension, but rather speaks of devotion to Krishna as a way of cultivating those attitudes to life that make for true freedom and finally liberation from the weight of attachment to the fruits of one's actions. That makes sense: devotion to Krishna is devotion to the one whose fantastic and decidedly impersonal theophany bespeaks the moral-causal, cosmic-karmic context for Arjuna's life that Krishna's teaching lays out. It is ironic that devotion to a personal image of God should be valued for its ability to cultivate awareness of the fundamentally impersonal wider context for human life, but no more ironic than seeking liberation in a morally deterministic universe. Both *work*. Moral determinism reinforces human responsibility and freedom in practice, even if the theoretical conflict is insoluble, just as devotion to a personal God in the presence of knowledge of an impersonal cosmos leads to liberated souls.

The Gita's system of symbolic material juxtaposes both personal and impersonal symbols and images for God calmly and scrupulously. The two kinds of characterization of the divine are reconciled only in practice, in the cultivation of the state of mind in which the virtues and limitations of each are appreciated. That is the theoretical reason for the acceptability of the perspectival management strategy. The reason for adopting a management strategy in the first place, by contrast, is practical: it is a matter of realism with regard to the fact that people are different and approach God in different ways. Without this perspectival way to balance impersonal and personal symbols for God, one of the modes of participation for striving after liberation might be crippled. And any balancing strategy that was more systematic than the calm, juxtaposing approach of the perspectival strategy would betray the fundamental insight that liberation is a matter of realization and not merely of conception.

PARADOX: PSEUDO-DIONYSIUS

The early medieval writings produced under the pseudonym of Dionysius (or Denys) the Areopagite (mentioned in the New Testament book of the Acts of the Apostles 17:34) constitute a small but influential corpus. I will not venture into the furiously complex debates over the authorship of these writings; nor into debates surrounding how large was the original corpus of which but four works and some letters have survived; nor into debates over the authenticity of parts of that surviving corpus; nor into the rich history of Pseudo-Dionysius's influence on Christian theology, especially in twelfth-century medieval theology and then in Saint Thomas Aquinas (who quotes Pseudo-Dionysius frequently) and subsequent scholastic theology. It is enough for my purposes to outline the balancing strategy evident in the symbol system of the Dionysian corpus.

Neoplatonic themes are omnipresent in these writings. Particularly important is the Neoplatonic idea of emanation and return, by which the unknowable One expresses itself in creation and then draws creatures back into itself (see chapter 3). In virtue of the emanation of the One into the created order, according to Dionysius, we must utter the divine names, which is to say we must make positive affirmations about the nature of God. For this, we ought to begin with the concepts that are most apt for expressing the divine (goodness, love, understanding, power, etc.) and then extend our naming toward the less apt, such as objects drawn from the rich diversity of sensible reality (light, father, mother hen, rock, water, etc.). This *via positiva* approach to the divine presupposes a fundamental participation of all of creation in its divine source and ground, so that to name is to involve oneself in the reality to which the name is applied.

The process works for salvation not because God can be named, but because the participation of creation in God is potentiated by aptness. That is, because some names are more apt than others for expressing the divine nature, a trajectory can be established from the more apt to the less apt and thus beyond even the least apt to the collapse of language in face of divine mystery. This trajectory guides the mature soul from devotional attachment to certain wondrous names toward a profusion of names, a never-ending chorus of cosmic naming, whose very fullness bespeaks the unnamable mystery to which all names are addressed in vain. It is actually a trajectory of ascent because the increasingly less apt names drawn from sensible reality are embraced for the sake of filling out the roaring of names, and so complete the soul's realization of the impossibility of capturing in names the mystery of the One.

Corresponding to the return of creation to its divine ground, for Dionysius, is the *via negativa*, by which affirmations about God are denied. This is a trajectory of ascent by which the least apt affirmations are denied first in a relentless attempt to discipline the imagination by driving it to silence. In due course, even the loftiest and holiest conceptual and scriptural names of God are denied and darkness descends upon the human soul. This darkness expresses the encounter with the divine abyss, to use one of Dionysius's powerful images. It is the same fecund abyss from which all being emanates, and which the *via positiva* attempts to name.

It is the more straightforward, open approach of the *via negativa* that causes Dionysius to prefer it to the *via positiva*. In fact, contrary to appearances, the *via positiva* is the more indirect approach to God. It calls at some point for a dramatic reversal of orientation as the soul discerns a nameless mystery in and through the cultivation of the great symphony of names. The *via negativa*, by contrast, requires no such reversal and leads directly to abysmal silence through consistently drawing attention to the failure of names.

Of all the surviving writings of the Dionysian corpus, *The Divine Names* is the one that most self-consciously exploits the *via positiva* approach, though references are made throughout to two other lost or fictitious writings. The first of these, *Theological Representations*, supposedly dealt with the names most appropriate to God: "good, existent, life, wisdom, power, and whatever other things pertain to the conceptual names for God." The second, *The Symbolic Theology*, supposedly discussed "analogies of God drawn from what we perceive," including images, tools, places, clothes, emotions, activities, and people (note that Pseudo-Dionysius describes the task of these writings in a number of places, including *Mystical Theology*, chapter 3; see Pseudo-Dionysius 1987, 139). Two other extant works, *The Celestial Hierarchy* and *The Ecclesiastical Hierarchy*, deal with the nature of perceptible symbols and how they lead the soul to deeper union with the divine through manifesting the hierarchies of reality—the hierarchy in the celestial sphere and its reflection in the ecclesial sphere. Another possibly fictitious work, *The Conceptual and the Perceptual*, is claimed to have done this, too. Its contention was supposedly that "sacred symbols are actually the perceptible tokens of the conceptual things. They show the way to them and lead to them, and the conceptual things are the source and the understanding underlying the perceptible manifestations of hierarchy" (*The Ecclesiastical Hierarchy*, chapter 2, in Pseudo-Dionysius 1987, 205). *The Mystical Theology* is the work of negative theology *par excellence*. It is necessarily much shorter than *The Divine Names* because negative theology drives toward the failure of speech much faster than theology *via positiva*.

Together the two parts of the Dionysian corpus present an important paradox: naming the divine and denying divine names both help the soul to attain a profound understanding of inexpressible divine mystery through driving the soul away from language altogether and toward silence. Consider, for example, personal metaphors for God. Dionysius distinguishes most clearly between perceptible and conceptual names, and it is not completely obvious into which category personal names fit. They are perceptual in the sense of corresponding to perceptual objects (fathers, kings), but conceptual in the sense of being abstractions from experienced relations (fatherhood, kingship). Nevertheless, it is clear that for Dionysius they do not possess the aptness and so the eminence of the more purely conceptual names, such as beauty, being, holy of holies, life, light, love, one, power, righteousness, salvation of the world, truth, and wisdom. Yet personal names such as father, friend, and lover still have their appropriate place in the *via positiva*, and so are a proper part of the process whereby the soul is drawn toward union with the object of such names. That process of personal transformation through mystical union necessarily involves the realized failure of all names. Attachment to any particular name fades in the cacophony of naming, and (we must infer) the personal names, being less apt than the conceptual names, more effectively summon the experience of dissimilarity that is crucial to realizing their failure.

For this very reason, in the complementary *via negativa* approach, the personal names would be denied before the less dissimilar, purely conceptual names are denied. One oddity about *The Mystical Theology* is that the personal names are included in the final section (especially kingship, fathership, sonship), which deals with denials aimed at establishing that "the supreme Cause of every conceptual thing is not itself conceptual" (this is the title of chapter 5 of *The Mystical Theology*; see Pseudo-Dionysius 1987, 141). That, I take it, is a consequence merely of the fact that there are but two short sections in which Dionysius crams in all of his denials, and the distinction between these two is the one between the perceptual and the conceptual that predominates throughout the corpus. In any event, the denial of personal names comes before the denial of loftier conceptual symbols, and both are necessary if the goal of union is to be achieved.

There is paradox aplenty here. The most obvious paradox is the one in which assertions that apply names to God are simultaneously true and false in significantly the same respect. But that is not the one to which I want to draw attention. A less obvious paradox is evident in the strategy Dionysius uses for balancing personal and impersonal (in Dionysius's case we should say "impersonal-conceptual") symbols for God. On the one hand, he (supposing Pseudo-Dionysius was a "he") allows that both sorts of symbols are "true" and "efficacious" while simultaneously insisting that both are "false" and "misleading." On the other hand, he orders the symbols by means of the concept of aptness or similarity, enabling him to assert that the impersonal-conceptual symbols are truer and less misleading than the personal symbols. And all the while he maintains that the intended object of our naming "is beyond assertion and denial. We make assertions and denials of what is next to it, but never of it, for it is both beyond every assertion . . . and beyond every limitation; it is also beyond every denial" (*The Mystical Theology*, chapter 5; see Pseudo-Dionysius 1987, 141). This establishes yet simultaneously undermines the basis for distinguishing more true from less true symbols of the divine.

This paradoxical balancing strategy permits Dionysius to affirm the superiority of impersonal-conceptual symbols over their personal counterparts while still preventing the impersonal-conceptual symbols from getting out of control, which would lead to the trivialization of personal symbols and the incomprehensibility of both personal spiritual development and many ecclesial practices. Anticipation of this result would be strong motivation for adopting a balancing strategy in the first place. And the fact that the balancing strategy must take a paradoxical form in Dionysius's case is due to his understanding of both God and religious symbolism.

SUBORDINATION: HUSTON SMITH

Huston Smith is a renowned scholar of religion who defended a decidedly unpopular view in the current climate of religious studies: the so-called perennial philosophy. He preferred to call it "the primordial tradition" to emphasize that this view is always present within, and confirmed by, traditional religious and cultic groups; it is not merely a form of intellectualism, as "perennial philosophy" might suggest. Smith argued that religious traditions, beneath their surface differences, have a common core—and that common core is the primordial tradition.

According to Smith, this primordial vision of reality expresses the deepest accumulated wisdom of corporate humanity about the nature of reality. Smith wielded this supposedly multimillennia-strong consensus against the modern West's infatuation with science. It is because "scientism" has taken over in the West that he believed it to be the only significant exception to the historical pattern that confirms the primordial tradition as the consensus of humanity about the ultimate nature of reality. Thus, Smith was frequently heard and read promulgating a twofold message. He prophesied against the scientific hubris of the West, while articulating the basic elements of the primordial tradition. Both tasks are undertaken with greatest clarity and efficiency in his *Forgotten Truth: The Common Vision of the World's Religions* (1992).

The primordial tradition affirms a hierarchical vision of a great scale of being, typically expressed in spatial metaphors. Smith's way of expressing this is to speak of "levels of reality." At the lowest level is the terrestrial plane, which is the realm of material, corporeal objects. Above that is the intermediate level, which is the realm of the psychic, of animate and inanimate phantasms and astral bodies, of demonic and angelic beings, of ghosts and other discarnate entities. It is primarily this realm that Pseudo-Dionysius charts in *The Celestial Hierarchy*. Above the intermediate plane, according to Smith, is the celestial plane, which is the realm of Plato's forms, of Jung's archetypes, and of the personal God of traditional Western theism. Personal metaphors are entirely appropriate here because the natural relation to be cultivated is one of love in which the distinction between soul and God is always maintained even in intense closeness.

Unreachably far above the celestial level is the Infinite, which Smith always spells with an uppercase "I". This is not another realm of being, but beyond being. It is what is left when all distinctions are removed, the sought-after goal of broken religious symbols, metaphors for divinity, trajectories of naming, and theological negations. It is the transpersonal One, the infinitely intense source of being without being a being, the mystic's dazzling darkness, the shining sea into which the dewdrop of each life silently slips, the abysmal ground of everything determinate. Simplicity and power of being increase as we move up the hierarchy of the primordial tradition, just as vulnerability and conceivability increase as we move down. Smith expounds an anthropology in which the levels of selfhood—body, mind, soul, and spirit—correspond to the levels of reality. Ultimately, then, *atman* is *Brahman* for the primordial tradition; the infinite human spirit is nothing other than the Infinite itself.

The distinction between personal and impersonal symbols for God is vital to Smith. He insists that affirmations made about the personal *theos* at the celestial level can be true without being the whole truth. So God really is mother, lover, king, friend, lord; and human beings are right to speak in those terms. But these truths must be contextualized by a full awareness of the great scale of being. The final truth cannot be spoken, though it be truest; the Infinite cannot be named, though the power of all names for divinity derives ultimately from it. The distinction between the personal God and the Infinite is well expressed in an Indian distinction: between the God with attributes (*saguna Brahman*) and the God without attributes (*nirguna Brahman*). The former is a personal God, the ultimate reality for theistic religious traditions; the latter is the ultimate reality for the primordial tradition that lies within each tradition and is shared among all traditions—especially among their mystical thinkers. The former is real, but less real than the latter; true statements may be made about it, but they are incomplete truths that point beyond themselves to the unspeakable Infinite.

The subordination of personal to impersonal symbols for God is obvious here, as is the inevitability that any relation between the two sorts of symbols would have to take this subordinationist form. What is not so obvious is why it is strategic: what is at stake for the primordial tradition in balancing personal and impersonal symbols for God in this way? When the primordial tradition appears in closed groups expounding esoteric teachings—as in some monastic communities, some forms of Gnosticism, and some sects—there is little interest in balancing mechanisms. The subordination serves to demarcate the deep truth about reality, and the reality of a contradictory view is explained by means of reference to the state or type of the human soul. The *jiva* of many lives may be able to see what the less experienced soul may not.

The interest in balancing mechanisms appears most strongly in what might be called "relatively egalitarian" forms of the primordial tradition. In these less esoteric settings, with many kinds of people bonded together in communities of worship and activity, there is the boddhisattva's interest in the cultivation of souls, as well as the need for a reasoned realism about the way symbols are wielded at every level of spiritual maturity. This implies that there will be the attempt to affirm the use of personal symbols for God, just as Smith does, while still scrupulously subordinating such usage to the larger scheme of levels in which the Infinite always lies beyond the realm of the personal God. In this way, and especially in Huston Smith, the hierarchical subordinationism of the primordial tradition is put to work as a strategic mechanism for balancing personal and impersonal symbols for God.

INTEGRATION: PAUL TILLICH

The final example to be considered here is that of Paul Tillich. I focus on part 2 of his *Systematic Theology*, and especially on the sections that deal with personal symbolism for God (see Tillich 1951, 163–289, especially 244–46, 286–89).

Tillich's discussions of divine symbolism are replete with balancing strategies, self-consciously adopted. This is a consequence of Tillich's heightened sensitivity to the polar structure of being. I explain this in several small steps. For Tillich, the self-world correlation is the basic ontological structure. It is expressed in polarities within being: the ontological elements of individualization and participation, dynamics and form, freedom and destiny. The first term in each of these polarities is the subjective element, corresponding to the subjective "self" term of the self-world correlation. Likewise, the second term in each of the polar elements expressed the objective "world" side of the self-world correlation. Second, since Tillich conceives of God as the ground of being, as being-itself, it follows that the self-world correlation and the ontological elements have their ground and unity in God. Third, the fact that human beings symbolize God as their ultimate concern out of the resources made available by being under the conditions of existence then implies that the self-world correlation and the ontological elements are crucial conceptual tools for analyzing symbolic language about God. Finally, the fact that the structure of being is essentially polar means that adequate symbol systems referring to God will have to be in balance. Most generally, symbols expressing the subjective side of the basic ontological structure will have to balance symbols expressing its objective side. More specifically, sets of symbols expressing the ontological elements will have to reflect the unity and balance that each pair of elements has within God. As Tillich says with regard to each particular polarity, it is "necessary to balance one side of the ontological polarity against the other without reducing the symbolic power of either of them" (244).

Tillich's adoption of balancing strategies is not only for the sake of having symbols in collective systems refer as truly as possible to God. He is also concerned with the distortions induced in spiritual life when theology allows its symbols for God to slip out of balance. For example, unless the family of symbols expressing the holy power of God (lord, king, judge, highest) is balanced with the family expressing the holy love of God (father, creator, helper, savior), distortions will result. Sentimentalism will emerge if the holy power of God is muted, and power unchecked by love is demonic. Tillich insists that "even the attempt to emphasize one over against the other destroys the meaning of both" (287), and he makes repeated remarks throughout his writings about the havoc such distortions wreak upon the religious life.

As we have seen, the tension between personal and impersonal symbols for God is fundamental for Tillich because it corresponds to the tension between the subjective and objective sides of the basic ontological structure (the self-world correlation). God is a self—but not only a self—and certainly not a self in the sense of being separated from other selves, for God is also the context for and ground of all selves. This tension between God as self and not-self is expressed more specifically with reference to the ontological elements of individualization and participation. Without personal symbols for God, Tillich insists that the individualization aspect of this tension cannot be expressed. Moreover, he insists that human beings cannot be ultimately concerned about anything that is less than personal. So how is God to be understood as personal? While acknowledging that this is a tricky question, Tillich argues that " 'Personal God' does not mean that God is *a* person. It means that God is the ground of everything personal and that he carries within himself the ontological power of personality" (245).

It appears, therefore, that Tillich's balancing strategy adopts an integrationist approach. He analyzes symbol systems for God against the background of a rich ontological analysis of being that has a distinctively polar structure.

Then he allows the ultimate unity of these poles in the divine ground of being to function as the motivation for balancing personal and impersonal (and other matched pairs of) symbols for God. Tillich's systematic integration of personal and impersonal symbols for the divine is arguably not as balanced as he says he would like because the personal side of God is far less prominent than the impersonal side in the system as a whole. That, however, does not alter his intention to maintain an evenhanded balance by means of an integrationist strategy.

From Four Strategies to a Classification of Strategies

There are balancing strategies other than the four illustrated here. However, what we have seen so far permits an argument—one not entirely arbitrary—to the effect that any other strategy would have to be related to the perspectival, paradoxical, subordinationist, and integrationist strategies in a particular way. Consider the following line of analysis.

First, to list the major premises of the argument, the implementation of any balancing strategy presupposes a means of judgment of the relative adequacy of the symbols to be kept in balance, for otherwise no sense of balance could be established. Such a basis for judgment will necessarily presuppose or implement or call for a relevant, wider theory that makes clear how arbitrariness is being avoided in the making of judgments. Such wider theories will have to comprehend either or both of two complex realities: the purported object of the symbols (God), and the wielders and wielding of the symbols (human beings and their religious activity and language).

Second, the basis for such a judgment may be readily apparent, or it may be obscure, owing to the need to subject the basis of judgment itself to multiple, superficially incompatible criteria of adequacy. In this latter case, the basis for judgment is both constructed and questioned even as it is applied, and the balancing strategy that results is paradoxical in the sense that the Dionysian strategy is.

Third, suppose, contrary to the Dionysian case, that the basis for the judgment needed to ascertain balance is readily apparent. Then a double distinction may be drawn concerning the wider theory such judgments presuppose. On the one hand, these judgments may be made with primary reference to parts of the wider theory that focus either on God or on human beings. On the other hand, this wider theory may promote an evenhanded balance or a lopsided balance between the symbols in question. When combined, these two distinctions permit a grid of possibilities to be imagined.

Fourth, when the balancing in question is between pairs of symbol families, as it is in the case of personal and impersonal symbols for God, there are two varieties of lopsided balance possible, along with the possibility of evenhanded balance. The resulting six (non-paradoxical) strategies are all independently conceivable, but the strategies described above blur over the edges somewhat. The perspectival strategy (from the Bhagavad-Gita) emphasizes judgments of balance made with reference to the state of the soul that wields the symbols, and permits an evenhanded balance to be achieved between personal (as in *bhakti*) and impersonal (as in *jñana*) symbols. The integrationist strategy (Tillich) likewise permits an evenhanded balance but depends more on a theory of God. The subordinationist strategy (Huston Smith) eschews an evenhanded balance and can be implemented using judgments that are grounded in wider theories of God or human beings. Smith himself uses both sorts of theoretical contextualization for his judgments simultaneously.

Finally, the strategies whose basis for judgment is paradoxical can also be analyzed using this pair of distinctions, but only with difficulty. For example, while it might be argued that Pseudo-Dionysius's judgments of balance stress the theory of symbol-wielding over the theory of God, the argument that he affirms impersonal-conceptual symbols over personal symbols is frustrated by the Dionysian self-deconstruction of the very basis for judgment that is implicit in such an affirmation. It is safest to resist subsuming the paradoxical strategy into the rest of the categorization, accordingly.

The resulting classification of balancing strategies can be diagrammed as follows:

NON-PARADOXICAL BASIS FOR JUDGMENTS OF BALANCE			
	Personal more significant than impersonal	*Personal as significant as impersonal*	*Personal less significant than impersonal*
Focus on God in the wider theory	[A]	Tillich	Smith
Focus on human beings in the wider theory	[B]	Bhagavad-Gita	Smith

PARADOXICAL BASIS FOR JUDGMENTS OF BALANCE
Pseudo-Dionysius

Note that this diagram can be generalized to encompass the balancing of any pairs of families of symbols. It would have to be modified, however, to express the complexities of balancing three or more symbol families. This is one indication of the misleading nature of the diagram. Another such indication is the fact that the names I assigned the four strategies discussed above run parallel to the categories of the diagram. I will continue to use the names because being able to refer to specific strategies with characteristic names is more useful than having an exhaustive classification. The classification is still useful, however, in that it makes evident what other balancing strategies might be employed, and it helps to formulate some of the fundamental issues surrounding the challenge of balancing symbol families in complex symbol systems.

Note, too, that it is not hard to think of examples where impersonal symbols for God are permitted as philosophical necessities, but are kept subordinated to personal symbols for God. Forms of religious piety that have a suspicious tolerance of philosophical categories might regard the impersonal-conceptual symbols for God as potentially dangerous to the soul, and balancing mechanisms would be introduced in the form of sanctions against excessive philosophizing in an attempt to cultivate most effectively the souls of believers. This would be a realization of the possibility marked [B] in the diagram. Less common in corporate piety but more common in theology (most contemporary conservative evangelical Christian theology, for example) is the insistence that impersonal-conceptual symbols for God are philosophical abstractions from the most basic truth that God is a supernatural "person." If it were held that such abstractions can be tolerated so long as they do not take over discourse about God, the result would be a balancing strategy of type [A].

Motivations for and Effects of Balancing Strategies

It is important to remember that some religious groups or thinkers abjure balancing strategies altogether, and simply ban the use of certain families of symbols. One example was given above: the esoteric social realizations of the primordial tradition, as in closed Gnostic communities. Examples of the opposite reactionary response would be forms of personal piety in which impersonal symbols for God are not tolerated but rather interpreted as dangerous incursions into religion from philosophy or from some other essentially alien source (the great liberal historian of theology Adolf von Harnack, for instance). Extreme forms of bhakti devotion, devotion to the Buddha, or Christian pietism illustrate this.

Even when these extreme reactions to the danger of religious symbols are not present, the sense that some danger attends the use of certain families of religious symbols usually still persists. There is good reason for this concern, of course, and the two points of view that have already been emphasized elsewhere will prove useful again here. On the one hand, in relation to the intended ultimate object of God-symbols, there is the legitimate concern that certain families of symbols threaten to distort the image of God presented in religious language. For example, according to the primordial tradition, while talk of God as personal is acceptable for people in a certain spiritual state or stage, it really does fail to express the higher truths about God, for which impersonal-conceptual symbols are better. On the other hand, in relation to the spiritual state of the wielder of symbols, there is the worry that the forming of the imagination under the influence of certain God-symbols may be counterproductive, in the sense of being spiritually or psychologically bad for wellbeing. For example, Tillich insisted that personal and impersonal symbols for God had to be maintained alongside each other to avoid the harms caused by demonic impersonal abstraction and sentimentally foolish personalism, under neither of which descriptions can God be the object of genuine ultimate concern.

These are the two main forms of anxiety that motivate balancing strategies: anxiety about truth and anxiety about efficaciousness of symbols for God. They are the moderate forms of reactions to the danger of symbols that in more extreme forms lead to the repudiation of the families of symbols that are perceived to be dangerous. Pseudo-Dionysius and Paul Tillich seem even-handedly concerned about both truth and efficaciousness in their adoption of balancing strategies.

The primary motivation of the Bhagavad-Gita and Huston Smith, by contrast, derives from another issue. In these cases, there seems to be considerable comfort with the aptness of certain symbols for certain types of people. Anxiety about souls in jeopardy from dangerous symbols or about the distortion of the truth about God seems greatly muted in these cases by comparison with Pseudo-Dionysius and Paul Tillich. The Bhagavad-Gita and the primordial tradition, however—in typical Indian fashion—take account of people's varying experiences of God, and validate the significance of those experiences for those having them by emphasizing their *aptness*. In this process of explanation, the challenge is how to make this validating move while still affirming a meaningful, consistent account of God and of the human soul. Balancing strategies, especially of the hierarchical and perspectival varieties, are well suited to that task.

Conclusion

We have seen that balancing strategies tend to affirm either that some *symbols* are less true or less helpful than others (Pseudo-Dionysius, Smith) or that certain *relations between symbol families* are less true or less helpful than others (Tillich and the Bhagavad-Gita). The judgments involved in these views underlie the implementation of balancing strategies. Two kinds of questions about the effectiveness of balancing strategies are suggested, accordingly. First, how accurate are the judgments pertaining to truth and helpfulness? And second, how effective are the balancing strategies themselves? Depending on the answers given to these questions, one strategy might appear superior to the others, or some new strategy might be suggested.

I confess that I am at a loss to know how to address these questions briefly, if it is possible to deal with them at all. For example, while I am convinced that the strategic preference for personal symbols of the divine ([A] and [B] in the diagram, above) can be justified only by the assumption that more theologically adequate symbols are not viable for the particular group or type of people in question, I do not know how to establish this conveniently. The argument required involves a complex comparative process in which the theoretical adequacy and practical efficacy of competing, large-scale interpretations of God, reality, and the religious life are weighed against one another. More profoundly, I agree with Pseudo-Dionysius that the basis for judgments bearing on the truth and helpfulness of symbols needs to be deconstructed precisely as fast as, and in the same sense that, it is made available by some encompassing theory of God or of symbol-wielding. But this agreement derives from an aesthetic preference for symmetry that is excited by the Dionysian tendency to handle symbols and criteria for assessing them in the same paradoxical way (see chapter 3). I do not know how I would go about establishing this through argument, even if I had unlimited space and time. For these reasons, I must be content to point out that balancing strategies can in principle be evaluated even though I cannot present the arguments associated with such an evaluation here—or possibly, with respect to some kinds of evaluation, anywhere (I have made an attempt at this in comparative phases of argument in Wildman 2009, 2017, and in the forthcoming *Science and Ultimate Reality*).

Another problem dogs the heels of attempts to evaluate the practical effectiveness of balancing strategies: our research techniques do not yet seem to have the required sophistication. The conceptual problem of designing adequate field instruments alone is daunting. It would be important to connect: (1) particular religious beliefs of individuals at a subtle level that detects and presses beyond mere reversion to the default formulations of their group, thereby seeing through so-called theological correctness; (2) personal histories of psychological-spiritual development; (3) what might be called "spiritual-personality" types, or at least preferences for orienting world-pictures; and (4) the structure and function of corporate activities of many different kinds as they bear on forming a religious milieu by means of a symbol system. Rough judgments can be made about the efficaciousness of balancing strategies, but they cannot have the reliability or longevity of the judgments that appropriate scientific instruments would permit.

With these caveats in place, I shall make some generalized evaluative remarks about systems of symbols and the balancing strategies that are implemented within them. First, it seems clear that balancing strategies have a certain degree of *prima facie* effectiveness. The use of symbols reflecting the value judgments underlying such strategies—in public rituals of worship, sacred texts, religious education, meditation, and acts of charity—really ought to have some of the desired effect on those participating. Human self-understandings and religious convictions are formed in part by the linguistic and social environment, as the sociology of knowledge has established. When the social-linguistic environment is itself formed by a balancing strategy of some kind, then those within its ambit will be subject to a strong tendency to conform. For example, Nietzsche's analysis of Christianity's hijacking of the symbols "Good" and "Evil," in spite of its extreme and slightly unstable character, is a sobering reminder that such environmental conditioning can have destructive effects. The emergence of saints in all traditions under the self-professed influence of traditional symbol systems is a forceful reminder that those symbols sometimes permit participation in that to which they refer with profound and positive consequences. And the existence of religious communities with distinctive styles and emphases is evidence that the way symbols are connected in systems—including by balancing mechanisms—does have an effect.

Second, however, it seems equally clear that it is not easy to make people and imaginations do exactly what any strategy or person stipulates—a fact for which we must never cease being grateful. Independent-minded people continually detect conceptual fractures in the models of God and world sponsored by symbol systems. Various forms of feedback in our experience of the world itself offer ways to test the adequacy of such models, and so of the symbol systems expressed within them. And people often have their own individual preferences that resist analysis in terms of what we can know of environmental influences. It follows that balancing mechanisms, or any symbolic conditioning processes, can be more or less, but never wholly, successful. Of course, religious groups vary tremendously in the extent to which they are prepared to impose upon their members a particular sense of how symbols ought to be related.

Third, many balancing strategies for religious symbol systems are profoundly related to a personal spiritual disposition or stage or state. The teenager who cannot help but conceive of God in personal terms may grow into a middle-aged adult with a balanced appreciation for a rich range of symbols of the divine, with a passion to disappear with Śankara and Smith into Brahman as a drop of dew into the shining sea, or with an ever intensifying fascination with God as person. Correspondingly, balancing mechanisms are often stratified in their application, imposing tighter limits for some people or some ages than others; the dangers of symbols are greater for the impressionable young than for the worldly wise elderly. Moreover, people learn to subvert the influence of balancing mechanisms in their religious group, willing to pay in the currency of cognitive dissonance for the freedom to develop their spirituality as they see fit.

Fourth, we have seen that a systematic process of symbolic checks and balances often serves strategically to control the supposedly potentially dangerous elements in a particular family of symbols. In religious groups for which this is a goal, the strategic mechanism tends to be highly effective, within the limits on effectiveness already described. However, when the aim is to keep personal and impersonal symbol families in evenhanded balance, the strategies seem to be significantly less effective. This remark is particularly dependent on personal observation, and so subject to the problems of bias and limited information. That said, it is borne out by a key difference between Tillich's integrationist and the Bhagavad-Gita's perspectival strategies. For both, evenhanded balance between personal and impersonal symbols for God is theoretically important. Whereas the Gita contains a comfortably plural portrayal of paths to liberation, Tillich's integrationist strategy sees things a particular way and tries to coordinate as many perspectives as possible into a consistent conceptual whole. Whereas the Gita's perspectival strategy is realistic about the fact that people approach God differently and remains content just to point people in the right direction given where they happen to be standing at the moment, Tillich's integrationist approach calls in principle for getting people to move together in more or less the same way. But that no more works in practice than Tillich pulls it off in his own system. Just as impersonal-conceptual symbols for God dominate in his system despite the theoretical evenhandedness between them, so the attempt to maintain a balanced appreciation for both personal and impersonal symbols for God in religious groups will always fail. Within the camp defined by the goal of theoretical evenhandedness, the move away from the Gita's strategic pluralism forces the introduction of a lot of theoretical overhead to try to keep very different families of symbols together. That theoretical overhead, even if it did its job perfectly in Tillich's system, is indigestible to most religious people.

Perfect balance might be an equilibrium state, but it is an unstable equilibrium; like an egg perched on the high point of an inverted convex metal bowl, the equilibrium can't be sustained. In practice, which is to say in the individual and corporate religious imaginations, either the personal family of God-symbols dominates over the impersonal, or *vice versa*, but evenhanded balance is rarely seen. This domination is explicitly recognized, approved and explained in the subordinationist and paradoxical strategies; it is recognized and approved but not really explained in the perspectival strategy; and it is recognized in Tillich's form of the integrationist strategy, but not approved. I believe this point could be extended to cover strategies of type [A] and [B], too. One family seems inevitably to gain ascendancy over the other.

This practical bias in favor either of personal or impersonal metaphors, where it exists, can be attributed to the psychological needs of people for conceptually relatively unloaded symbol systems that tend on the whole to be projected extensions of their own self-consciousness. In that respect this practical bias is inevitable and actually useful. But, to make the strongest normative claim of this essay, the religious group in which the practical bias is not subverted within the reigning symbol system itself by means of some strategic balancing mechanism threatens to force its members or itself aground. It presents an unappetizing forced choice as its members mature: between denying the impulse to move toward a more adequate view of God by becoming fanatically one-sided, or abandoning the group in search of greater realism and balance. It is unsurprising, therefore, that major religious symbol systems both have a characteristic emphasis—usually on the personal but sometimes on the impersonal—and also subvert that emphasis within the symbol system itself by means of strategic balancing mechanisms (even though this is not always recognized by priests or theologians). And the very fact that it seems impossible to avoid this practical bias and its attendant dangers is one indication of the importance of strategic metaphors in religious symbol systems.

Chapter 6

Eclipsing

Introduction

IN CHAPTER 4, WE SAW HOW A VARIETY OF SYMBOL SYSTEMS PRODUCE SIMILAR magic in regard to blame deflecting—something extraordinarily subtle yet absolutely vital—in quite different groups of religious language wielders. In chapter 5, we saw how a wide variety of symbol systems employ balancing techniques to maintain a healthy tension between competing personal and impersonal metaphors for ultimate reality. In this chapter I train my critical eye on a single symbol system as a whole. The target for analysis is the symbol system of liberal theology, especially in Christianity but with parallels in other major theistic traditions such as Judaism, Islam, and Hinduism. My aim is to show how an entire symbol system can weave a different kind of magic: *eclipsing the very ultimate reality it purports to describe.*

If that kind of magic seems to point to a defect, or a mistake, in the symbol system, then it has to be remembered that defects are pervasive but outright mistakes are extremely rare in religious symbol systems. If a language game performs a particularly puzzling kind of magic, it is more efficient to ask what vital problems are being solved through that magic than to assume stupidity or inattentiveness on the part of language wielders. In fact, the eclipsing magic of liberal theology is potent and its social outworking extremely important in any wider field of religious and theological life worlds.

To my way of thinking, liberal theology is a striking achievement of religious symbol-system building. It is honorable through being devoted to human well-being, noble through preserving its own kind of wisdom despite plummeting numbers in Western liberal and mainline churches since World War II, and intellectually sophisticated particularly in regard to its hermeneutics (interpretation) of sacred texts. In specifically theological terms, however, the symbol system of

119

liberal theology betrays significant conceptual fractures. I think those fractures are inevitable if liberal theology is to perform the special kind of magic that is its native genius. There's a fascinating story behind that conclusion.

~≈~

The journey of liberal theology in the last couple of centuries is akin to the person who enters a mirror maze with high hopes of finding a graceful and quick way through. Beginning with a clear plan about how to navigate the maze, he winds up confused, disoriented, and surrounded by useless self-images. He unwittingly passes through the same places over and over again, never gaining a relevant perspective for guiding decisions about where to go next. For some of these lost souls, the overseer of the maze comes to the rescue, perhaps after sensing rising panic, and for the sake of public safety escorts the exhausted liberal theologian out of the maze and into the sunshine, whereafter the shattered explorer swears never again to wander the pointless and confusing halls of liberal theology. Of course, most liberal theologians perpetually wander the maze, fascinated by the images they encounter, not particularly interested in the sunshine outside, and quite content with their experience.

At least that's one way of seeing things. There is enough truth in this image that I hope even liberal theologians can, with me, smile wryly and acknowledge the point—that liberal theology has been and remains a fascinating process of world-exploration that rather often yields unwitting repetition, intellectual disorientation, and unseemly self-satisfaction. But there are other ways of caricaturing the journey of liberal theology. One of those alternatives encodes insight roughly equal to that of the mirror-maze caricature. Here it is.

The journey of liberal theology in the last couple of centuries is akin to the courageous reformer who correctly diagnoses a profound problem in the surrounding social context and sets out to transform her community. The envisaged revolution requires that she name the problem, after which she meets determined resistance from entrenched defenders of the community's familiar principles of operation. They assert their authority in an attempt to suppress her prophetic unmasking of conventional dissembling and social control. Enough people get her message, however, that the reactionaries maintain their steely grip only on some of their followers. Others essentially reaffiliate—in intellectual beliefs and spiritual affections, and sometimes in social loyalties as well. Thus, the fruits of our revolutionary's efforts are the establishment of a putative counterculture, partly within but mostly outside the mainstream social world that she set out to change. For some reason, the countercultural social organization perpetually shrinks, regardless of the energy she invests in maintenance and growth, which she finds enormously frustrating. Meanwhile the gloating majority culture seems to get new affiliations more or less by default and with relatively little effort. Yet her supposedly countercultural social alternative to the apparently self-sustaining majority social world never completely disappears, mainly because her group receives a steady stream of defectors from the majority group, each one disillusioned with the same dissembling and social control that drove her to launch the prophetic revolution in the first place. Meanwhile, all her prophetic energy is now taken up with institutional maintenance, and every night she goes to bed wondering why she is spending her precious days the way she is.

So there we have it—two images pointing, in the delightful way only caricatures can, to the ambiguous heritage and perpetual promise of liberal theology. In only slightly more judicious terms, liberal theology tends to be correct in what it criticizes, good in its moral affirmation of radical inclusiveness and equality, and true in its intellectual interpretation of symbolism and its correlative deconstruction of mythologized beliefs and authoritarian social structures. I say "tends" to be correct, good, and true advisedly. At the level of details, liberal theology often succumbs to an incoherent mélange of concepts. Despite its notable record of moral courage, it often lacks the moral clarity required to carry through the revolution it perpetually invites. And these problems arise because the social survival of liberal theology depends on the exercise of social control and the deployment of colorful conceptual confusions that the very thoroughgoing critique it recommends would in fact undermine.

My aim here is to explain these colorful assertions in a way that makes some degree of intellectual, historical, social, psychological, and evolutionary sense. I begin with a discussion of what liberal theology gets right, more or less. I then move onto what liberal theology gets wrong, more or less. Finally, I discuss what liberal theology can and cannot achieve, more or less. The "more or less" phrase in each of the three section titles is meant to indicate that I will be working at a high level of generalization, driving at salient insights that persist even when historical details tend to go in a variety of directions simultaneously. The generalizations I offer have significant problems, but they also convey insights sufficiently useful to warrant this level of analysis.

~≋~

By the phrase "liberal theology" I mean to refer to:

1. the multiple streams of thought described in Gary Dorrien's *The Making of American Liberal Theology* (see Dorrien 2001, 2003, 2006);
2. the European threads running from Enlightenment figures such as Kant and Schleiermacher to the Liberal Protestants Ritschl, Herrmann, and Harnack,

and beyond, and to the Catholic Modernists Tyrrell, Loisy, and beyond (this history is thorough documented in Welch 1972, 1985; Reardon 1970; Livingston 1997, 2000);

3. the theological aspects of the Liberal, Progressive, and Reform movements within Judaism, which Michal Meyer documents in his *Response to Modernity* (see Meyer 1988); and

4. the theological elements within the more recent development of Islamic modernism (see Cooper, Nettler, and Mahmoud 1998; Kurzman 1998).

Most of these strands of intellectual tradition on both sides of the Atlantic:

5. attempt to engage cultural wisdom and to accommodate traditional beliefs to it in such a way as to remain faithful to a particular faith tradition—with engagement and fidelity understood differently in different settings;

6. date back to the European Enlightenment, with some having earlier links to the Protestant Reformation;

7. share in various ways the Enlightenment wariness toward externally imposed authority and superstition;

8. share the Enlightenment hope for a peaceful future based on science, technology, medicine, the overcoming of tribalism, the rejection of in-group-out-group exclusion, the collapse of unjust hierarchies, the refusal of fanatical aggression, and the affirmation of a moderate form of religious belief and practice that sustains people in meaningful lives while enhancing creative cultural expression.

In Western Christian contexts, we do not achieve deep understanding by contrasting liberal theology with evangelical theology, or indeed liberalism with evangelicalism. The proper contrasts are between liberalism and conservatism, or between liberalism and fundamentalism. Contrary to more recent narrow usage, the word "evangelical" is shared property within the Christian heritage. As the nineteenth-century Protestant battles between modernists and conservatives indicate, most on both sides thought of themselves as evangelicals and the relevant questions were the meanings of engagement with contemporary cultural wisdom, fidelity to extant traditions of belief and practice, and scriptural hermeneutics. This led to disagreements among evangelicals regarding the nature of reality, authority, history, morality, and church. The later sequestering of the word "evangelical" by conservative evangelicals, and its meek surrender by liberal evangelicals, misleads with regard to the longer history (see Wildman and Garner 2009).

What Liberal Theology Gets Right, More or Less

I earlier telegraphed three things that liberal theology tends to get right, and I discuss each of these in what follows. Obviously, these are value judgments, not merely historical or descriptive statements. I am writing here as philosophical theologian, after all, not as historian or cultural anthropologist. Little that is theologically or philosophically interesting can be said about this subject that does not attempt evaluation. I will not make cases for all these evaluations, however. I offer them as a declaration of my own determinate location as a liberal-evangelical philosophical theologian, and also as a prelude to the analysis of the ambiguity of liberalism.

~≈~

First, *liberal theology tends to be correct in what it criticizes.*

When David Hume argued that we never have a good reason to believe that miracles occur, he was correct. When Hermann Reimarus quietly complained about the theologically biased quality of historical work into the historical Jesus, he was correct. When Immanuel Kant said that theologians could prove the existence of God neither from patterns in nature nor from the realm of ideas, he was correct. When Friedrich Schleiermacher pointed out that theologians routinely fail to notice how the qualities of their religious experiences directly impact what they are prepared to accept as theologically true, he was correct. When David Strauss noticed the pervasiveness of legendary and mythical elements in the Hebrew Bible and New Testament, he was correct. When Adolf von Harnack rejected the centrality of a sacrificial atonement for making sense of the significance of Jesus Christ as a manifestation of divine love, he was correct. When Alfred Loisy refuted the deductive theory of Catholic doctrinal development, he was correct. When Ernst Troeltsch attacked the absoluteness of Christianity and the special pleading used to justify it, he was correct. When Paul Tillich diagnosed anthropomorphic God concepts as a form of idolatry, he was correct. When Eugene Borowitz disparaged the rigid understanding of covenant that eliminated the possibility of authentic individual religious expression as a Jew, he was correct. When Rosemary Ruether drew attention to the fundamentally sexist conceptual and social structures of the Christian tradition, she was correct.

Liberal theology has tended to be on the correct side of most of the major points of conflict with conservative theology. In regard to conflicting metaphysical visions of reality, liberalism has been correct to be suspicious of supernaturalism, and of the credulity that goes along with conservative affirmations of supernaturalism. In regard to conflicting visions of authority, liberalism has been correct to be suspicious of overly definitive and absolutist conceptions of authority, and of the psychological coercion and dangerous forms of social control that go along with conservative affirmations of such conceptions. In regard to conflicting visions of history, liberals have been correct to be suspicious of dismissal of the historical process of cultural growth and development as irrelevant to salvation, and of the neglect of social justice that goes along with conservative affirmations of this dismissal. In regard to conflicting visions of morality, liberals have been correct to be suspicious of the fondness for hierarchies, in-groups, and purity judgments in religious ethics, and of the discriminatory social practices that go along with conservative affirmations of such principles. In regard to conflicting visions of religious community, liberals have been correct to be suspicious when an emphasis on purity of doctrine supplants unity in love as the key to communal identity, and of the ecumenical disasters that go along with conservative affirmations of doctrinal purity.

It is because liberalism tends to be on the correct side of these debates that thoughtful people keep flowing leftwards from out of majority religious cultures, seeking a religious home where they can be themselves and express their honest opinions, without fear of reprisals from conservative defenders of religious identity with an overdeveloped sense of loyalty to purity of doctrine and practice.

~∾~

Second, *liberal theology tends to be good in its moral affirmation of radical inclusiveness and equality.*

While frequently muddled or undecided on metaphysical questions, liberal theologians have tended to be impressively consistent on moral matters. The reason for this appears to be rooted in the intellectual coherence and practical feasibility of the liberal alternative to what can be thought of as the evolutionarily derived moral framework that has guided human (and indeed possibly some pre-human hominid) groups over long evolutionary time scales. Jonathan Haidt has offered the clearest statement of this evolutionarily derived moral framework, and the best diagnosis of how it helps to make sense of the average ethical differences between conservatives and liberals (see Haidt 2001; 2007; Graham, Haidt, and Nosek 2009).

Haidt argues, based on compelling experimental and survey data, that we have species-wide, and probably partially genetically rooted and heritable, moral intuitions, and that ethical reasoning serves those reflexive moral feelings by furnishing for them a rational framework and narrative coherence. Very few human beings display the ability to use moral reasoning to change their fundamental moral intuitions. But many people can develop conditioned responses that help regulate the effects of deep-seated intuitive moral reactions. We are not slaves to our moral impulses, therefore, but can organize social forms of life in which we regulate them and thereby transform personal and corporate behavior. Nevertheless, those moral intuitions are extremely powerful.

Haidt identifies five cross-culturally universal domains of moral intuition that naturally stimulate appreciation for moral virtues. Most are shared at some level with higher primates. Their evolutionary origins are difficult to support with clear-cut evidence, given the sorts of data available from the far past, but their cross-cultural and even cross-species applicability does seem quite clear.

1. The harm domain is associated with feelings of compassion, virtues such as kindness, and vices such as cruelty and neglect.
2. The fairness domain is associated with feelings of gratitude and anger, virtues such as trustworthiness, and vices such as cheating.
3. The in-group domain is associated with feelings of pride and belonging, virtues such as loyalty and patriotism, and vices such as betrayal.
4. The authority domain is associated with feelings of respect and fear, virtues such as obedience and deference, and vices such as rebellion and disrespect.
5. The purity domain is associated with feelings of satisfaction and disgust, virtues such as cleanliness and chastity, and vices such as tasteless and unnatural behavior.

Haidt's research suggests that self-identifying liberals have been socialized to down-regulate morally loaded feelings that spring from the in-group, authority, and purity domains. Liberals learn to associate feelings of disgust with cruel treatment of people who seem different, and so they endeavor to be tolerant. Similarly, liberals link in-group feelings with racism and xenophobia and authoritarian feelings with sexism and abuse, so they stay on their guard against these feelings. Liberals still have feelings from these three domains but try to prevent those moral feelings from determining their moral judgments. Instead, they emphasize the domains of harm and fairness. In emphasizing the virtues of doing no harm and being fair to others, liberals intuitively support a simpler and less textured moral system. Haidt calls it a "thin" morality.

By contrast, self-identified conservatives treat all five domains with roughly equal importance, making for a "thick" morality. This means, for example, that conservatives tend to trust that their feelings of disgust indicate the morally wrong whereas liberals would be suspicious of the moral value of such feelings. Similarly, loyalty to one's group and deference to figures of authority are virtues prized in conservative moral frameworks because these virtues help to sustain the valuable institutional social arrangements that help us to flourish.

The work of moral psychologists such as Haidt, Marc Hauser, Joshua Greene, and others helps to make sense of the way liberals creatively construct a socially borne alternative to the evolutionary default moral framework of human life. The conservative approach has proved its usefulness over time, but the liberal approach is far superior in cosmopolitan settings where it is necessary for people to deal routinely with strangers who don't comprehend their in-group hierarchies and purity practices. Moreover, the principles of equality and distributive justice are much better served by the liberal "thin" morality than by the conservative treasuring of distinctions derived from in-group-out-group awareness, hierarchical deference, and purity rules.

Evidently, the evolutionary stabilization of human morality supports more than one system of moral principles, but the conservative system requires less maintenance energy than the liberal system in most social settings. Only in relatively rare cosmopolitan socioeconomic contexts is it worth the social trouble to devote the significant cultural resources necessary to teach people to regulate their moral instincts and thereby to support the thin morality that liberals prize. But the high-energy, thin alternative to the low-energy, thick evolutionary default setting for human moral life is intellectually coherent, practically potent, and highly relevant to the cultural conditions of modernity and postmodernity. That's why liberals have tended to be on the right side of debates over inclusiveness and equality.

⨯⨯⨯

Third, *liberal theology tends to be true in its intellectual interpretation of symbolism and its correlative deconstruction of mythologized beliefs and authoritarian social structures.*

Arguably the most important intellectual contribution of liberal theology has been its articulation of a sophisticated hermeneutical alternative to the plain reading of religious texts, beliefs, practices, and imaginative worlds. There is good evidence that most religious people in all traditions and at all times treat their beliefs with poetic license to various degrees. Few people think God is actually "up" in the sky, wherever that might actually be on a near-spherical planet. Despite this, a surprisingly large number of people actually believe that Elijah really ascended on a fiery chariot to God and that Jesus really ascended upwards to God, as if God really were "up" somehow. Liberal theologians hold that poetic license must be applied to religious texts and beliefs more often than most religious people suspected over the centuries, and especially when the goal is to make accurate historical and metaphysical sense of the world.

Liberal theologians also offer a persuasive rationale for this viewpoint—namely, that secular scientific and historical understanding can make a positive contribution to purifying religious belief and practice of errors and excesses. Implicit here, and only occasionally made completely explicit, is the belief that cultural developments manifest divine truth just as divine revelation does, and also that religion is a partially problematic phenomenon that requires purification, even as it remains an indispensable means of human engagement with ultimate reality.

Unfortunately, most liberal theologians have been better at naming and theorizing the problem than at articulating the constructive alternative that liberal theology represents. The problem has been variously named "mythology," "credulity," "superstition," "idolatry," "anthropocentrism," or "anthropomorphism," with the correlative theological goal being demythologization, hermeneutical sophistication, skepticism, iconoclasm, theocentrism, critical self-awareness, or something similar. The names are fine as far as they go. What is really needed, however, is the theory of religious symbols that can explain how religious symbols succeed in effectively and truly and authentically engaging people with ultimacy even when the person wielding them does so without being aware of their myth-laden or idolatrous character. Here as always, few liberal theologians go all the way and theorize the underlying hermeneutical dynamics (but see Neville 1996 for an exception). Most are reluctant to make explicit the outrageous but unavoidable implication of their viewpoint—that our knowledge is actually progressing and that, despite our perpetual moral confusion and bad behavior, we know better than the ancients did what in a sacred text is likely to be true regarding history and nature. While the timidity is disappointing, the view itself is deeply true.

What Liberal Theology Gets Wrong, More or Less

Earlier, I hinted at three things that liberal theology tends to get wrong, and I discuss each of these next. Once again, note that these are evaluations, particularly the first two. I trust they draw some measure of support from the explanations and arguments presented on their behalf.

⋙⋘

First, *liberal theology often succumbs to an incoherent mélange of concepts.*

I offer here an example of liberal theological incoherence. In so doing I am necessarily selective. The selection made may suggest that science dictates what theology can and must do, but this is a misleading side effect of the chosen example. Religion and humanistic insights of all kinds can and do rightly contest the attitudes and practices and sometimes even the theories of the human sciences and the natural sciences. In longer presentations, the refusal of reductionisms of both the scientific and theological varieties can be made perfectly clear (I have tried to live up to that principle in Wildman 2009, 2010, 2011. 2017).

There is an infamous dispute within each of Hinduism, Judaism, Christianity, and Islam over the theological implications of evolution. While this dispute rises on the back of the liberal-conservative disputes I described earlier, it has its own special quality. Liberal theologians take the line, as usual, that secular scientific and historical knowledge is valuable and consonant with our understanding of God. Thus, they seek to harmonize traditional beliefs with scientific knowledge and will confidently declare that "God creates through evolution." That is fine as an initial hypothesis, but it is shocking how few liberal theologians think through the implications of this superficially amiable declaration.

Consider Charles Darwin, who began his scholarly career as a convinced believer that God intentionally conceived, designed, and created the world in roughly the form Darwin encountered it. As a young man, he read and accepted the still-famous design arguments of his countryman William Paley (1802). After all, he couldn't explain the wondrous structure of the eye any other way; he had to assume a personal, benevolent, attentive, and active designer God. As his studies widened and deepened, however, Darwin's theological views slowly shifted. Though he never discovered the mechanism by which traits are trans-mitted across generations, which we know as DNA, he was confident that trait preservation and transmission occur, and that random variations of traits make organisms more and less fit to survive the rigors of any given environment. He believed that this process of trait inheritance, random variation, and natural selection in competitive environments is powerful enough to explain the origin of species, which is the name he gave to his most famous book (Darwin 1859). And in that book and several others, he assembled a formidable array of evidence to support his theory—evidence that is extraordinarily difficult to explain apart from the evolutionary hypothesis.

Unsurprisingly, Darwin's view of God changed as the secrets of the natural world opened before his uncanny gaze. God was no longer necessary to explain the particulars of the world and its teeming life forms. Rather, God's domain was the creation of the potentialities of the world-as-a-whole, a world that answered to the description that the theory of evolution provided. Unsurprisingly, to Darwin, God gradually seemed less personal, benevolent, attentive, and active. Surely such a loving, personal deity would have created in another way, a way that involved less trial and error, fewer false starts, less mindless chance, fewer tragic species extinctions, less dependence on random symbiotic collaborations, fewer pointless cruelties, and less reliance on predation to sort out the fit from the unfit. Darwin arguably never lost his faith in God. Rather, believing that God created through the evolutionary process, his growing knowledge of that process dramatically transformed his view of God. And this left him ill at ease with the anthropomorphic personal theism of his day, and with friends and colleagues who believed in a personal, benevolent, attentive, and active divine being.

Theists who casually assert that God creates through evolution—as if there is no theological problem with this—should pause and consider Darwin's faith journey. Darwin was theologically more perceptive than many of the liberal theologians who have endorsed his scientific views. He knew that saying God creates through evolution puts enormous stress on belief in a personal, benevolent, attentive, and active deity. Evolution casts a pall over the moral clarity that most people want to see in the God they worship and serve. Darwin felt the difficulty acutely. Tragically, many liberal theologians since Darwin have only casually struggled with the problem, after which they easily blend evolutionary theory and belief in a personal, benevolent, attentive, and active God as if there is no problem.

Many conservative theologians feel the problem more sharply, and some take a stand against evolution precisely to avoid implications for God's nature that they cannot countenance. A God who really did create through evolution would be morally unrecognizable to them, a kind of heartless gambler over the lives and well-being of Earth's creatures, and not at all like the loving and wise parent they trust and serve. This would contradict their morally clear and homey worldview, which is borne up by a God of pure compassion and perfect goodness. Because they take on authority the proposition that God is personal, benevolent, attentive, and active, they know with confidence that Darwin must have been wrong, both in his science and in his theology.

Now, in my view, conservative-evangelical theologians who reject evolution in favor of creationism, or who embrace the neo-creationism of Intelligent Design theory, make a serious error in judgment. Nevertheless, they may understand what is theologically at stake in evolution far better than most of their liberal-theologian counterparts who casually resolve the issue by declaring that God creates through evolution, without pausing to think through what that must mean. Where the conservative theologians display acute sensitivity to the coherence of theological concepts, too many liberal theologians are careless with the prized value of conceptual coherence.

⁓

Second, *liberal theology often lacks the moral clarity required to carry through the revolution it perpetually invites.*

While often displaying impressive moral courage, a distressingly large number of liberal theologians seem unprepared to follow through on the moral obligations they incur because of their working theological commitments. But the same is true in a different way with conservative theologians. To make this clear, what would "following through" look like in the case of the evolution and creation example just discussed?

For a conservative evangelical theologian, following through would mean dreaming up a theologically coherent alternative narrative of creation that could ultimately prove scientifically credible. An example of just such a theologically coherent creation narrative is C. S. Lewis's creation story, which is presented in a lesser known volume of his Narnia Chronicles called *The Magician's Nephew.* The children in that story are present when the great Lion Aslan creates Narnia and its creatures. The method of creation is beautifully intimate and personal: Aslan sings in a majestic voice, with spectacularly complex undertones and rippling overtones, and the world awakens around him. Each creature struggles up and out of the Narnian soil, awakening to a new world, personally called into being by the fatherly Lion God himself. Lewis grasped the point that Darwin also felt so forcefully: the God Lewis believed in could not create in a way much different than Aslan did. Good literature is able to test the coherence of the "God creates through evolution" idea. So long as God is conceived as a personal, benevolent, attentive, and active being, like Aslan, the literary acid test shows that God cannot and would not create through evolution. They just don't fit. But Lewis's alternative narrative does fit.

Conservative evangelical Christians who resist evolutionary theory for theological reasons are shrewdly targeting a problem for their God-infused worldview, perhaps the sharpest problem that worldview has ever faced. They are not tiptoeing around, pretending that the God they trust every day somehow creates through evolution. They construct a theologically plausible alternative narrative—most recently Intelligent Design theory—and then try to show that it has the scientific chops to take on evolutionary theory. Of course, it does not have any scientific credibility whatsoever, and that's where the conservative response to evolution falls on its face, and also where conservatives fail to follow through with intellectual consistency.

On the side of liberal theologians, the embarrassing pratfall happens much earlier. Their theological narrative is incoherent from the outset because they train themselves not even to feel the contradiction embedded in the idea that a personal, benevolent, attentive, and active deity creates through evolution. Intellectual coherence begs for this God, or evolution, to go. Now, for the most part, liberal theologians are in no doubt about the exceptional robustness of the theory of evolution, even if tragically few of them really know anything about it. After all, it is as stable a scientific theory as the atomic theory of matter. For liberal theologians, therefore, the choice of God or evolution *should* lead to a conclusion opposite to that of conservative theologians. God the creator simply cannot be a personal, benevolent, attentive, and active deity. Liberal theologians can preserve those affirmations symbolically and poetically, but they do not refer to a divine being with intentions and awareness, with feelings and intelligence, with plans and powers to act, and with a moral character that humans can recognize as good. Rather, these symbolic assertions refer to the ground of being itself, to the creative and fecund power source in the depths of nature, to the value structures and potentialities that reality manifests. They refer to the God beyond God, which is to say the truly ultimate reality that hovers behind and beneath and beyond the symbolic Gods we create and deploy to satisfy our personal needs, to make sense of our world, and to legitimate the exercise of social control.

Now, this is theologically coherent! It is just as coherent as the conservative creation narratives. And it has the excellent virtue that it takes evolutionary biology with proper seriousness, which neither conservative theologians nor liberal theologians manage to do very often. With this option available, therefore, why don't more liberal theologians move in that direction? Why don't they finish their thought, follow through, see the implications of their ideas, and commit to them? The reason amounts to an indictment of liberal theology. To follow through would require more than just acute sensitivity to the coherence of theological concepts. It would take peculiar moral clarity as well, because so few people are spiritually attuned to the abysmal ground of being rumbling in fecund creativity, morally impenetrable, imponderably beautiful, and defying rational grasp. Liberal theologians are, in general, quite nice people, and they don't like offending anyone or hurting feelings. And that is what following through would do. It would hurt. Moral clarity is difficult to come by in this world at the best of times, so we do well to be slow to judge, lest we are caught in the hypocrisy of our own standards. Nevertheless, I venture to say that liberal theology has tended to lack the moral clarity needed to fulfill the revolution of majority-culture religious frameworks promised in its basic ideas.

⁓⊙⁓

Third, *liberal theology is socially self-defeating and survives symbiotically in relationship with authoritarian and myth-laden forms of religious belief and practice.*

We are now at the point where we can draw our first diagnostic conclusions about the peculiar status of liberal theology as a modern movement of thought. Its fondness for conceptual unclarities serves an important double function. On the one hand, the insensitivity to conceptual muddles masks the lack of moral clarity I just described, which allows most liberal theologians to live with themselves happily inside the maze of mirrors, which is where their failure to follow through leaves them. On the other hand, it avoids hurting the very people who are supposed to be supported and nurtured by liberal theology—ordinary religious people seeking a meaningful religious framework that embraces cultural wisdom from many sources and that helps them grow in faith while encouraging individual creativity.

When liberal theologians overcome the insensitivity to conceptual imprecision and truly follow through, they become quite radical, declaring the death of God and uncovering the social construction of religion. The majority of liberal theologians concludes that the radicals go too far, sacrificing the traditional mediating liberal theologian's virtue of graceful balance between theology and culture—sacrificing it in the name of fidelity to the alien criterion of conceptual consistency. But this critique of radicalism is a mere diversionary tactic in the mirror world of the liberal theologian; it does not address the issue most profoundly at stake in the confrontation of traditional religious and modern secular perspectives on ultimate reality but merely finesses it.

The criteria employed in this finesse are the same criteria that allow insensitivity to conceptual incoherence to mask liberal theology's moral unclarity. They are criteria that prioritize the survival and flourishing of liberal religious communities, regardless of the intellectual cost. So the liberal theologian continues to affirm the comforting comprehensible personal God that we fondly construct in affluent democratic capitalist cultural contexts, the God of endless love who co-suffers with us, the God who wouldn't hurt a flea and especially not me, because this is what the community requires. And the price paid—anthropomorphic conceptual incoherence and inconsistency with the implications of other forms of knowledge such as evolutionary biology—is judged acceptable because nothing less will sustain the community.

Liberal theologians tend to make these judgments about social feasibility reflexively without much evidence of what is really possible in religious communities, but I think they are basically on target. Thus, nobody should be surprised that most liberal religious denominations shrink; people sense that something is rotten at the conceptual core of liberal religion even when they prefer it to the alternatives. Most liberal pastors, priests, and rabbis still do not know how to preach a clear religious message of good news, not because they lack intelligence but because it is genuinely unclear what such a message would be. Most liberal religious communities are dominated by people whose appreciation for emotional and spiritual connectedness is pronounced enough to overcome their discomfort with the conceptual problems at the core of liberal theology. Rationalists who get their kicks from ideas rather than human connections either belong to conservative religious communities, where at least the ideas are clear even if they are fantastic, or else they stay away from religion altogether.

Younger children can't understand the subtleties of the message because it depends on sophisticated hermeneutics requiring years of schooling. When they get older they get almost no help in deconstructing and reinterpreting the symbols they absorbed as children because few if any of the adults around them know what to make of their religious beliefs either. Liberal religious groups lose most of their children in early adolescence when it dawns on the kids that what they hear at church doesn't make anywhere near as much sense as their oversimplified middle-school social studies textbooks. Most liberal religious communities have almost zero conversions of people in the sensitive teenage years. Teenagers learn a treasured lifestyle and sometimes return to it when they have children of their own, but few develop a conceptually coherent faith—at least until the persistence of committed habits of participation over a lifetime yield the fruits of wisdom in old age. The new members that keep most liberal religious communities afloat are disenchanted conservatives who love the freedom of liberal communities so much that they are willing to tolerate the conceptual muddles they are confronted with in every sermon and prayer. And the people who become liberal theologians are much more often conservatives who went through some sort of disenchantment than people raised within a liberal setting from a young age. Most liberal church people don't even feel comfortable with the idea of their children becoming pastors or priests because they don't have as much respect for that profession as they used to.

Groups survive best whose identity can be grasped, remembered, and narrated by children. Psychological studies of what children can appreciate and remember predict that the comic-book-like minimally counterintuitive grand narratives of conservative religions will have a decided advantage over the subtleties and intellectual sophistication of liberal theological narratives (these results are discussed in Atran 2002; Boyer 2001; Boyer and Ramble 2001). Thus, liberal theology is socially self-defeating. It is too difficult for kids to understand, and most adults don't really understand it either. But people can sense that something is incoherent in the story with remarkable accuracy, even when they can't say precisely what it is. Myth-laden beliefs and practices are better for sustaining religious communities even though those beliefs are less true then what results when those beliefs are processed through the sophisticated hermeneutics of liberal theology. It follows that liberal theology depends on majority culture conservative religious groups for its survival. The robust social strategies of conservative religion are more nearly self-sustaining, and liberal groups can live reasonably well by receiving their alienated castoffs with open arms.

An interesting question is whether this relationship is parasitic or symbiotic. I think we have here a symbiosis, where the dependence of liberal on conservative religious communities is more obvious. The reverse dependence is subtle but important. Without liberal religion, conservative religion would lack the natural enemy it needs to consolidate social identity, and conservative extremism relative to the wider culture would make an entire religion culturally suspect. It is indeed a symbiosis. So liberal religious communities will continue to shrink but they will not vanish. People need a place to take cover when the bright sunshine of authoritarian and myth-laden forms of religious belief and practice becomes overbearing. Liberal religion offers a welcome place of respite, even with its defective narratives and its questionable moral clarity.

What Liberal Theology Can and Cannot Achieve, More or Less

The picture of liberal theology that emerges from this analysis, if correct, is intriguing. I am describing a profoundly ironic, almost paradoxical, language system in which the quest for justice and truth at the heart of the liberal theological project endangers the social resources needed to sustain the quest. Yet I am also identifying a symbiotic mechanism whereby the social vehicles of liberal theology survive by means of receiving the disillusioned defectors from the conservative religious world and energizing them despite their disenchantment. Finally, I am hinting at a form of high-energy, high-education, high-culture sociopolitical organization in which liberal theology is at home in a way that more authoritarian and mythological forms of religious belief and practice never can be. I discuss these three propositions here.

~⊷⊷~

First, *there is a profoundly ironic, almost paradoxical, reality in which the quest for justice and truth at the heart of the liberal theological project endangers the social resources needed to sustain the quest.*

Groups need hierarchies and relationships of deference to run efficiently. Groups need out-groups to foster in-group solidarity through costly in-group signaling. Groups need purity rules to get people to conform to group norms and to appear acceptable to one another. Groups need recruitment mechanisms that allow outsiders to join and to be grateful to be a part. Groups need clear identity narratives that a child can appreciate if they are to survive down the generations. Groups need cosmologized versions of those narratives to bolster the authority of imperfect leaders when their stupidity provokes damaging criticism. These are the low-energy defaults within the evolutionary landscape of human group life. And yet groups founded on liberal theological principles effectively undermine every single one of these principles. Liberal theology's quest for justice and truth therefore endangers the social resources needed to sustain the communities that liberal theology serves.

For liberal theology to fulfill its promise, it must inevitably plunge into a kind of radicalism that makes all this uncomfortably clear. For liberal theology to avoid that outcome inevitably requires arresting thought on its natural trajectory, leading first to conceptual incoherence and then to traditions of discourse in which conceptual fuzziness is tolerated and even replicated to the point of desensitization. To return to our two caricatures, liberal theology's mirror-maze existence is directly correlated with its noble determination to supplant authoritarian and superstitious forms of religion.

~~∞~~

Second, *there is a symbiotic mechanism whereby the social vehicles of liberal theology survive fluidly through receiving disillusioned defectors from the majority social world and energizing them despite their disenchantment, while simultaneously saving religion from becoming culturally despised by elites who reject conservative religious social practices.*

These social realities mean that, at least for the foreseeable future, and at least in most cultural contexts, liberal theology must remain in a symbiotic relationship with conservative theology, just as liberal and conservative religious communities are symbiotically related.

In one direction, conservative groups are more nearly aligned with low-energy default patterns for evolutionarily stabilized human belief and behavior, so they define the majority religious culture in most circumstances. But without the legitimation that liberal intellectual culture supplies, conservative religion often appears ridiculous or dangerously credulous to the wider culture, and especially to its culturally powerful elite voices. And without the religious haven of liberal religious communities to mitigate the resentment of disaffected conservatives, the authoritarianism and superstition so rampant in conservative religious groups would produce not just defectors, but dangerous enemies with every reason to attack conservative religious identity in the wider culture.

In the other direction, liberal religious groups depend on conservative religious groups for the sheer institutional buoyancy of conservativism, for the steady stream of frustrated immigrants fleeing the hostile shores of conservatism, and for conservatism's ability to win the new converts that make an entire religion socially viable and culturally relevant. Liberal theology also depends on semi-mythic statements of conservative doctrine that function both as easy targets for liberal theological deconstruction, and as decoys to deflect attention from the intellectual inadequacies of liberal theological constructions.

I see no possibility of totally escaping this symbiotic relationship at the present time. The fundamental reason for this is that the religious truth is misaligned with evolutionarily stabilized individual and corporate interests. To discover the truth about religious matters, therefore, is usually to interfere with the mechanisms that allow religious groups—and indeed any group—to flourish.

≈

Third, *there is a form of high-energy, high-education, high-culture sociopolitical organization in which liberal theology is at home in a way that more authoritarian and mythological forms of religious belief and practice can never be.*

The fact that conservative theology and religion runs more nearly with the evolutionarily stabilized grain of human cognition and sociality than liberal theology and religion do means that conservativism requires less energy than liberalism for its sustenance. Liberal theology and liberal religious groups require far more energy in every aspect of social life, save for the defense of institutional authority. When the message is hard to understand, it must be explained. When the reading of sacred texts requires sophisticated hermeneutics, training must be provided. When institutional budgets must be fought for and competent religious leaders are scarce, minimally trained volunteers are indispensable, with associated costs in identity maintenance. When instinctive tribal moralism must be perpetually intercepted and challenged, there will be conflict and division. All of this takes energy.

This in turns defines the conditions for picturing a more nearly self-sustaining form of liberal theology and liberal religious community. A symbiotic partner for liberal theology and liberal religion is inevitable because the terminus of liberal theology being misaligned with evolutionarily stabilized mental and social tendencies makes liberal theology inescapably socially self-defeating. But it is conceivable that liberal theology and religion could find its symbiotic partner in a sociopolitical structure rather than in conservative theology and religion. In that case, it would be necessary for the symbiotic partner to be a high-energy enterprise, a high-culture achievement, appealing to high-education people. This envisaged wider sociopolitical culture would so prize education, rich cultural expression, and the thin morality of liberal compassion and justice that many of the requirements for the flourishing of liberal theology and religion would already be met. In that new symbiosis, liberal religion would supply a venue for the exploration and celebration of the moral and spiritual and aesthetic depth dimensions of human existence, under the rubric of whatever symbolic forms prove ready to hand at the time.

This possibility has been partially realized in a few places, here and there, such as the cosmopolitan coastal regions of the United States, but only ever partially. The symbiotic relationship with conservative theology and religion is still at center stage, and unlikely to be displaced for some time. Moreover, as soon as disaster strikes, eliminating the preconditions for the flourishing of high-energy cultural creations, this possibility probably vanishes, and human social life reverts to its low-energy defaults, with hierarchical, superstitious, authoritarian, purity-conscious in-groups defining themselves by contrast with alien outgroups. There are no in-principle limits to how far human beings can go in attempting to fashion cultural products that fly in the face of the low-energy default patterns stabilized through evolutionary pressures, but the practical challenges are daunting indeed.

CONCLUSION

The inevitability that liberalism should be in symbiotic partnerships either with conservativism or secularism derives not from any failure of liberal institutional imagination but from the very nature of the truth to which liberal theology draws our attention, in its sadly half-hearted way. To see the face of God is to become instantly aware that the social construction of reality is genuine, and that its purpose in significant part is to hide from that terrifying divine visage, to eclipse it with our very sacred canopies and language games. Because liberal theology allows a modicum of the threatening dark side of the divine to show forth, liberals have good tools for deconstructing everyone else's authoritarian deflections and anthropomorphic theological defects. But nobody escapes divine judgment, not even the annoyingly enlightened liberal theologian.

In other words, the dark truth that liberal theology has a flimsy grasp on is, like Śiva, as destructive as it is creative. It unmasks everything, and so is poorly fitted to sustaining any civilizational project, all of which require dissembling, deflection, distraction, and the defusing of desperation. The ultimate destination of liberal theology—the dark place to which it points but dare not actually go—is a type of mystical awareness in which the cognitively all-surpassing, morally impenetrable, and aesthetically overwhelming qualities of ultimacy are spurs to worship. That dark place must be eclipsed to sustain institutional life, and thus it can only be pointed to indirectly, through conceptually incoherent shrouds of evasion.

When we draw close to this dark place, in the midst of the blazing sunshine of the social construction of reality, we find a shady spot under the leafy boughs of an institutionally impossible tree, floating above an impossibly profound abyss. In that strange place, people gather who see ultimacy most clearly for what it is. They can build nothing and sustain nothing, at least not under the tree. But they can be with one another, speechless and joking, watching and listening. Here there is no liberalism or conservatism, no institutions and no cultural expressions, for it is the place of rest from all such exertions. But it is also a peculiarly demanding resting place because of its impossibly natural rules. There is no dissembling there, no deflection or distraction, and desperation is never defused; rather everything is allowed to be what it will be, in the presence of the few who gather there.

This shady refuge can never be institutionalized; people can always find it in the interstices of ordinary and extraordinary institutional achievements. Its language about ultimate reality requires no eclipsing because there is nothing to defend or protect. It is the underside habitation of spiritual beings in every religious and cultural tradition that has ever existed. It is a fecund place, spilling over with the wisdom of not taking ourselves so seriously. It unobtrusively nurtures the bright topsides of constructive institutional ventures. The traditions of ideas and poetry that describe this place are another way to find it, and those traditions would perish were it not for the dominant top-side religions that bear forward everything with them, including the deep underside traditions that are almost indistinguishable from one another across religions and cultures. To speak of this shady place is to utter the last word before plunging into the abyss of infinite darkness into which all human ventures plunge, into which all human beings plunge, in due course.

This is the perpetual promise of liberal theology—its hinting at the shady underside of the brightly lit topside traditions of religion and culture. It hints, yes, and then the institutional commitments of liberal theology and liberal religious communities eclipse the promise, preventing them from following fully realizing it. But liberal theology hints truly, and sometimes even beautifully, despite its eclipsing. When all is said and done, in a world like ours, it is arguably better to be lost and happy in a mirror maze than to be clearly oriented in the bright light of a world of delusions.

Part 3

ULTIMACY MANIFESTATIONS

PART 3 *is phenomenological in character. Each chapter picks out a slice of life—loneliness, intensity, bliss—and describes how these liminal situations conjure ultimate reality in our experience and thereby engage us with it. The shared claim is that such liminal experiences manifest the character of ultimacy, so these are yet other ways to eff the ineffable. The continental tradition of philosophy is most prominent here, with the emphasis on phenomenology and indirect manifestation of ultimacy in intense, uncommon life situations. Chapter 7 on "Loneliness" is religious philosophy in the phenomenological, literary, and theoretical styles. Chapter 8 on "Intensity" displays religious philosophy in the phenomenological, theoretical, and analytical styles. Chapter 9 on "Bliss" illustrates religious philosophy at the junction of the phenomenological and analytical modes.*

CHAPTER 7

LONELINESS

INTRODUCTION

LONELINESS ... NOT BEING ALONE BUT BEING LONELY. PONDER IT WITH ME. I think meditating on loneliness takes us deeply into the character of reality—first into the nature of human existence, and ultimately into the abysmal divine ground of existence. It is a phenomenological pathway toward effing the ineffable.

The human experience of loneliness is intimately connected with many other experiences, including individuation, identity, change, freedom, relation, difference, alienation, and love. This is not difficult to show. Take individuation, for example. To become self-consciously distinctive as a person inevitably involves awareness of being different from others, with a unique history, character, and destiny—and this induces in most people feelings of both confidence and loneliness. Again, to be free to choose is to have the capacity not only to constitute oneself from within and to influence others, but also to isolate oneself from an alternative history of possibilities and thereby to close oneself off from the other—and this is a lonely experience for many people.

This point has been made many times before in a variety of ways. In recent decades, the poetic meditations of Henri Nouwen and the systematic ontology of Paul Tillich have achieved an unusual pastoral realism through acknowledging the intimate connections of loneliness with other aspects of the human condition. Likewise, many forms of mystical theology speak of loneliness in conjunction with the ascent of the soul to union with God. In such accounts, typically, loneliness is regarded as a necessary but undesirable concomitant of desirable experiences and activities. If we recognize and welcome these desirable experiences, then we must also accept loneliness—not welcome it, perhaps, but *come to terms* with it as a painful part of human life. In fact, in principle, loneliness is to be overcome, and, if possible, eventually experienced only as a dim memory in some hoped-for,

141

future glory. Were the fullness of life's potential to be realized, thinks Nouwen, separation and being alone would not induce loneliness. Tillich imagines the unobstructed luminosity of New Being as the harmony of the elements of being under the conditions of actual existence in which the loneliness associated with separation and alienated freedom is overcome. And many mystics, while thoroughly realistic about the rigors of loneliness, affirm that it drives us toward, and is finally overcome in, the intimacy of divine union.

I would like to take a step beyond this oft-stated, standard interpretation of loneliness to ask whether loneliness is a proper object of praise, whether it has any intrinsic virtue. Now, to be necessary for desirable experiences is, of course, a kind of indirect virtue, even as belching in some cultures is a virtuous necessity (I am told) for the proper expression of gratitude after a hearty meal. Indirect virtue of this sort seems to be a feature of many experiences and activities that we have no reason to call virtuous in themselves. Perhaps loneliness falls into this category; there are certainly reasons to think so. The loneliness of the mystic's "dark night of the soul" is surely a necessary aspect of the movement toward union with God. Mystics who conceive of this blissful union as antithetical to loneliness will still regard loneliness as an indirect virtue because of the role it plays in drawing them toward the final goal. Tillich and Nouwen, presumably, would deny that loneliness is intrinsically virtuous because they assume that—unlike faith, hope, and love—it does not abide forever, it does not have a fundamental place in reality. Moreover, loneliness is often so emotionally painful that it induces in us a range of self-protective psychological responses from denial to displacement, so it appears to be positively threatening and not at all the kind of thing we usually think of as having intrinsic value.

It seems, therefore, that the cards are stacked against the case I wish to make. Nevertheless, I shall try in this chapter to seek out the intrinsic virtue of loneliness, thereby to discover if there might be any reason for cultivating it, any basis for praising it.

GROUND CLEARING

To begin, three items of conceptual ground clearing are in order, to make room for the other things I wish to say. First, we need briefly to consider what a virtue is. For my purposes, it is appropriate to begin with the ancient Greek insight that virtue (*arete*) refers to the excellence with which the proper natural character of a thing is realized. To speak of loneliness as a human virtue, then, is to suppose both that loneliness is part of the proper natural character of a human being and that we can be better or worse at being lonely. Both suppositions are debatable, and I argue in what follows that both are correct. There is another dimension to virtue, however. Suppose that the proper natural character of a thing is thought of in relation to some transcendent reality, such as Plato's Form of the Good in which all virtue participates, or Aristotle's Unmoved Mover that knits the natural purposes of all things into a cosmic teleological organism, or Augustine's God the creator of all determinate reality. Then virtue would have more profound connotations, and it would be necessary to ask whether a given virtue derives ultimately from this transcendent reality, or whether on the contrary it belongs to the proper natural character of a human being yet in such a way as not to reflect the essential character of that transcendent reality. I consider these alternatives in closing.

Second, it is important to anticipate an obvious objection—namely, that loneliness cannot belong to the proper natural character of human beings, let alone be susceptible of cultivation as a virtue, because it is merely an emotional state. Emotional states such as sadness or happiness can never be virtuous because they are thoroughly contingent, according to this point of view. It is true that some people do attempt for a period of their lives scrupulously to cultivate a certain emotional state as if it were a virtue, such as the excitement associated with adrenaline rushes. But ninety-eight-year-old versions of the same people tend to look back on such life goals as passing phases; they are lots of fun but not the kind of thing that can be cultivated in the course of an entire life. The biochemistry of the brain changes with time, for one thing, but the judgment of old age has general applicability: emotional states are too variable to be properly dignified, feasible objects of human cultivation. And if you can't cultivate it, you can't be excellent at it, and it can't be a virtue. Loneliness is like happiness or sadness or excitement in this respect, according to the objection.

This objection is not as forceful as it might seem. To see why, consider the fact that loneliness is usually expressed in emotions, but not the same emotions in all instances, even within the same person. In itself, loneliness must be interpreted more abstractly as a state of being. States of being express relations between human beings and their proximate and ultimate environments, and so are rightly submitted to norms of truth, goodness, and beauty. If a state of being corresponds to the proper natural character of a human being, then it is a proper object of human cultivation and striving. Loneliness is a state of being and not merely an emotional state, so it is not completely deranged to consider whether it is part of the proper natural character of human beings, and so whether it can be cultivated as a virtue.

Finally, a remark about the task of seeking out "the nature of loneliness" seems prudent. To the extent that I am correct to suppose that loneliness is a state of being, investigating the nature of loneliness is essentially an ontological task and only in subsidiary ways a psychological or biochemical task. Whatever is said in such an ontological investigation must do justice to the human experience of loneliness, and that will be one concern in what follows. But care is also needed so as not to be misled by superficial features of the human experience of loneliness. The nature of loneliness might be quite different than its popular reputation.

CORRECTING A BIAS TOWARD THE PLEASANT

The ground somewhat cleared, let us take a step forward. It has been said that we should think about whatever is true, noble, right, pure, or lovely; whatever is admirable, excellent, or praiseworthy. This advice of Saint Paul is first rate, but in some cases we need to think hard before we can decide whether something has these marvelous characteristics. In particular, to make the case that loneliness is a state of being with intrinsic virtue, I need to attack a hidden bias that prejudices my chances. This bias makes loneliness a leper in the colony of those human states of being that have a strongly emotional cast. Anxiety gets similar treatment. To show that there really is a bias at work here, I contrast loneliness with that paragon of virtues, the Boddhisattva's inspiration and the greatest of them all: love.

Love is a word with a dissonant horde of connotations and emotional connections. We must discriminate among the emotional responses associated with love in order to discern the nature of love. Does love dignify human beings and their aspirations? Or does it destroy or distort in a haze of confused transference and codependent clinging? Is Mother Teresa's work on behalf of Calcutta's poorest or a teenager's crush the superior model for love? Judging the appropriateness and profundity of emotional responses is tricky. The presupposed criteria are complex yet familiar, for they resemble the considerations that guide us in making judgments of artfulness of living and saintliness of character.

The need for judicious discrimination to sort through the dissonant array of emotions associated with love has led many to conclude that the emotional content of a state of love is usually misleading when the goal is detecting the presence of love in its more profound forms. Some go so far as to speak of love not as an emotion but as a decision. I think the more effective strategy is to regard love as a state of being with connections to the willing, feeling, and thinking capacities of human beings.

Now, once love is deemed really to be occurring in a superior form, is there some distinctive, pure emotional response associated with it? Surely not. Love is famous for being emotionally complex even when it is most ennobling; there is agony and wretchedness right along with satisfaction and ecstasy. Love drives us tormented to our knees even as we are swept away by the bliss of communion. Love is as pure as driven snow in its selflessness and yet flush with lustful desires to merge that are colored by urges to destroy self through absorption into the other.

Likewise, it is important not to be misled by the emotions that accompany the state of loneliness. Just as the droopy-eyed, pounding-heart caricature of love fails to furnish workable criteria for detecting its virtuousness, so the wholly negative, drawn-faced, wrenching caricature of loneliness can be thoroughly misleading. Emotions are merely initial hints inviting further exploration of the thing felt; they are not reliable guides to the nature of the thing, be the thing love or loneliness. Only closer analysis can disclose the nature of loneliness. That is my concern in the next section, but now I must complete the argument that the task of discerning the nature of loneliness is complicated by a widespread bias.

If emotional states are such misleading indicators of the nature of the states of being giving rise to them, why do almost all people regard love as desirable, but loneliness as more or less abhorrent? Why do we call love a virtue and seek to cultivate it, at least nominally, yet flee from loneliness as if it were some spectral horror with the power of very life and death over us?

Because of a bias, of course—a bias toward the pleasant. Human beings are biased in their self-assessment of emotional responses, elevating the pleasant over the unpleasant. This has disastrous results. When everything must be pleasant, it is not possible to represent accurately the full blast of powerful feelings occasioned by the higher forms of love, and the result is the popular trivialization of love in order to avoid its properly painful aspect. Likewise, the bias toward the pleasant results in the marginalization of loneliness, because loneliness-as-virtue takes too much discipline to discern and too much courage to cultivate. In every sphere of life, patience to see without denial through the unpleasant to the good, the true, and the beautiful is hard to find, and even harder to cultivate in oneself. Of course, the same applies to seeing through the pleasant to the good, the true, and the beautiful; the way things are is more important than the way things feel, but feelings determine most human motivations and desires.

Whence this bias toward the pleasant? I think its origin can be plausibly explained as an evolutionary adaptation. This particular bias is effective in helping human beings cope with their potentially deadly and always tricky environment, so that they can stabilize their social surroundings for long enough to raise children to maturity, and their children in turn can bear children. More precisely, while the bias toward the pleasant does not help to tame natural disasters or marauding invaders, it is a great asset for managing the threat of social chaos.

Pleasantness keeps people calm in the short term, so cultivating the pleasant in our social environment and in the wispy fecundity of our own imaginations minimizes the destabilizing influence of the more extreme, negative emotions. Uncontrollable external threats are bad enough; if we can just keep the parts of our environment that are closest to us calm and happy—that is, us and our neighbors—then we might have half a chance of feeding ourselves safely, reproducing successfully, and having our kids grow up in relative security. In view of the evolutionary advantages it confers, the bias toward the pleasant has the potential to help explain the origins of both the projective impulse of human beings that is amply evident in their world-making activities, and the prohibitions and taboos associated with the ethical norms active within societies.

As with everything else in life, we need to critique the bias toward the pleasant in light of more complete knowledge of the world. So, despite the specter of reductionism hovering around its adaptive role in evolution, a deep question persists: Are we biased toward the pleasant because ultimate reality is actually pleasant and the unpleasant is merely an aberrant detail that only theodicists worry about? Or are we biased toward the pleasant because of an accident of our moral and biological histories? In the latter case, the unpleasant and the pleasant may both await us in the depths of reality, and we shut off a part of ourselves when we allow the bias toward the pleasant unchecked reign over our imaginations. This is a theologically loaded point, obviously, and I will return to in a slightly different form it as I conclude.

A STORY ABOUT LONELINESS

If emotional caricatures betray only hints of the presence of loneliness, but mislead as to its nature because of an ingrained human bias toward the pleasant, then we must work hard to discern the true nature of loneliness beneath its bad reputation. We ought to be thankful, I think, that this problem of needing to see the essence of things through the veil of appearances despite misleading habits has been long recognized. Pythagoras, Parmenides, Plato, and Plotinus are the great ancient heroes of this line of work, though every discerning philosophical mind does it. In our own time, the art or science of phenomenology is the expression of this great heritage of refusing to be fooled by the familiar and promises pay dirt for a mining task like ours: detecting the nature of loneliness. To go deeper, then, I think we need to engage in a kind of phenomenological analysis.

There is a long-standing tradition of pseudo-phenomenology that permits phenomenological amateurs such as myself to keep talking. This time-honored alternative to the more technical forms of phenomenology has the rather untechnical name of "storytelling with commentary." It is quite innocent of the rigors of real phenomenology, as experts from Husserl to van der Leeuw would be quick to point out, but it is much more entertaining, and can produce interesting results despite there being a better way for those able to take it. It is to a story that I turn, therefore, followed by the inference of many conclusions that will be less secure than I would like because only real phenomenologists can produce serious arguments for them.

THE EPIC OF GILGAMESH

The Epic of Gilgamesh is an Akkadian tale, probably from the early second or late third millennium BCE (I'll refer to the Speiser 1969 translation; references are in the tablet.column.line format). I think we can learn a lot from it about loneliness. On another occasion I might be prepared to argue for the adequacy of the interpretation of this story that I offer here. My purpose here, however, is to use the story is a vehicle for thinking about loneliness, so I will set aside the concern with justifying my interpretation and simply fold the story into my interpretation of it.

Gilgamesh is a legendary king of marvelous strength and beauty. He has no equal, and so no true friends, and he is a restless, unstable, arrogant ruler. Gilgamesh's subjects in Uruk grow frustrated with his abuses of power and beg the gods to intervene by creating a rival capable of contending with him. The goddess Aruru responds in subtle fashion by creating a wild-man double of Gilgamesh named Enkidu. As the narrative unfolds, it becomes clear that Aruru's intention is far more complex than simply creating the rival for which Gilgamesh's complainants begged.

Upon hearing from a hunter of this man who roams the woods and eats with the creatures, Gilgamesh sends a harlot along with the hunter to tame Enkidu. The harlot's womanly charms and her wisdom combine to achieve this goal, and she convinces Enkidu to return with her to Uruk, there to meet Gilgamesh. Meanwhile, Gilgamesh is having disturbing dreams, which his wise and loving mother interprets for him. She says that Gilgamesh's restless spirit is recognizing a glorious but frightening possibility—namely, that his previously unacknowledged yearning for a true companion might be met in Enkidu, despite the probable rivalry between them. When they eventually meet, predictably, the two great men lock in furious battle, neither able to overcome the other. Their mutual rage subsides, and then Enkidu speaks the deep truth to Gilgamesh: "As one alone thy mother / Bore thee" (2.6.31). How wonderful to find one's equal, to be understood! And then, "They kissed each other / and formed a friendship" (3.1.19).

Gilgamesh's restlessness, once the apparent result of being alone in his greatness, is now transformed into a desire for heroic adventure with his new friend, showing that it is deeper than merely being alone. Gilgamesh conceives of a plan to slay Huwawa, a terrible creature appointed by the gods to guard the Cedar Forest. Enkidu attempts to dissuade him, but Gilgamesh convinces his friend to join him in the perilous adventure. Perhaps Enkidu agrees because he is grief-stricken at the loss of his Love, the wise and beautiful harlot women who tamed him. Perhaps he agrees out of irritation with the wise but boring elders of Uruk who attempt to dampen Gilgamesh's enthusiasm, saying, "Thou art yet young, Gilgamesh, thy heart / has carried thee away. / That which thou wouldst achieve thou knowest not" (3.5.9). Gilgamesh's restlessness was too powerful to be checked by the wisdom of probabilities, so he and Enkidu set out against the elders' advice.

In the ensuing confrontation, the two friends eventually subdue Huwawa. This achievement of greatness sparks an offer of marriage to Gilgamesh from the fickle goddess Ishtar, which Gilgamesh declines in insulting fashion. In a rage, Ishtar sends the Bull of Heaven to wreak vengeance on Gilgamesh, but the two friends slay the bull. Now the gods become concerned that things are getting out of hand, and they decree that Enkidu should die; Gilgamesh, however, shall live. Enkidu learns by a dream of his fate, and here we come to one of the most moving passages in the epic (7.2.17). Enkidu is stricken by illness and lies down before Gilgamesh.

As his tears were streaming down, ([Enkidu] said):

> O my brother, my dear brother! Me they would
> Clear at the expense of my brother!"
> [. . .] "Must I by the spirit (of the dead)
> Sit down, at the spirit's door,
> Never again [to behold] my dear brother with (mine) eyes?

Enkidu's horror of dying causes him to curse the wise harlot woman who brought him into this life from his abode with the beasts of the field. His gratitude for Gilgamesh's companionship, however, causes him to relent and bless her instead for the very same act.

After much agony, Enkidu dies, and Gilgamesh is swept into a frenzied, bitter grief. Gilgamesh's identification with his dead friend yields to a folding of his grief into a larger grief for the eventual loss of his own life: he, too, will die. Thus, once again Gilgamesh's restlessness drives him out of Uruk on an even greater quest. This time he will try to find the ageless hero of the flood, Utnapishtim, and to discover from him the secret of everlasting life.

On his way to find Utnapishtim, he meets an alewife called Siduri. In getting this far in his journey, Gilgamesh's identification with Enkidu has strengthened both emotionally and physically: Gilgamesh has lost his clothes and dwells with the animals, even as Enkidu did before he was tamed by his harlot Love. Thus, when first she lays her eyes on him, Siduri the alewife is suspicious that Gilgamesh is a wild killer. He eventually convinces her of his sincerity, however, and in their conversation she utters perhaps the most famous words in the myth (10.3.1):

> Gilgamesh, whither rovest thou?
> The life thou pursuest though shalt not find.
> When the gods created mankind,
> Death for mankind they set aside,
> Life in their own hands retaining.

The alewife goes on to encourage Gilgamesh to accept his fate as a creature of pleasures, staying within the bounds laid down by the gods. But Gilgamesh's restlessness, now tinged with rage and terror, cannot accept such advice, so Siduri directs him to Sursunabu, the boatman for Utnapishtim. Sursunabu explains how great are the dangers associated with crossing the sea, particularly the waters of death. Nevertheless, after much striving and further adventures, Gilgamesh eventually reaches Utnapishtim.

Utnapishtim reflects with Gilgamesh on the inevitability of death, and then Gilgamesh asks him about his youthful appearance and great age. By way of explanation, Utnapishtim tells him the story of the great flood, for after the flood the gods had counted Utnapishtim and his wife among their number. After all Gilgamesh's efforts to find him, therefore, Utnapishtim merely confirms Gilgamesh's worst fears: we are utterly powerless before death. Gilgamesh then falls into a trance-like sleep for seven days, exhausted from his adventures, overcome by grief and frustration. When he awakes, his host tells his boatman to take Gilgamesh to a place where he can clean up a bit before he finally leaves for good. Utnapishtim's wife, however, asks her husband to give a parting gift to Gilgamesh, whereupon Utnapishtim, in a complete reversal of expectations, tells him a secret of the gods: an underwater plant with sharp thorns to prick the hand that contains within itself the secret of life.

Gilgamesh immediately dives into the waters of the deep, locates the plant, and makes plans to recover his youth by eating it. Bidding Utnapishtim and his wife farewell, he sets out for home. After he travels many leagues, the story reaches its splendid climax (11.1.285):

> Gilgamesh saw a well whose water was cool.
> He went down into it to bathe in the water.
> A serpent snuffed the fragrance of the plant;
> It came up [from the water] and carried off the plant.
> Going back it shed [its] slough.
> Thereupon Gilgamesh sits down and weeps,
> His tears running down over his face.

MARKS OF LONELINESS

Three characteristics of loneliness are illumined by the story, and I shall say a word about each.

First, loneliness is dynamic, with a driving restlessness at its heart. It is not merely the state of being alone, which can be described without any hint of internal dynamism. It is restless aloneness, ever driving beyond itself toward action.

To explain this, first notice that Gilgamesh's restlessness directs the entire story, from his abuses of power and his fascination with Enkidu to his longing for adventure and his quest to cheat death. The story even furnishes a rationalization for Gilgamesh's restlessness in Enkidu's insightful words to him: "As one alone thy mother / Bore thee." Gilgamesh's restlessness flows from being singular. Furthermore, the story's structure and characters are organized to draw attention to Gilgamesh's driving restlessness and the loneliness underlying it. For example, Gilgamesh appears to have been loved even when his abuses were hated; he was the object of unbroken reverence. The people complained to the gods about Gilgamesh, but they did not hold his abuses against him forever. Rather, it is as if they understood his agony and realized that Gilgamesh's dangerously uncontrolled reaction to it was a passing phase. In this way, hearers and readers of the story are invited to understand Gilgamesh also. As another example, notice how all the wisdom lies on the side of the people, usually the women: the wise harlot woman whom Gilgamesh was prepared to sacrifice, Gilgamesh's wise mother, the wise alewife, the wise elders of the city. Gilgamesh, by contrast, is driven to foolishness by his restlessness, and the narrative surrounds him with figures whose pacific steadiness illumines his inner life. These literary strategies, taken together, make the story a study in the dynamism of loneliness that permits us to identify with Gilgamesh and his struggles.

To be a king means that abuses of power can be a means of self-expression. As self-indulgent and irresponsible as this is, this is what happened with Gilgamesh:

his lack of restraint was his personal reaction to being singular and without equal. He was conducting a kind of cosmic sound test: "Testing one, two, three: I am violating human rights here, doing the worst that I know with all the callousness I can muster, in an effort to get attention; someone please stop me so that I will know I am not alone, so that the agony of my loneliness will abate." This is the dynamism of loneliness at work. We might not be kings or uniquely strong and beautiful, but all of us are lonely, because each of us is singular. It is to be expected, then, that most of us sense the same dynamic character of loneliness that made Gilgamesh so restless.

Note, however, that the dynamic drive of loneliness can be expressed in two ways, both of which are evident in the Gilgamesh epic. On the one hand, the state of loneliness motivates action aimed at self-preservation. In this case, loneliness is represented as a threat, an enemy that must be overcome lest its triumph ravage us. Loneliness is death up close and personal, its rot and decay placed close to eye and nose. It is the prolepsis of extinction, and it evokes a fighting reflex in human beings. In the early part of the story, Gilgamesh's restlessness is represented as a consequence of his distinctiveness, but it is disclosed in the unfolding of the story to be a terror of death. This shows that the singular distinctiveness of each human being presages death. Finitude connotes not only the terminus of a finite life span, but also the distinctiveness of a finite life expression. The end of life and the distinctiveness of a life evoke one another, and both prompt aggressive, self-protective reactions.

On the other hand, the dynamic drive of loneliness can lead to a desire for self-annihilating extinction, a yielding to the claim of death expressed in being singular, a longing for absorption into the dark arms of loneliness. Thus it is that Gilgamesh falls into a dreamless trance-sleep upon hearing that Utnapishtim cheated death only at the whim of the gods. His quest had failed, and there was nothing further he could do but surrender. In this surrender there was a coming-to-terms for Gilgamesh, a release of his grief and frustration, and a grasping at comfort through a cessation of striving. The dynamism of loneliness can drive to what can properly be described as a psychologically appropriate death wish, a longing for extinction, for absorption, for the peace of nihility.

In both ways, therefore, loneliness is a state of great moment. Its dynamism brings to it the gravity of ultimate self-determination, either through the adventure of great deeds unconsciously aimed at conquering death, which is the silent, patient enemy intimated in the contours of loneliness; or through the calm resignation of coming-to-terms with that enemy, of befriending it through a self-annihilating, death-neutralizing merger.

The second feature of loneliness illumined by this story is its presence even in the heart of intimacy. It is Gilgamesh's mother who first shows us this: in the king's restless dreams there is a longing for intimacy that stretches beneath the surface of his fascination with a potential rival. Just as this longing for intimacy colors the lonely restlessness of Gilgamesh, so his intimate brotherly companionship with Enkidu bespeaks the insatiable thirst of loneliness. What intimacy promises to sate, it only further awakens, even as drinking salty seawater worsens the state of thirst that prompts it.

Gilgamesh's discovery of a friend did not fully calm his restless spirit. Rather, it caused Gilgamesh to lift his eyes from the self-loathing motivating his abuse of power up toward great adventures. The restlessness was transformed by intimacy, but not removed. The friendship between Enkidu and Gilgamesh was forged in those adventures. They made their mark, violating ancient taboos of fear that dominated the hearts of the masses, subduing great monsters together, each encouraging the other when the task seemed too great.

Their courage even drew the attention of the gods. But strength of intimacy steels the soul even against the greatest of threats, it seems, and Gilgamesh was emboldened to rage against all the powers that be. In his delight at spurning the goddess Ishtar's affections, he once again found himself unconsciously throwing down the gauntlet to the gods, even as he had done as the unjust ruler of Uruk. This time, however, his heady cosmic cry was different. In my words: "Nothing can stop us now, not even the gods who wield the power of death. We shall conquer loneliness and its veiled threat of death. We shall become larger than death through being larger than life." The intimacy of friendship was necessary for such glorious courage, for Gilgamesh without his brother had been a pitiful, self-destructive, and dangerous man. But if intimacy is necessary for courage, then intimacy bespeaks the underlying presence of loneliness with which that courage contends.

Loneliness haunts intimacy. It is the space marked out by the geometry of sensuously entangled limbs. It is the silence out of which irrupts a tender word and into which it drifts. It is the indiscernible edge of the fierceness of desire, the invisible motivation of mutual achievement, the ghastly interest on a lifetime's investment in becoming profoundly familiar with another. Loneliness haunts intimacy because loneliness is the most intimate state of being. It is preeminently what you have when you have only yourself, and therefore finds in intimate attachment only a kind of vain distraction. Even this appears in the story, though subtly. Gilgamesh needed adventure more than his friend did, and Enkidu, being more satisfied by friendship than Gilgamesh, tried to dissuade Gilgamesh from hunting down the guardian of the Cedar Forest. Gilgamesh needed intimacy badly, but not even the greatest intimacy could help him come to terms with the threat of loneliness. To rely on intimacy as an escape from loneliness is a vain hope, a maneuver guaranteed to fail. The wonder of intimacy must be received as pure gift, not as for-the-sake-of anything. Intimacy is finally unable to hold off the horror of loneliness.

All of this becomes completely explicit in the story, of course, as Gilgamesh's raging bravado causes the gods to curse his friend. Death comes tumbling out of their intimacy as dice from a shaker. Gilgamesh is thrown into grief by the end of his intimate friendship, and this is as it should be. It is his attachment to intimacy that transforms his grieving into desperate terror, that makes his own anticipated death seem such a shocking surprise, that brings insanity dangerously near, and that drives him on a new journey of shamanic identification with his dead friend. Is the moral of the story, then, to avoid intimate friendship? No. It is rather to resist the attachment to intimacy that makes of it a desperate denial of loneliness.

The story illumines a third aspect of loneliness—namely, that loneliness has the implacable weight of fate. Consider the exquisite agony of Gilgamesh's loss of the thorny plant that held the secret of rejuvenation. The gods, it seems, are flexible with adventurous heroes only up to a point; the basic rules don't vary. As the alewife put it: "When the gods created mankind, / Death for mankind they set aside, / Life in their own hands retaining." It is amazing that the gods can be sufficiently well organized to achieve the remarkably high enforcement rate of this rule familiar to us all, but they appear to manage somehow. They apply the rule even to Gilgamesh, in whose creation they themselves had a part. Only Utnapishtim and his wife are excepted, and that exception serves to underline just who is ultimately in charge of human life and death.

It is no accident that the plant is buried deeply in water, that Gilgamesh had to cross the Waters of Death to reach Utnapishtim, or that a water serpent stole the plant. Water is the dominant ancient Near-Eastern symbol of chaos, and the serpent—at home in the water—is the agent of chaos. Close up, chaos looks to be unpredictable and dangerous, wildly fecund and untamable. But from a distance, chaos takes on more of a static character, a consistent given in life, the condition for the possibility of most things of interest. Unnervingly threatening close up, necessarily ubiquitous from a distance, chaos is the ground of the implacability of loneliness. Just as, in the long-distance narrative perspective, there was never any doubt that restless Gilgamesh would fail to cheat death, so, from the perspective of narrative proximity, something frustratingly random was going to have to happen to cause that failure. This is the role of the thorny plant. The plant's discovery bespeaks the strength of human ingenuity and the dynamism of loneliness that drives it. The fact of its loss demonstrates the impossibility of overcoming the finitude of loneliness and death. The manner of its loss highlights the fact that the frustration of loneliness is driven home in the arbitrary details of life. And the entire episode underlines the fact that loneliness is a state of being inexorable in its outworking.

THE NATURE OF LONELINESS

According to this reading of the Epic of Gilgamesh, to be a singular being is to be the progeny of loneliness, to determine one's life is to express the dynamism of loneliness, to enter into companionship is to explore the contours of loneliness, to become overly attached to intimacy is vainly to attempt to cheat the price of loneliness, and to live and die is to illustrate the unswerving implacability of loneliness. These are marks of loneliness from which we must infer, if possible, an interpretation of loneliness as a state of being expressing the proper natural character of human life.

Interpretations of the nature of loneliness along these lines do exist, but it is a case of an embarrassment of riches: so many philosophers and poets have broached the topic, often in passing, that it is difficult to enter the discussion briefly without appearing rude or redundant. Nevertheless, some assessment of these views of the nature of loneliness needs to be ventured to evaluate my claim that loneliness belongs to the proper natural character of human being. To that end, it seems to me that interpretations of human loneliness can helpfully be described with respect to two issues: locus and status.

The locus of an interpretation of human loneliness refers to its placement in the metaphysical geography of the human being. There are lots of proposals here. For example, it is arguable that, whereas spatial consciousness underlines the expansion of self into larger communities, time consciousness drives home the persistence of self in distinction from everything and everyone else. Loneliness is thus located in human consciousness of time (Edmund Husserl and Martin Heidegger in rather different ways). Alternatively, a Cartesian or Leibnizian understanding of human consciousness makes of human beings essentially individual monads, and this singularity of consciousness can be seen as the locus of loneliness (Ben Lazare Mijuskovic). Again, the vicissitudes of life are constant reminders of the instability of companionship and communion; loneliness is one of the painful kinds of suffering experienced because of this (from Buddhism 101). And from the Epic of Gilgamesh we see yet other possibilities for locating loneliness within the geography of human life: in finitude and death, in freedom and individuation—and each of these has interesting philosophical connections.

I am relieved to point out that my case does not depend on taking a stand in relation to this welter of possibilities. In fact, I am inclined to be suspicious of the arguments I have seen for these points of view, for they depend upon settling metaphysical questions that, if answerable at all, demand at the very least decades of diligent cross-cultural comparison with a view to truth-seeking about the nature of reality and human life, and such a venture has only in recent times even become conceivable. It has certainly not yet been undertaken fully effectively. But there are impressive attempts. For example, Ben Lazare Mujiskovic (1979) employs the monadic Cartesian understanding of consciousness to interpret loneliness, but the metaphysical context for this case (itself argued for in the equally interesting Mujiskovic 1974) is too focused on Western assumptions about humanity and reality to hold off the natural objection that important alternatives have been overlooked.

Of course, the most direct way to show that loneliness belongs to the proper natural character of human being is indeed to produce a convincing account of the locus of loneliness that delivers this result for free, but this is much more work than needed for so modest a job. It is enough to show that one of these accounts must be correct, or perhaps a number of them in complementary fashion. And for this, the status issue is of more use.

The status of an interpretation of human loneliness refers to whether loneliness is regarded as essential or incidental to human nature. If the former, then loneliness belongs to the proper natural character of human being, and the question of its cultivation as a virtue can be raised. If the latter, then loneliness is merely an inessential byproduct of the stresses and frustrations of human life, one that in principle can be overcome. If my pseudo-phenomenological analysis of loneliness has anything to commend it, then it follows that loneliness is as profound an experience as humans ever have. The various marks of loneliness to which I have drawn attention are too deeply embedded in human experience—beneath differences of sex, culture, and history—for loneliness to be a contingent concoction of other, more fundamental experiences. It is true that modernity is intensively individualistic and readily suggests alienation, existential estrangement, and loneliness. But loneliness has so rich a presence in human life that any feasible world-construction inevitably registers it, though perhaps in a different way than modernity does. Likewise, there are undeniable variations between (as well as within) male and female interpretations and enactments of life, and that doubtless means that some marks of loneliness typically show up in the lives of men and others typically in the lives of women; nevertheless, in all cases lone-liness is profoundly present.

To say that loneliness is as profound an experience as human beings have (note: not uniquely profound) is not to demonstrate that loneliness is essential to human being. But it does decisively shift the burden of proof to those who would argue that it is an inessential characteristic of human life. This challenge is taken up in number of ways. In each case, a principle of discrimination is invoked to justify the interpretation of some fundamental human experiences as essential to human life and others as admittedly central in actual experience but not essential to human nature as such. One famous principle of this kind is the Christian conception of the Fall: loneliness is part of fallen human nature, but not part of perfect human nature. A psychologically more useful variation on this theme is Tillich's distinction between essential being and being under the conditions of actual existence. According to one use of this principle, lone-liness is the result of the disruption of the polar elements of being in existence, but New Being's actualization of essential being under the conditions of exis-tence involves no such disruption.

Note, however, that the application of such principles threatens to be arbi-trary: Why ought not the fallen state coincide merely with the suffering associated with loneliness? Why might not loneliness be regarded as a primitive element in the structure of being, and the rupturing of being under the conditions of exis-tence as producing not loneliness itself but only fear and denial of loneliness? Other philosophical and religious traditions have functionally similar principles, but I think the same problem applies. These principles provide a rationalization for the claim that loneliness is not an essential characteristic of human being, but each rationalization is incomplete, lacking instructions about how it is to be applied to the various fundamental experiences of human life. This makes such principles particularly vulnerable to the bias toward the pleasant.

If these discriminating principles all fail decisively to render loneliness inessential to human being—and I am betting they do, though this would be a complex case to make in detail—then we are left where we started: loneliness is as fundamental to human life as, say, love. The simplest explanation of this is that loneliness and love are co-primal in the constitution of human being (along with possibly other characteristics). The only way justifiably to break this equitable symmetry is to make appeal to some larger interpretative scheme that allows a principle of discrimination to apply without arbitrariness, or at least with no more arbitrariness than is already present in the larger interpre-tative scheme itself. From this it follows that the question about the essential character of loneliness in human being cannot be resolved without recourse to the metaphysical-theological question of the place of loneliness in a larger interpretative scheme.

THE GROUND OF LONELINESS

To move further, therefore, it is necessary to reflect on the ultimate ground of loneliness; only in this way can we complete the examination of its nature, and so the determination of its praiseworthiness. Let us recognize that our inquiry terminates right here in the case that reality in its broadest sense is centerless and ungrounded, for then there is no court of appeal by which the testimony of experience to the primal character of loneliness (or love) can be refuted. Finalizing the question of its status as a virtue would then be accomplished simply by deciding whether one could be better or worse at loneliness—and surely even the baldest practical criteria indicate that excellence at loneliness consists in resisting the disruption associated with fear and denial of it. A virtue it would be, therefore— though, as always in such world pictures, virtues in themselves are only more or less interesting social constructions with no special significance beyond their distinctive function.

Suppose, however, that speaking of a ground is possible because reality in the broadest sense is ultimately grounded—even if nothing both literally true and conceptually completely clear can be said about this ultimate ground. In that case, one question becomes crucial: does loneliness express something about the way things ultimately are? An affirmative answer to this question implies that loneliness really does belong to the proper natural character of human being, as its fundamental position (with, for example, love) in the realm of human experience suggests. In this case, therefore, loneliness is praiseworthy because it bespeaks the essential character of its ground. A negative answer to this question would imply that the ground of reality is not congenial to loneliness, that the lonely state of being is an affront to the ultimately real, that loneliness is essentially something to be repudiated rather than praised. An intrinsic virtue in the first case, in the second case it would be at best an indirect virtue, a necessary accompaniment of human life struggles, and of the quest for union with this ultimate ground. These two positions mark out one of the most intriguing choices in religious-existentialist ontology.

Both options take with appropriate seriousness the agony of the lonely soul. Neither has any surreptitious dependence on the bias toward the pleasant, or for that matter on the less common bias toward the unpleasant. Adjudicating this case is extremely difficult, as a result. To appreciate the difficulty, consider the explanatory pattern each option adopts in trying to account for two features of mystical experience: the dark night of the soul and the bliss of ecstatic union. The second option sees the dark night of the soul as that infinitely lonely state of desperate abandonment that creates in the soul an infinite desire for union with its ultimate ground; it is the necessary journey through the purging fire on the way to a blissful state of union that is essentially its opposite. By contrast, the first option sees the dark night of the soul as the complement of the bliss of ecstatic union; the longing of one participates in the ecstasy of the other because loneliness and blissful union are necessarily codetermining; the agony of loneliness and the ecstasy of union are eternally commingled, but it is the fear of loneliness and the grasping after union that combine to make the dark night of the soul so distorted and tortuous.

It may well be the case that both positions produce adequate explanations of everything within their compass, and that people are drawn to one or the other merely for reasons of personal taste. Thus, one might be forgiven for thinking that we have here equivalent theories of the place of loneliness in the ultimate scheme of reality with no possibility of making a rational decision between them, and nothing of significance riding on the decision. In such a circumstance, agreeing to disagree would be a most satisfying outcome. Something of great significance *is* riding on the decision, however: the conceptions both of loneliness and of the ultimate ground itself are genuinely different in the two cases. This is an important consideration in world-building and world-interpretation of all sorts.

To speak of loneliness as a state of being essentially at odds with the ultimate nature of things is to admit discriminations about that ultimate nature—discriminations of an essential sort. Now such discriminations are frequently possible. For example, if we were to say that the ultimate ground of reality is not hateful, this would be unproblematic—more like saying it is not a lump of quartz crystal—because hatefulness is not universally fundamental in human experience. This would be an appropriate part of a *via negativa* approach to describing this ultimate ground (see chapter 1). But there must be good reasons for making *essential* discriminations about the ultimate ground of things. Consider three such candidate reasons.

First, we might appeal to human experiences. But the appeal to human experience involves vicious circularity: we say the ultimate ground of reality is not congenial to loneliness (or love) because (we claim) it is not essential to human nature, yet we can justify the claim of its inessentiality to human nature only with reference to its incongeniality to ultimate reality.

Second, we might appeal to revelation. But the appeal to a body of special revelation in which this ultimate ground is said to disclose its nature is also problematic, but for reasons of hermeneutical complexity. The case that the Qur'an, the Vedas, or the Bible establishes decisively for the corresponding theistic traditions that loneliness is ultimately incongenial to God is, I think, impossible to make out. A particular theological system may stipulate this point, but these sacred writings are more ambiguous and open to multiple construals. In each of these cases, the imagery is complex and allows loneliness to be conceived as equiprimordial with love in the divine life.

Third, we might appeal to tradition. But the appeal to a tradition of theological interpretation risks creating a vicious regress of justification. We know that the ultimate ground is essentially incongenial to loneliness because our theological tradition says so; our theological tradition is justified in saying this . . . because of our experience? (no, loneliness is universally fundamental in experience); . . . because the ultimate ground is really like that? (no, that is viciously circular); . . . because of divine self-disclosure in a body of special revelation? (no, that is not hermeneutically viable); . . . because mystics say so? (no, there are mystic voices on both sides of the issue); . . . well then, because our theological tradition says so. There is the regress of justification. This might be an indication merely of an impressively coherent worldview, in which case the regress would be benign. But it is vicious if it is used to resolve a debate between comparably coherent interpretations of the relationship between loneliness and the ultimate ground of reality, which is the case here.

These reasons are not good enough (individually or jointly) to justify making essential discriminations about the ultimate ground of reality regarding loneliness. As in the case of our analysis of the status of loneliness in human nature, there is a symmetry here that is hard to break. There is no justification for breaking symmetry by denying equiprimordial status to loneliness and love in human nature (see chapter 3 for another example of unjustifiable symmetry breaking). Likewise, there is no justification for breaking symmetry by declaring that ultimate reality expresses itself in love but not loneliness, whereby loneliness would be a distorted representation of the ground of all being that must be conquered in the name of fidelity to that ground. The simplest explanation is the best one: loneliness and love are equally primordial in essential human nature and both bespeak the ground of reality. As far as I can see, this simplicity is the main decisive advantage my position holds over its alternative. It is not hard to imagine someone rejecting this advantage to avoid an undesirable feature of the attendant interpretation of the ultimate ground, but such a rejection cannot be justified independently; it must be a matter of personal preference—and in that case care needs to be taken so as not to smuggle in the influence of the bias toward the pleasant.

At this point, I should remark that we have stumbled across good names for these two views. The *symmetric* view, to which I am inclined for its simplicity; and the *asymmetric* view, which I have argued requires a symmetry-breaking principle, of which there are no effective instances. The debate between symmetric and asymmetric views of ultimacy is a rich one in the history of metaphysics (again, see chapter 3). To adopt the symmetric view is to take Schelling's view over Hegel's, refusing to make an essential discrimination between the original ground and final end of the cosmos so as to express the purposeless singularity of existence. It is to affirm the Neoplatonic flight of the alone to the alone. It is to interpret Jesus's cry of dereliction on the cross as echoing in the eternal heart of the divine life itself. It is to see the lonely alienation of difference as the necessary concomitant of divine self-expression in Isaac Luria's vision of the contraction of the shekeina. It is to read with Thomas Altizer the merciless loneliness of Friedrich Nietzsche's self-conscious deicide as equivalent to loving divine self-giving.

The relation between the symmetric and asymmetric views has a special function in this debate: they may be seen as stark alternatives, but they may also be coordinated in interesting ways. The perennial philosophy, as in Huston Smith's thought, interprets the symmetric view as the higher and more comprehensive view, with personal inclinations and lower maturity of soul determining the preference for the less comprehensive asymmetric view. When creation *ex nihilo* is taken with ultimate seriousness, as in Robert Neville's thought, the asymmetric view reflects the primordial indeterminacy of God as understood apart from the determination of both the world and the divine self in creation. Creation itself is in this case a kind of symmetry-breaking principle, rooted in inexplicable divine will, an act without an actor; but it is not a principle of the sort necessary to support the asymmetric view of the ultimate regarding loneliness and love. The symmetric view has a privileged place.

The symmetric view does have a distinctive aesthetic flavor. It asserts that the abysmal ground of all being is expressed in every state of being, from love to loneliness, and from joy to anxiety. Nothing is alien to the fecund darkness that illumines the being and beings springing from it, precisely because it lies deeply beneath all its manifestations and defies description. We have no cognitive grasp of the abysmal ground of being, so if an element of our experience such as loneliness is a fundamental state of being at all, then it participates in the ground of being. The symmetric view entails that a lonely ground grounds loneliness, even as a lovely ground grounds love. Loneliness springs as such from the fertile abyss that is our first love, our first loss—and this we can affirm until it spins away into the darkness of our ignorance, ultimately missing its mark like all such characterizations.

CONCLUSION

The cultivation of loneliness consists in coming to terms with it so as to limit the effects of fear and denial of loneliness. It amounts to a kind of befriending of a monstrous transcendent otherness, an otherness preeminently expressed for human beings in the infinitely transcendent ground, but also present within this ground itself. It requires cultivation of the discernment of love even within the heart of loneliness, even as we inescapably encounter loneliness in the heart of the most intimate love. In this we may truly be more or less excellent, so it is fitting to regard loneliness as a virtue. We regard love as a virtue for precisely the same reasons.

One way of seeing this is to consider the import of the Christian doctrine of God. God is Trinitarian in character, which is to say, God possesses (so to speak) an internal dynamism of difference-in-unity. But what is the effect of this affirmation, if not to ground otherness and loneliness within the heart of the divine life, right along with intimacy and love? The Trinitarian model exhibits all the elements of loneliness: distinctiveness driving internal dynamism, intimacy of union, and implacability in the form of the eternal character of the Trinitarian relations. At other times I am inclined to think of Christian theology's way of accounting for loneliness as one of the few philosophically commendable reasons for a Trinitarian doctrine of God, but here the connection works in the opposite direction: the Trinity bespeaks primordial loneliness along with primordial love.

In view of this, how are we to live with loneliness? I know I am not wise enough to answer this question, but I want to try anyway. How do we cope with loneliness? Not out of dulled horror driven by an ingrained bias toward the pleasant. Nor out of crass denial that the ground of our very being configures itself in the lonely shapes of our lives. Nor out of despair, for to live without loneliness is instant death due to the vanishing of the dynamic possibilities of free self-determination. Rather, we should follow Gilgamesh's heroic yet oddly ordinary example of allowing the dynamic restlessness of loneliness to have its seasons in our lives. In this way, as with Gilgamesh, loneliness slowly transforms us into compassionate rulers, humble listeners, great adventurers, truer companions, freer wanderers, and deeper grievers.

The Buddhist affirmation of the universality of suffering (*dukkha*) helps here. Loneliness is arguably a form of suffering connected with the vicissitudes of life, or *viparinama-dukkha*. Accordingly, loneliness, like suffering, is as ultimately rooted in the nature of things as anything can be in the Buddhist vision. But the pain of suffering (and so of loneliness) is not inevitable, for the third noble truth speaks of the cessation of suffering (*nirodha*). Rather, the pain of suffering is due to our attachment to it. The negation of suffering is not a repudiation of the fundamental character of loneliness, but rather the inevitable retraction of a cognitive claim before the incomprehensible nihility of *nirvana*. This negation is thematized early in Buddhist consciousness, but much later (if at all) in Western traditions. We live with loneliness, we befriend it, by overcoming our aversive attachment to it. Likewise, we live with love, and cultivate it, by overcoming our grasping attachment to it. Attachment as aversion or grasping always distorts and causes pain. That pain is a reminder to us that things are not as they might be. Thus, we must regard loneliness and love as virtues, and cultivate each by overcoming our attachment to them.

Our experience of loneliness can be a joyous participation in the loneliness springing forth from the heart of existence, and a mode of our companionship with unspeakable mystery. In the end, when the deathly promise of loneliness is fulfilled in our own lives, gently easing us back into the abyss from which we once rose, the words of our farewell to the familiar things of life, whether recognized by us or not, shall be words in praise of loneliness.

CHAPTER 8

INTENSITY

INTRODUCTION

INTENSE EXPERIENCES HAVE LONG BEEN OF INTEREST TO SCHOLARS OF religion because they seem to be one of the power sources for generating religious beliefs and practices. Social needs, economic conditions, and evolutionarily stabilized cognitive-emotional tendencies also play roles, as the sociology of religion (spring especially from Durkheim 1954 and Weber 1930) and bio-cultural accounts of the origins and functions of ethical and religious systems (springing from works such as Atran 2002 and Boyer 2001) have shown. Yet even the most reflexive social process has some manifestation in the lives of individuals, so the personal-experience level of analysis is also important.

Because individual experience is welded to both sociality and biology, theories of the social origins and nature of religious beliefs and practices have a reciprocal relationship with theories of intense experiences. For example, religious people often make reference to intense experiences when explaining why they believe what they believe and do what they do, and that fact is vital for the interpreter of religion. But what those people experience, believe, and do also needs to be interpreted in terms of the life world of their particular religious community and the relationship of that social microcosm to wider socioeconomic forces.

That makes studying intense experiences complicated, to say the least. My approach here is to bracket social and economic considerations (I have taken them up elsewhere; see Wildman 2011). Instead, I'll focus on the phenomenological characteristics of intense experiences and the intricate stresses they induce in language when we try to describe their significance for us. I'll then ask what might possibly be inferred from the fact of their occurrence, from their existential potency, and from their language-defying character.

Note that regular participation in identifiably religious activities is misleading as an indicator of the presence of intense experiences. Almost everyone has intense experiences; those who don't are definitely the exceptions to an impressively general species-wide rule. Sometimes those who have them deem these experiences to be religious and consonant with the norms of their religious groups. Other experiences occurring to religiously involved people provoke cognitive dissonance, while nonreligiously involved people often lack any framework at all for making sense of their intense experiences.

It is no surprise that some of the most creative exertions in effing the ineffable arise at precisely this point in human life. How can we express the meaning of those intense experiences? Even saying how they feel and what they make us think we know stretches language to the limits. Describing intense experiences, reflecting on what it means to be "given" over to them in our very minds and bodies, and understanding their ineffability is the theme of this chapter.

∽◦∾

The study of religious, spiritual, anomalous, extreme, liminal, and peak experiences in recent decades has showered insights upon those who seek to understand human beings as a species whose members' subjective lives are conditioned by the irregular occurrence of such experiences. Here are some of those insights in regard to intense experiences.

1. Intense experiences feel important to, and command the attention of, almost every person who has them.
2. Intense experiences occur unpredictably and with wide variations in frequency in the population.
3. Intense experiences are extremely diverse in kind.
4. Intense experiences often provoke religious interest, belief, and activity.
5. Intense experiences often are appealed to as justification for religious interest, belief, and activity.
6. Intense experiences often serve as touchstones for a person's self-interpretation.
7. Intense experiences can provoke cognitive dissonance and so can be marginalized in a person's self-interpretation.
8. Intense experiences occur to people on a spectrum of mental health from the desperately ill to the perfectly healthy.
9. Intense experiences range along a spectrum of affect from the pleasant and important to the terrifying and repellant.
10. Intense experiences lie along a spectrum of intention from occurring spontaneously to being intentionally cultivated.

11. Wisdom traditions include techniques for refining the ability to have intense experience more often and more potently.

12. People sometimes ingest chemicals to induce intense experiences, both within and beyond existing wisdom traditions.

13. The recurrence of certain intense experiences strengthens judgments of their importance and meaningfulness.

14. Intense experiences that are recurrent, intelligible, and desirable within a group can consolidate that group's identity.

The diversity of intense experiences is only hinted at in this list of the ways such experiences condition human life. Sir Alister Hardy has presented one of the most comprehensive lists of types of intense experiences, though even this list seems incomplete (see Hardy 1979). Many less comprehensive lists have been generated in various places and from various perspectives beginning with the classification of psychologist William James (see James 1902). Attempts to classify such experiences have been legion since then, each effort carrying starting assumptions and limitations. These categorizations and typologies demonstrate the possibility as well as the attractiveness of trying to make sense of the wealth of intense experiences by means of the organized classification of survey, physiological, and life-history data.

Other students of intense experiences have tried to analyze a particular subclass of them as thoroughly as possible. This is the approach both of scientific studies of neurological disorders that consistently produce specific subjective experiences and of psychological studies of certain types of intense experiences (see Cardeña, Lynn, and Krippner 2000). This approach is particularly helpful in managing consequences for health and well-being of identifiable types of recurring experiences.

My own first attempt, made with neuropsychologist Leslie Brothers, takes a strongly multidisciplinary approach but draws basic distinctions based on neurological considerations (see Wildman and Brothers 1999). Subsequently I integrated this early effort with an approach informed by evolutionary biology, cognitive psychology, the social sciences, and religious studies (see Wildman 2011).

Yet another approach proves interesting to the phenomenologist who seeks the "deep read" on intense experiences. The impulse in this case is to identify the common core features of intense experiences, those features that recur in various combinations in each and every intense experience. The ambitious aim of this procedure is twofold: to cast light on causal factors of intense experiences and to set in place a strong basis for a philosophical or theological interpretation of intense experiences.

Identifying common core features of intense experiences serves the aim of understanding causal factors by means of the (somewhat architectural) assumptions that rich diversity can be explained as variations on a small set of recurring structural elements and that the causes of recurring structural elements are likely to be the most easily identifiable (Lévi-Strauss 1963). Similarly, the quest for common core features promotes the aim of creating a compelling interpretation of intense experiences by means of the assumption that we can understand their significance in terms of the individual contributions to judgments of significance made by those common core features. A comprehensive structural analysis of intense experiences seems well out of reach at the present time. Yet, it would be prejudicial to neglect such structural similarities as actually exist in the data in the name of some misplaced commitment to the fundamental intangibility of the depths of human experience. Looking for structural commonalities while never forgetting the roles of social context, personal formation, and individual differences seems most prudent.

～≫～

Here I follow the phenomenological approach just described: one that seeks structural commonalities across the diversity of intense experiences. I'll try to identify and describe common core elements that arise with varying strengths and in manifold combinations in a wide range of intense experiences. The kind of core elements I seek out bear on the emotional valence of intense experiences and their production of specific linguistic and bodily impulses, which I label the pressure to silence, the pressure to speak, and the pressure to move. Others have adopted different phenomenological strategies (see below for a comparison of my results with those of others).

Doubtless my approach is defective in a variety of ways. But it does seem to have several virtues. First, its list of common core features of intense experiences is rich enough to invite comprehending disagreements among other phenomenological efforts as incomplete perspectives on a more complex whole. Second, it recognizes some experiences of nonreligious people as intense experiences, correcting a pattern of neglect evident through a great deal of phenomenological work on intense experiences. Third, it steers close to evolutionarily primary neurological and physiological factors and away from evolutionarily secondary conceptual and cultural factors, thereby both maximizing its usefulness for causal analyses of the origins of our capacity for intense experiences and minimizing exposure to the shoals of cultural relativism and problems of translatability and commensurability. These characteristics promise to enhance theoretical depth and breadth perception, and thus to improve subsequent interpretations of the causation and significance of intense experiences.

I begin with a discussion of the three impulses or pressures that I use to distinguish the common core elements of intense experiences. I then present the five common core elements, which I dub depth, horizon, scale, complexity, and mystery. I compare these results with those of related efforts. I then ask the philosophical theologian's insistent question: what is manifested in and through intense experiences, and through the limits of language encountered in trying to speak of them?

Language under Pressure

THE PRESSURE TO SILENCE

One mid-November morning some years ago, I made my first visit to the Vietnam War Memorial in Washington, DC. The design was unsettling, with the path plunging into the ground before arcing through and back up and out again. The mass of names, a veritable horde of them, swarmed around me as I slowly paced this gash in the earth. A young man traced a name on the wall. A few children were playing a short distance away. I could hear cries of "catch it!" and teasing and laughter as I walked.

Though it was not part of my experience, I thought of the controversy surrounding the Vietnam War. I had heard stories of people losing lifelong friends, ministers being run out of churches, and parents alienated from their own children, all because of their different perspectives on the war. I had seen films of crowds surrounding returning U.S. soldiers, some holding "Baby-Killers" placards, many shouting their disapproval, and a few even spitting on the fortunate who survived. I had read about the difficulty that returning soldiers had in weaving themselves back into the fabric of society, and the high psychic cost of the war both for veterans and for the nation as a whole.

I pondered the sense of humiliation that burdened and perhaps still burdens some in the United States about the war. For some this humiliation was about not being able to stop communism from spreading in Vietnam. For others it was about the "policeman" role the United States and its allies played in deciding what should happen in Southeast Asia. For still others it was about losing a war to which the North Vietnamese were so committed that their human losses alone were probably an order of magnitude greater than those of the armies allied with the South Vietnamese. For yet others it was about the undignified way in which public debate about the war was conducted across the United States, the shameful way that courageous American soldiers were treated, and the political shortsightedness of anti-war sentiment.

I thought of my country of origin, Australia, going to war on its Southeast Asian neighbor as an act of loyalty to its gargantuan cross-Pacific ally. The confusion about the war in Australia was complicated by other factors. Australians were one step further removed from the war than the American public, for whom the spread of communism was a more prominent issue, one more clearly worth fighting about. Yet Australians bordered Southeast Asia and had to concern themselves with regional developments, and the US Navy and Marines had come to the rescue during World War II as Japanese troops headed south towards New Guinea and Australia. A country with memories of the rank incompetence of British commanders causing the pointless deaths of thousands on the shores of Turkey in World War I, however, is always anxious when serving the interests of an ally even when it has interests of its own at stake.

I thought of Vietnam. I had never been there and had not then seen the shocking figures on Vietnamese casualties of the war, but I knew about defoliants, the horrific fate of some small villages, and the resentment toward the interfering West. I knew about Vietnam's reputation as a paradise and how the war dramatically changed the landscape, at least for a while. I thought about the grief over lost children affecting many more Vietnamese families than in the United States and its allies combined, rumbling through the generations as such unrelenting sorrow does.

These thoughts drifted through me as I walked the path. They were registered wordlessly, as feelings rather than as a series of thoughts. This wordlessness was the only way to let the furiously diverse perspectives on the war coexist in my imagination. I was silent for a long time afterwards. Just as I did not speak for more than a day after seeing the film *Gallipoli*, a retelling of some of the most tragic events of the Great War remembered ever after in Australia and New Zealand on Anzac Day (April 22), so I stayed silent for the rest of the day as I wandered about Washington. This silence was no ritual act of respect to the fallen; at least it was not primarily that. Mostly it was an attempt to allow the enormity of the events space to breathe in my imagination, an air space that words would close off as soon as they began to intrude, which they would all too soon.

This pressure to silence was strong, then, and welcome. It is always welcome. It has the dimensions of home and the colors of winter. It is the full silence of thick, windless snowfall. It is fire-in-the-hearth relief from the harsh, time-bound linearity of language. It is an antisocial withdrawal from inane chattering, which in that state grates on my nerves and includes almost everything spoken or written. It is restful, then, but tinged both with a patient grief that anticipates the inevitability of silence broken and with a slightly desperate vigilance. When in such moods, my reentry is unpredictable. It might be a smile and a courteous, simple reply to a child's question. Or it might be a selfishly savage attempt to defend my silent habitation, which is of course instantly destroyed by so harsh a move. These days, I try to smile.

Looking back on that emotional journey through the War Memorial and rethinking remembered currents of the stream of my consciousness at that time, I am impressed by an abiding conviction—namely, that a rational piecing together of these perspectives on the Vietnam War would be in bad taste. Floating along the silent flow of the river of feelings and ignoring the paddling option of thinking things out now seems to have been absolutely necessary for the significance of that experience to have had a chance of sinking in, of transforming me, of being honored in me.

The intensity of things sometimes conjures the pressure to silence. Rushing upwards from the unfathomable depth of our experiences, the pressure to silence engulfs us—we who are blessed with such a facility for language that we are used to being able to say almost anything to the point of being cavalier, unknowing victims of linguistic hubris. The shock of the pressure to silence is partly surprise at the sudden unmasking of language as a sinister adjunct to a subtle social habit of using language to paper over the painful intensity of things. This habit lulls us into a flatly comfortable world, defined by predictability and colored merely by aspirations for relatively harmless, well-controlled excursions into the terrible and the blissful and other extremities.

The pressure to silence is also about the need to acknowledge the failure of something. This might be the failure of language to capture that which we wish to express, but this risks misdescribing the situation as having chiefly to do with expressibility. It is perhaps more centrally the failure of the *will to express*. Whenever making the effort to speak the intensity of our experience strikes us as futile, as a distraction from action, as imprudent or immodest, as distasteful or dangerous, we are liable to be pressed to silence. Poets might dare to speak under such circumstances, but poetry is all the more dangerous for its hazardous aspirations, its winking disruption of the blanket of calm warmth that language wraps around our societies. All these considerations are independent of the question of whether we can express everything we can think, with or without the aid of specialized languages and expert discourse communities to maintain them. From this it follows that the pressure to silence is not one thing in every instance, but rather is complex and shaped by context. Unsurprisingly, then, it is also constrained by the intensity that evokes it.

Feeling the pressure to silence and yielding to it in situations like the one I have described is my way, and I know that it is not the only way. I vividly recall a car trip back to Krakow after visiting Auschwitz and Birkenau, a far more overwhelming experience about which I dare not speak at all—a very different sort of pressure to silence than the one I felt at the Vietnam War Memorial. That return journey was filled with the agonized and highly intellectual verbal processing of a friend as he struggled to come to terms with what he had seen. I was suffocating for want of silence even as my friend yielded to another pressure, familiar to me only in more mundane situations, to talk it out and to think it through.

Though I suspect that my friend was as desperate for comfort as I was, the ways we responded to the existential crush and went about getting what we needed were quite different. We human beings are such diverse creatures! One seeks to defer to the intense through silence while another bends the full power of intellect to a similar goal. In fact, both the pressure to speak and the pressure to silence are familiar to most people, and it is probably a blend of circumstances and personal style that determines which is activated.

There is a strange relationship between the pressure to silence and the pressure to speak. To see this, consider the familiar paradox that mystical writers of the apophatic sort have to embrace. Whereas their self-appointed task is to describe an object of experience that drives the mind away from familiar categories and words and toward something like undifferentiated unity or perfect emptiness, the medium available to them for expressing the idea of such experiences and for maintaining traditions of such expression is verbal. The paradox is obvious in the stating but prodigiously subtle in the outworking. The stresses induced in language by the end that apophatic mystical writers force it to serve are extreme. The great exponents of such writing have been similarly extreme in the creative production of techniques for getting the point across without vitiating the infinitely delicate final goal. Some have analyzed many of these techniques at the level of syntax and grammar (Sells 1994; Knepper 2005). There are also techniques at the level of symbol systems, such as balancing mechanisms (see chapter 5) and conceptual trajectories (see part 2), and techniques depending on the historical play of symbolic transformations (see Pelikan 1996, 1999; Neville 2001).

The question to be asked in light of these phenomena is this: why do apophatic mystics bother to speak at all? Why not allow the pressure to silence free rein and just stop talking about such matters? Well, some do embrace silence in just this way; some members of silent religious orders are one example, and another might be those Sufis who cultivate disciplined, joking, storytelling evasions of talk about ultimate matters. Mystical writers do not choose these paths, however; they experience a pressure to speak that is powerful enough to compete with the pressure to silence that their writings describe. Note that this has nothing to do with the *via negativa* or the *via positiva*, both of which are ways of speaking that represent themselves as paths toward deep visions of God and ultimately toward differently modulated silences (see chapter 1). It has to do with the motivation of mystical writers. Most apophatic mystical writers manage to intensify the paradox of their bothering-to-speak-at-all by speaking mostly of the pressure to silence and saying relatively little about the pressure to speak. Yet it is the pressure to speak of the pressure to silence and that which provokes it that drives them into the position of intense creativity and makes their writings so memorable.

What, then, is this pressure to speak? By way of contrast, consider that there is a generalized habit among human beings of speaking, for diverse purposes and with effects of varying value. This is a biologically basic side effect of a triple correlation: the development of vocal tract physiology, the creation of systems of language, and the evolution of the neural capacity for symbolic reference and other cognitive requirements of language. The pressure to speak as I mean it here refers not to this more-or-less unrestricted urge, however interesting it is—and it is fascinating—but to something every bit as distinctive and complex as the pressure to silence.

The pressure to speak derives from this basic capacity for language as a specialized response to extraordinary conditions. My friend in the car trip away from Auschwitz and Birkenau felt one form of this pressure to speak; the poet experiences another; the prophet is driven by another; and the scholarly inquirer is subject, as I am here, to yet another. Each develops special techniques as subtle as those of mystical writers for speaking about that which, when felt most intensely, is difficult or impossible to capture in words and can even defeat the desire to speak. The poets play with language and become the high adventurers of trope. The inquirers create specialized discourses and cultivate traditions of knowledge. The prophets battle beneath the interminable wet blanket of oppressive social convention with masterful rhetoric. The worshippers speak and sing in ritualized ways whose expressive and transformative power finally turns more on blessed repetition and emotional potency than on cognitive content. These specific forms of the pressure to speak are distinguishable from the generalized urge to speak by context. Just as things show up as differently intense in different contexts, so human beings experience pressures to respond, in silence or by speaking, to that intensity.

THE PRESSURE TO MOVE

Distinguishing the pressure to speak from the pressure to silence seems to demand that we distinguish between the pressure to move and the pressure to stillness. While there is a point to this, I will collapse this sensible distinction and speak inclusively of the pressure to move because there is no extended tradition of thought demanding recognition of the pressure to stillness as there is demanding the pressure to silence. This difference in intellectual heritage may reflect the linguistic distinctiveness of our species, so that the cessation of speech is more notable than cessation of movement, which we share with an enormous number of other animal species. Besides, we comprehend stillness as a kind of movement, so the possibility of no-motion is registered in what follows.

The evolutionary context is the most promising framework within which to interpret human movement. The neural hardwiring for movement refined in the evolutionary process is our inheritance: our central nervous system has everything from distributed processing that provokes the muscular contraction away from danger without having to waste time in centralized cognitive processing, to a flight response that triggers such cognitive confusion that the direction of our movement is as unknown to us as it is unpredictable to a dangerous foe. Our species has an enormous range of instinctive movements from locomotion to facial expressions. We have formidable dexterity that, combined with cognitive abilities, allows us to compensate for relative weaknesses in the strength and agility departments with tools and culture. It is by means of those tools and cultures that we have organized ourselves to penetrate and usually dominate most of our planetary home's diverse ecosystems. Our movement is geared to emotional states almost as much as to perception and cognition. We feel through moving and move in response to feeling in an incredibly fine-tuned feedback process. Without that embodied feedback process we could never master the perpetual tumbling that is walking, nor learn to balance well enough to move in any other way, nor figure out how to compensate for our endlessly moving sense organs so as to stabilize perception.

Our brains develop in the early years on the basis of a complex hardwired connectivity of feedback processes among perception, emotion, and movement toward a prodigiously subtle set of finely adjusted neural connections that make all of our movements possible, from the subconscious rhythm of breathing and other autonomic bodily processes to the masterful elegance of the dancer or the breathtaking power of the athlete. Indeed, the very aesthetic criteria by which we assess beauty, economy, and elegance of movement themselves derive from this same conjoining of hardwiring and learning that makes us able to move and to recognize movement in others. Nothing makes this clearer than the mirror neurons that cause our brains to react to the perception of moving human beings in the same way our own brains would fire if we ourselves were moving, save that other neural processes necessary for activating movement do not occur. We appreciate the movements of others literally by experiencing them to some degree in our own minds. This is how we judge beauty of movement as well as estimate the motivations and intentions associated with movements we see.

It is no wonder, then, that we have characteristic impulses to move when we undergo intense experiences. Of course, speech is a special kind of movement, and the pressure to silence and the pressure to speak have been described. Beyond this, however, the pressure to move is extremely powerful. It is a visceral reaction to intensity that manifests itself in an enormous variety of ways, from sitting quietly and alert to the furious movement of limbs and torso in wild dancing, from the violent physical outburst to the joyous sprint. All of these physical movements are modulated by cognitive considerations. For example, prudence may determine that one's anger be expressed in a white-hot stare rather than bodily assault, and a cultured environment may determine that a subtle hand movement enters a bid at an auction even though such a movement would not be noticed elsewhere. One group may interpret falling down in a religious act of worship in a most positive light whereas another group might read such movement as a medical emergency.

The diverse range and contextual variations of movement complicates the identification of correlations with intense experiences. In the final analysis, the plausibility of associations between core features of intense experiences and various movements depends on identifying underlying primitive neural structures and controlling for the effects of considerations from personal style to social context. We are significantly in the dark because research on this topic—from associations of intense experiences with particular movements to the neural entanglements of emotion and movement—is in its infancy. I think something can still be said, however, and I also think something ought to be said, because the associations between feeling and movement play a vital role in intense experiences.

Intense Experiences

FIVE CORE FEATURES OF INTENSE EXPERIENCES

The intensity of things evokes the pressure to silence, the pressure to speak, and the pressure to move in a variety of ways because intensity has more than one face. In fact, it has at least five faces, which I shall distinguish using names, some of which have fascinating lineages in the phenomenology and philosophy of religion and in theology: depth, horizon, scale, complexity, and mystery. It is the different qualities of the pressure to silence, the pressure to speak, and the pressure to move that serve as the first-level justification for a phenomenological distinction among five faces of intensity. While the rationale for using the word "intensity" needs to be furnished, and I'll come to that later, it is most efficient first to outline these five faces of intensity and to connect them with the various forms of the pressure to silence, the pressure to speak, and the pressure to move.

This is effectively an atomic theory of intensity, explaining its complex manifestations through simpler component aspects. The names I am using for these five basic aspects of intensity are not random. "Depth," "horizon," and "mystery" are terms partially stabilized by existing discussions in the phenomenology of religion or theology; "scale" and "complexity" as used here may be less familiar ideas. I shall attempt to describe these five faces of intensity by means of their inscription in intense experiences, their correlations with human feelings and activities, their links to social institutions and ritual processes, and their characteristic associations with forms of the pressure to silence, the pressure to speak, and the pressure to move.

∼≈∼

First, depth is registered in feelings of intense, objectless fear or joy. Associated mental states typically have no direct object. The primary activity invited is that of surrender, with consciousness of being at the mercy of something that may or may not be worthy of trust, but which is trusted nonetheless, inevitably. This is the import of Yahweh placing Moses in the cleft of the rock for his protection, David dancing in the temple, and Śiva dancing in destruction across the face of the earth. In such situations, our ultimate environment shows up as deadly and yet gracious, though there is absolutely no rational cause to believe that grace can be counted on in the situation. Thus, surrender is the natural response. This is the founding experience of grace in religious life, regardless of the doctrinal framework furnished for it. Attempts to understand are irrelevant in this state.

No social structures are associated with the recurrence of these kinds of feelings, but in small communities the achievement of this awareness is prized and rewarded with admiration and respect. Liturgy registers the reality of this experience of depth in praise, whether verbally or musically, and especially in adoration, where the particular cognitive content of what is said or sung fades, allowing something akin to a trance state to predominate. Repetition of songs and mantras as well as rhythmic vocalizations and synchronous bodily motions can help relativize cognitive content on the way to such states of consciousness.

The pressure to silence associated with the experience of depth is that of surrender to fear and joy, which involves the prohibition of pretenses to control such as language typically connotes. The pressure to speak associated with the experience of depth is that of playful babbling, incoherent singing, glosso-lalia, screaming, and mumbling—the forms of speaking that deconstruct the illusion of control associated with the cognitive grasp of language. The pressure to move is especially interesting here: the experience of depth seems to be the consistent inspiration for solo dancing, trance dancing, and synchronous rhythmic movement.

⁓ᴥ⁓

Second, horizon is registered in feelings associated with recognizing difference, such as fascination, alienation, fear, disgust, or hate. The experience of horizon can be aggressively internalized as failure to recognize oneself or a part of one's body, with the associated sense of panic or violation. It can also be spectacularly externalized into powerful senses of presence, which may be hostile or benign. The mental states in which horizon is realized always have logical objects and thus are intentional states, but the objects may be either diffuse or specific. The primary activity associated with horizon is engagement, which can cover everything from defending and fighting to dialoguing and flirting. Understanding this response involves interpretation, comparison, and dialogue.

Politics is the institutional sphere in which this experience in human life is most directly registered, and the typical social form that presupposes it is the group that represents special interests. There are legitimation processes associated with any group's perpetuation and function; the legitimation processes of special-interest groups are essentially ideological and self-protective. Liturgy responds to the prevalence of this human experience with confession, intercession, and supplication. Consciousness of ourselves and our own pain and interests and concerns is centralized in such liturgical acts, but they also engage us with the Other as essential to our own well-being.

The pressure to silence associated with the experience of horizon is that of fearful and fascinated recognition of difference, a pregnant silence in which words are necessary yet all words are premature. When engagement demands the breaking of the dangerous silence, the pressure to speak takes the form of the language of politics, words that serve the end of surviving and thriving: "diplomacy," "prophecy," "negotiation," "rhetoric," and "persuasion." These special kinds of verbal dance are akin to the pressure to move evoked in experiences of horizon as dancing: flirtatious dancing, body-grinding dancing, teasing dancing, the ballroom tango, and the candlelit balcony waltz of lovers.

☙❧

Third, scale is registered fundamentally in feelings of awe, which can involve oceanic calm or the anxiety of agoraphobia, vastness or emptiness, and which leads out into feelings of benevolence, compassion, wideness of heart, or loss of self. The panoramic appreciation of the nature mystic is typically dominated by scale; the natural world becomes vast and all encompassing, abundantly fertile and creative, from the very large to the very small, and from the very far to the very near. The feeling of emptiness is correlated with this feeling of vastness because, as the appreciation of the vastness of reality widens, the filtering of that reality through personal interests lessens, to the point that utterly succulent vivid awareness coincides with emptiness of self.

The need to register the mutual determination of vastness and emptiness is the reason why this face of experience is better called "scale" than either "vastness" or "emptiness," though "scale" is admittedly a bit obscure (but then "depth" and "horizon" would also seem obscure were they not stabilized by extant habits of discourse).

While intense experiences of scale are sometimes terrifying and can skittle psychic stability, they can also induce peacefulness, equanimity, and wideness of heart. It is just as the Buddha taught: the realization of vastness or emptiness evinces compassion, for the reason that everything appears related in an all-encompassing vista, so that my interests are viscerally experienced as merged with those of every being everywhere. The mental states associated with experiences of scale are typically objectless, as with experiences of depth. But experiences of scale are distinguishable from experiences of depth both because of the feelings involved and because the basic urge in response to scale is not to surrender (as in depth) but to behold, an essentially selfless reaction. As with experiences of depth, attempts to understand experiences of scale are irrelevant because they interfere with beholding.

No social institutions exist in specific recognition of the prevalence of experiences of scale; both they and experiences of depth are essentially deconstructive impulses within human social life, unmasking self-protection and mocking clever legitimation strategies. Liturgy responds to the presence of experiences of scale in human life with songs of grandeur, heart-stoppingly glorious architecture, and awe-inspiring language.

The pressure to silence in this case prohibits words in the name of making us small so that the universe can expand in our imaginations, consuming us. The pressure to speak shows itself as unselfconscious, rippling laughter on the way to speaking "Om," when it is the word that comprehends all and evokes all. Yielding to the pressure to move in this case leads to dancing alone among trees, dancing alone under the stars, running in trains of hand-holding friends streaming like wind gusts across grassy hills, or else sitting quietly in the open-bodied lotus position.

⌇

Fourth, complexity is registered in feelings of confusion, disorientation, irritation, surprise, and wonder. A mental state in which complexity is dominant has an object. The object might swarm around us, as the world does for the airplane pilot in twisting freefall. Or else the complexity of this object might be newly noticed, evincing oohs and aahs and stimulating curiosity. The primary activities associated with experiences of complexity have to do with the satisfaction of curiosity, the relief of confusion, and the solving of problems, all of which lead out into serious attempts to control and understand that which irritates or provokes curiosity. Understanding in this case involves inquiry and associated activities of model building, experimenting, testing, and exploring.

Liturgy addresses the prevalence of experiences of complexity with the reading and exposition of sacred texts, with educational and inspirational public speaking, and with moments of pastoral care. There are many social institutions whose reason for existence depends upon the recurrence of experiences of complexity, from educational and research institutions with explicit missions to understand, to family and community institutions implicitly devoted to controlling the problematic environment of human life. These institutions protect and provide resources for solving theoretical and practical problems; for comforting the confused, orienting the lost, and soothing the irritated; and also for giving free rein to wonder and curiosity.

It is here that human beings are at their creative best, transforming overwhelming confusion into social arrangements that steady the spinning world and inventing technologies that control and alter the environment for human life. This describes the pressure to speak but the pressure to silence hovers nearby. We are driven to respectful silence by wonder: the cell under a microscope, Jupiter's moons through a telescope, a finely tuned ecosystem, or the proof of Pythagoras's theorem of right-angled triangles. We are compressed into silence by the suffocating confusion of complex problems: the production and fair distribution of food on planet Earth, the endlessly rebellious teenager, the inner workings of our own minds, or the way long chains of amino acids consistently fold into the same-shaped protein when in the right cellular environment. In no sphere of intense experiences does the pressure to silence yield so quickly to the pressure to speak. But the pressure to silence hovers beneath and at the boundaries of human confusion and our prodigious efforts to solve problems. The pressure to move is as powerful as the pressure to speak in this case, and gives rise to making, molding, and crafting; poking, prodding, and exploring; looking under, around, and through; weighing, testing, and measuring; finding out, finding more, finding *it*; researching, recording, rethinking, and retracing steps. The whirlwind of movement spins as fast as the words flow.

～⊛～

Fifth, mystery is registered in feelings of ignorance and incomprehension. Whereas the experience of complexity yields to curiosity through positioning the object as a tractable problem, the experience of mystery involves being stopped in one's tracks. The object in this case always seems diffuse, beyond our control, and cognitively impenetrable. This is so whether or not the object really can, with right effort and skillful means, be specified, controlled, or understood. The primary activity associated with mystery is reverence, which involves recognizing that the mystery must be set apart and made holy. Attachment to mystery is common, which leads to rationalizing its incomprehensibility by distinguishing between secular and sacred, creating rules that protect the sacred and defend it from incursions of the merely curious, and delineating ritual space and time within which the mystery can be savored with proper reverence. Religious institutions are the social forms that most directly recognize the recurrence of experiences of mystery in human life.

Ritual, sacrament, vestment, and symbol are the lifeblood of the liturgical recognition of mystery. Hierarchy and authority are the concomitants of institutionalizing commitment to the defense of mystery. Hierarchical authority can be used to suppress and resist incursions of the curious by framing them as lacking the requisite appreciation and respect for the mystery and carelessly trampling on that which deserves reverence. Reverence is enormously captivating. At the heart of institutionalized religion lies not merely Nietzsche's priest, cruelly sucking the life out of the weak and dependent, but also people captivated by mystery, at times perhaps obsessive like the desperate lover, but revering that which is more valuable to them as mysterious than as comprehended. And though many former mysteries have proved to be tractable for inquiry in recent centuries, the primal mystery of our existence remains, undergirding all life and evincing reverence from all who sense it.

The pressure to silence in this case is the silence of reverence. Whereas the silent wonder of complexity yields quickly to the chatter of inquiry, the silence of reverence is difficult to interrupt for lack of any motivation to do so. The pressure to speak in this case is driven by the needs of sacrament and liturgy, authority and legitimation. The pressure to move in this case is a power source for ritual: the raising of the hands just so, the pouring of the milk just so, the delicately tuned timbre and inflection of voice, the simple but elegant economy of movement, and the impeccably careless casting of rose petals.

∽⊱⊰∾

These five faces of intensity are neither exhaustive nor mutually exclusive any more than are the sorts of pressure to silence, pressure to speak, and pressure to move that they engender. Nor are the associations with emotions and kinds of human activity strict; there are other ways of slicing the intensity pie. These limitations in systematic comprehensiveness do not affect the point of the exercise, however, which is to notice something of how the internal variegations of the pressure to silence, the pressure to speak, profound feelings, and human actions are correlated. This correlation is the most basic evidence for intense experiences having these five characteristics that recur in our experience. The second level of evidence is the stability of this phenomenology of intense experiences across cultures, eras, personalities, and mental capacities. That I cannot formally test here, but it has guided the description and will continue to test and correct it (see Andresen 2001; Andresen and Forman 2000).

COMPARISON WITH EXTANT PHENOMENOLOGIES OF INTENSE EXPERIENCES

The approach to intense experiences taken here comprehends a number of other phenomenological attempts to articulate common core elements of intense experiences. These have usually been aligned with attempts to establish a pattern of inference from basic human experiences, however analyzed, to theories about their causation (a task not taken up here but see Wildman 2011) and significance (a task to which I turn presently). It is valuable to consider how the descriptive phases of some of these previous attempts relate to the present effort. I have made a representative selection of a large group of thinkers, but the group is rich enough to illustrate my claim that the five faces of intensity create the possibility of understanding these efforts as partial perspectives on intense experiences, adequate for the particular aims of each thinker, but finally limited in scope.

First, Friedrich Schleiermacher (1928) contended that a "feeling of absolute dependence" pervaded thought and action in the sense of being a condition for their possibility. Schleiermacher's controversial way of speaking about dependence, as a feeling rather than as an ontological state, provokes a distinction between a real metaphysical relation of dependence, on the one hand, and feeling as a way of detecting this metaphysical relation, on the other. In terms of the analysis of intense experiences given here, Schleiermacher's dependence is most closely related to depth and horizon. When we are aware of our pervasive dependence, we are at the mercy of something wondrous by which we are fascinated and to which we might be inclined to surrender, which is the depth form of intensity. We are simultaneously vividly aware of that on which we are dependent as utterly other, which is the horizon form of intensity.

Second, Rudolf Otto's phenomenology of the irrational dimensions of religious experience leads to its analysis as encounter with the holy (see Otto 1917). This holy corresponds in the current scheme to a blending of the depth, scale, and mystery forms of intense experience.

Third, Paul Tillich's investment in depth psychology and Neoplatonism led to his use of such images as depth, ground, and abyss to describe the ultimate that is disclosed in human existence (see Tillich 1951). Human beings are anxious, alienated, and in need of the courage to be. In this case, we hear the accent on the depth and horizon forms of intense experience.

Fourth, Karl Rahner (1978) offers a beautiful analysis of human freedom, whereby the moment of choice is disclosed to be an infinitely graced presentation of the depths of being, inviting movement toward the horizon of future possibilities. These are the elements of depth and horizon melded together, much as in Tillich. Yet our ignorance of the source of this grace, the formal impossibility of grasping or controlling it, is strongly emphasized in Rahner, thereby drawing in the mystery form of intense experience.

Fifth, Gordon Kaufman (1993) emphasizes the fact that human beings are biohistorical creatures, evoking or provoking awareness of an unendingly complex dependence on a biological web of being and an endless entanglement with the historical constraints on and possibilities of human existence. Here we see especially the scale and complexity forms of intense experience woven together in a scientifically sensitized portrayal of human nature. Despite the title, *In Face of Mystery*, Kaufman's interest in the mystery face of intense experiences is not especially pronounced; his is the silence of wonder that yields to inquiry rather than the silence of reverence that yields to protection of mystery.

Sixth, the study of mysticism has sometimes refused generalizations about mystical experience in the name of historical contextualization (famously, see Katz 1978, 1984, 1992, 2000). Other students of mysticism point to a convergence between mystics of all traditions on the strength of mutually resonant phenomenological descriptions of mystical experiences (see Forman 1990, 1999; Smith 1992). Huston Smith has even gone so far as to propose a South-Asian styled theory of spiritual personality types that seeks both to explain divergence among mystical experiences and to protect his perennial-philosophy account of their unanimity about the nature of ultimate reality (see Smith 2000). The present effort walks an empirical line between the historicists and the perennialists, seeking commonalities where they may be found and searching for differences with equal eagerness. That these five features of intense experiences recur across cultures and eras is an empirical claim. That these five features of intense experiences reflect the character of that to which the experiences are responses is a theological claim, yet one that I think might be partly tractable. That these five features of intense experiences are vague and differently specifiable in different historical and psychological contexts is sufficient, I think, to account for the fascinating variation among intense experiences.

Seventh, recent neurological studies of religious experience have the potential to illumine a phenomenological description of intense experiences. So far, however, the goal has been chiefly to find neural correlates for a narrow range of intense experiences and the possibility of correcting and improving a broad phenomenological description does not yet exist. It is interesting, nonetheless, to ponder how intense experiences interpreted in relation to neural imaging scans fit with what has been said here. For example, Andrew Newberg proposes a correlation between the lessening of brain activity in specific brain areas (such as what he and Gene d'Aquili call the "orientation association area") and subjective reports by Tibetan monks of experiences in which the world is perceived as vast, as somehow free of filtering through the ordinary categories of language, and as productive of benevolence and compassion (see d'Aquili and Newberg 1999; Newberg, d'Aquili, and Rause 2001). This would be an instance of an intense experience of scale.

Finally, in other work Brothers and I have identified basic characteristics of two classes of intense experiences (see Wildman and Brothers 1999). Short-term episodes involve sensory alterations, self-alterations, sense of presences, compelling cognitions, and powerful emotions; while long-term experiences involve existential potency, social embedding, transformation of behavior, transformation of personality, and transformation of beliefs. We intend this neuropsychological categorization to be comprehensive so its relation to the phenomenology of this essay is an important question. Short-term episodes are most relevant for comparison with the phenomenological analysis of the five faces of intensity. That analysis describes a range of cognitions and emotions associated with short-term episodes. It casts some light on sensory alterations. It says less about alterations in sense of self and the sense of presences but it does describe the cognitive and emotional coloring of those spectacular experiences, particularly in relation to intense experiences of horizon.

Intensity as Such

FROM INTENSE EXPERIENCES TO INTENSITY

The philosophical theologian is predictable at times. This is one of those times. Most philosophical theologians want to know what is manifested in intense experiences. That is, they want to know about *intensity as such*. But is it even possible to move beyond the use of the adjective "intense" to refer to the quality of certain experiences and begin using the nominalized "intensity" to describe that to which intense experiences are in some sense a reaction?

The adjectival usage doesn't seem particularly controversial. The nominal form, "intensity," is more problematic. It might be called "profundity" or "richness," perhaps, though these terms have their problems. The main liability of the term "profundity," beyond its semantic proximity to the word "depth" already being used to name one of the faces of intense experiences, is that it suggests an intellectual state by means of its familiar association with ideas. That would be misleading. The main problem with "richness" is its invocation of balanced appreciation and evaluation, with the corresponding diminution of the element of immediacy suggested by "intense." I have tried to describe those moments when we human beings feel most vividly alive, whether in terror or wonder, or most open to and aware of the environment of our lives, whether constructively or destructively; such experiences are often, even typically, out of balance. So I'll stay with "intensity."

Intensity involves a combination of the vertical dimension of vivid awareness—the intensity of feeling vividly alive—and the horizontal dimension of openhearted connection—the intensity of relationship with other living beings and even with the cosmos itself in some sense. These dimensions occur with varying weightings in the faces of intensity. Depth, for example, is most strongly associated with the vertical dimension, whereas horizon is most strongly associated with the horizontal dimension. Scale is a mixture of both, as are complexity and mystery. Note that complex experiences featuring many of the faces of intensity can be intense even when they are limited in one or the other dimension. For example, the ecstasy of obsessive fulfillment, as when lovers feel the need for nothing besides each other, involves openheartedness that is genuine but tightly constrained, being limited in scope to each other and focused by obsessive attachment; the vertical dimension is the most evident in that manifestation of intensity. Similarly, great servants of humanity in their ordinary activities are open to the needs of others to a prodigious extent that would collapse the lesser souls of most people, yet intensity of feeling (the vertical dimension) is limited in the everyday exercise of compassion. "Intensity" seems to register both dimensions at once about as well as any English word does.

⸎

Can we safely extend the reference of "intensity" from a name for the general quality of intense experiences to a name for that to which intense experiences are a response? That is, can the characterization of intense experiences as environmentally conditioned, as a response to *something*, justify using the name "intensity" for that environmental *something*? This is the heart of the philosophical theologian's question about these special experiences. Can we build on a phenomenological analysis such as the one offered here in the direction of rich theories of intense experiences that will illumine questions of their causation and their moral and epistemic significance?

To put the promise and the problem of this possibility in its most pointed form: if there are stable patterns of inference from intense experiences to the nature of intensity, then we have discovered something important about the world, something of enormous interest to philosophical theologians. Indeed, a theory of intensity might be forthcoming that would have the proportions of a philosophical-theological account of ultimate reality. Rather than sneaking this possibility into the imagination by means of clever usage of the word "intensity," I think it is wise to reflect on the overtones of this way of speaking, to flush the hidden metaphysical controversy into the open, and to inquire explicitly about the feasibility of the associated type of inference.

Ordinary people routinely draw inferences about the moral and metaphysical nature of reality on the basis of their intense experiences, particularly those meeting the approval of a group to which they belong. A few philosophical theologians have endorsed this common-sense procedure by shifting the debate from experience to perception (see especially Alston 1991). They argue that ordinary perception is just as epistemically dubious as extraordinary perception, and then propose to allow the corporate wisdom of socio-linguistically located discernment procedures to do for extraordinary perception what trial and error in everyday life does for ordinary perception.

Other philosophical theologians have criticized the defenders of common-sense inference from intense experiences. These critics urge recognition of contextual and epistemic complexities, much as always has been done within the traditions of the hermeneutics of suspicion. These critics have also urged that ordinary perception is far more reliable than extraordinary perception because the former is subject to more robust fidelity conditions (such as survival of the perceiving organism) than the latter, even when the latter benefits from sophisticated discernment practices operative within a socio-linguistic community (see especially Bagger 1999).

If critics such as Bagger are correct to be sharply skeptical of extraordinary perception by contrast with ordinary perception, then the sort of inference constructive philosophical theologians seek to make from intense experiences to the nature of intensity seems futile. There is no point inferring anything about reality from delusions; it's just not an attractive intellectual activity. If common-sense reliabilists such as Alston are correct, by contrast, then the constructive philosophical theologians have an embarrassment of riches, with allegedly robust chains of inference leading to bluntly contradictory conclusions about the nature of reality. (Alston tries to deal with this problem of pluralism in his otherwise carefully argued book, but I think his effort on this front does not rise above the well-intentioned.)

⤬

My own view is that Alston and Bagger are both extreme. If Bagger's fallibilism is to be taken seriously, as I think it should be, then the question about the feasibility of inference from intense experiences to the nature of intensity can and should be framed in *empirical terms*. That is, the possibility of this sort of inference can be neither established nor rejected definitively in advance so we need to try and see. When we do try and see, we learn quite a lot. For example, on the one hand, the result that inference from intense experiences can produce metaphysical conflict is strong evidence that inference should proceed with great caution, attending both to the vagueness of terms used and to the contextual specifications of general categories. On the other hand, when inference from religious ideas rather than intense experiences is properly sensitive to considerations of vagueness and context, it has proved possible to achieve sensitive interpretations of those religious ideas that do not provoke the specter of unlimited metaphysical conflict (see Neville 2000a, 2000b, 2000c). So what would happen if a similarly sensitive form of inference were attempted from intense experiences rather than from religious ideas?

This is not the place to try and see (see Wildman 2011, which does try and see). But I expect partial success with the limiting factors being (1) the irresolvable vagueness of terms used in self-descriptions of intense experiences, (2) the lack of stable correlations between neural states and self-reports by which vague categories might be stabilized, and (3) our poor understanding of the large role played by social context in conditioning self-reports of intense experiences.

At root, the problem is our limited understanding of the ways intense experiences are like and unlike perception. The value of likening intense experiences to perception, as Alston and Bagger both well understand, is that our understanding of how perception produces reliable knowledge claims is then made relevant for making sense of knowledge claims arising from intense experiences. This analogy, if it holds up in the right respects, ameliorates all three of the limiting factors above. But the hard truth seems to be that intense experiences are only partly like perception; they are far more entangled with emotion and embodied responses and far more reflexively productive of confusing cognitive-emotional side effects than perception is—and thus the limiting factors listed above are genuinely difficult to remove.

On the positive side, and against Bagger's incompletely empirical variety of skepticism, I am urging that partial success in inference might be possible. What would partial success mean? I think that inference could be stabilized to the point that we could produce a vague characterology of Intensity as Such, thought of as that to which intense experiences are a response, as perceived in and through intense experiences. This hazy vision of the nature of the Intense in the world would be quite vague and not immediately connected with particular traditions of wisdom about ultimate reality, primarily because it would be generated within the socio-linguistic community of a certain sort of phenomenology and expressed using the technical language of that community. But translation ought to be possible, at least so as to allow this characterology of Intensity to constrain any philosophical-theological account of ultimate reality, even if such an account could not decide among the best of the alternatives. That would be a valuable outcome.

It wouldn't be enough for Alston and it would be too much for Bagger but that's always the way it goes with extreme views.

~∽∾~

Theorizing Intensity as Such on the basis of intense experiences should be subject to criteria of adequacy, as with all theories. These criteria include aesthetic virtues such as judiciousness, completeness, and importance, in addition to Whitehead's famous four theoretical virtues of applicability, adequacy, coherence, and consistency. Failure to realize any of the (let us say) seven virtues of theory building sometimes proves costly. The parsing of intense experiences introduced above refuses the virtue of completeness and so risks arbitrariness. The concept of intensity itself seems to have been pulled out of thin air, too, thereby defying other demands of systematic theory building, particularly the demands to realize the virtues of applicability, judiciousness, coherence, and importance.

I am plainly acknowledging limitations of the bold venture to build philosophical-theological interpretations of Intensity on the basis of intense experiences. So it is important to note that these limitations are themselves curtailed in significance. Theory building sometimes postures at being completely systematic when the object of the theory is in fact far too complex for the available theoretical terms to manage. The theory may register fragments of what is important about the object in question but little more, and the overall theoretical picture can become quite distorted in the presence of a claim to completeness. In such circumstances, the concern to be completely systematic and orderly needs to be subordinated to the more basic concern to be faithful to the object, which can be accomplished to some extent by means of the juxtaposition of singular perspectives as rich and complex as existing theoretical terms allow. This shift to blessed rage from self-deceptive order can be confusing but at least it permits intellectual work to continue with proper sensitivity to the object in question. Recognition of the pluralism of religious ideas is, of course, one of the standing examples of this strategy in action. Another is the response to the way big-deal theories of religion seem too distorting: most scholars repudiate them in favor of the mostly unresolved juxtaposition of a horde of micro-queries.

I would say that theories of intense experiences face a similar challenge: it is fatuous to attempt *complete* parsings, *exhaustive* typologies, and *one-to-one correlations* with other theoretical elements, such as phenomenologically distinguishable forms of the pressure to silence, the pressure to speak, and the pressure to move. Yet whatever can be said to minimize arbitrariness in the formulation of the concept of Intensity as Such should be said, for the refusal to attempt to realize the seven virtues of systematic theory building is its own kind of retreat from understanding. That sort of refusal might be made in the name of deference, an honorable kind of yielding to the pressure to silence. But deference alone neither satisfies the curiosity that drives theory building, nor protects our interpretations from ideological blindness. So theory building is useful and important and, to avoid the wishful thinking of both obsessive theory builders and zealous theory avoiders, we should strive to say what we can say without saying too much.

⁓

There may be ways to stabilize the conception of Intensity further. Information theory might prove useful for supplying a kind of theoretical quantification of Intensity, for instance, with increasing intensity in the horizontal and vertical dimensions corresponding to increasing richness of information. Something similar might be achieved with the aid of a metaphysics styled after Charles Peirce's semiotics. In such a metaphysics, the basic ontological units are signs and sign transformations, whereby the associated ontology incorporates interpretation, causation, and potentially even consciousness at a more basic level than physicalist ontologies, yet without (what I take to be) the metaphysical liabilities of the related process ontologies.

Such semiotic ontologies evoke a metaphysical vision of reality as a flux of semiosis, with signs standing for other signs and the patterns of sign transformation marking the causal connections that underlie both physical causation and relations of significance that are detectable by organisms with sufficiently complex nervous systems. The density of sign transformations and the scope of their distribution serve in such a metaphysics as qualitative indicators for intensity of feeling and openness to other beings, respectively. When sign transformations are especially dense and especially richly distributed, as they are at certain memorable moments for conscious beings, reality is richly registered and its intensity is evident. Thus, intensity increases with the density and breadth of distribution of sign transformation.

Such an abstract approach to intensity may not seem worth the trouble yet this is one way to say what can be said about that which inevitably escapes the net of systematic theory. It helps to give serious answer to the charge of arbitrariness that I have been entertaining against the concept of Intensity. I think that such a metaphysical vision is also capable of registering the distinctions between the forms of Intensity that provoke the phenomenologically distinguishable types of pressure to silence, pressure to speak, and pressure to move. But that is a task for another time.

INTENSITY AS MANIFESTATION AND REVELATION

If inference from experience and experience-based language to religious realities is possible—I argue that it probably is, acknowledging many difficulties—then a phenomenology of intense experiences and a sound analysis of religious language should trigger reformulation of traditional theological doctrines. To see how that might look, consider how the theme of revelation might be reframed by the foregoing discussion. The result is a close kin of Ray Hart's interpretation of revelation (see Hart 1968), though tied more closely than Hart's to the actual experiences of people—as might be expected from an empirically minded philosophical theologian. The theme of revelation serves as a useful case study because it sheds light on what might count as an adequate theory of Intensity as Such. It also conveniently allows me to address the famous Barthian objections to any attempt to draw inferences about ultimate reality (for Barth, God) from created reality.

Something important happens when a person appreciates how profound things are. I spoke earlier about the wonder tinged by confusion or disorientation that is associated with realizing that something is prodigiously complex, or the fascinated awe associated with being grasped by the scale of things. I also argued that people might experience either a pressure to silence or a pressure to speak under such circumstances, and perhaps both at once in different ways. The pressure to silence is necessary for beholding and deferring, for wonder and reverence. The pressure to speak serves the interests of coping and can satisfy curiosity when it yields to inquiry. These feelings, reactions, graspings, and responses are *important*. They unmask our situation, they partly disclose what reality is; they are, all this is to say, *revelatory* moments.

Such revelations wake up lives that formerly were under the spell of the blind normalcy of conventional reality. They inspire great acts of devotion and courage in ordinary people apparently not cut out for great works. They provoke outrage at social conditions that once were taken for granted. They can trigger behavior changes overnight that therapeutic processes can take years to accomplish. They structure human values and commitments more profoundly than anything else. They are more than important; especially when subjected to proper rational consideration, they are the best and brightest guides to life that we humans have.

We need not suppose that anyone or anything decides to reveal the nature of things to us in these intense moments. It may simply be a matter of waking up from the slumber of comfortable delusion (another way the world shows up for us), after which we see the world differently and in a way that is decisive for our values, choices, actions, and self-understandings. It is important to point out, however, that intense moments of revelation sometimes feel as though they are from beyond us, even sent from outside us to us and meant for us personally. (Sometimes they are accompanied by visions or auditions or visitations.) This feeling of revelation-as-intentional-message is most naturally explained, at one level, by supposing that our intense experiences are in fact gifts from beyond ourselves, labeled for us personally, and lovingly given by One in a position to do so.

Is this really the way revelation is? I think it more likely that the revelation-as-intentional-message feeling is a side effect of some of the phenomenological characteristics of intensity, read against the background of our ordinary experience in which most realizations occur in relationships with other people, and helped along by our cognitive tendency (shared with many Earth animals) to attribute mental states to ambiguous phenomena. But I'll set that puzzle aside for now on the grounds that it is better settled in the context of a comprehensive portrayal of the ontological conditions for the possibility of Intensity (I deal with these questions in detail in Wildman 2009, 2011). For now, it is enough to notice that revelation is a good name for what happens in intense experiences and one good reason for judging intense experiences to be important.

～⊱⊰～

Another question about revelation bears on the truth of any information about the world thought to be disclosed in intense experiences. This is tricky, too. We should take care to admit that we are talking about the disclosure of information when we speak of revelation—not only information, to be sure, and not necessarily intentionally delivered information, but information about the way things are is discovered nonetheless. When Richard Dawkins gazes at a spider web or a not-yet unwoven rainbow and experiences (so I imagine and so he asserts in other words) a powerful experience of intensity, this has to do with the way the world is in spider webs and rainbows (see Dawkins 1996, 1998). This revelatory moment includes propositions about this world we inhabit—for Dawkins, propositions about the world's value and its beauty, at least. Other propositions may follow, perhaps about how human beings should conduct themselves in relation to this valuable world or about how spider webs and rainbows work in detail.

This exploding cascade of propositions differs from person to person, which is clear evidence that revelatory events are dense with significance that is drawn out only interactively, as it were, with the cooperation of the one by whom this revelation is experienced. As Paul Tillich says, revelation is a fusion of subjective ecstatic receptivity and objective miraculous event (Tillich 1951). It is the necessary involvement of the recipient of revelation that underlies the philosophical theologian's instinct to insist that revelation in its inmost core is non-propositional and, thus, not a matter for judgments of truth.

This can be granted as an abstraction from our actual experience of revelatory moments, or perhaps as a regulative ideal that can serve to protect us from a kind of naïve and dangerous expectation that revelatory moments bring specific messages to us from beyond. In practice, however, revelatory events are not neutral to questions of truth; they stimulate some propositions and not others and the world is regarded in particular ways and not others in the wake of such moments. Moreover, people can compare what they learn from such revelatory moments and thereby generate consensus about the world to a certain degree, at least within traditions that perpetuate reflection and debate about revelatory moments, and possibly more universally than that.

The world is revealed as being something-in-particular in intense experiences, albeit with such density of significance that the formulation of this something-in-particular can only ever be fragmentary, scattered into perspectival shards that reach for reunion in vain. This is the something-missing about revelation, the aporia that provokes the sense of mystery and the conviction that that which is revealed, whatever it is, cannot be grasped fully and is only ever received as somehow unknown and unknowable. Among Christian intellectuals, Luther understood this with exceptional clarity and testified to it in his characterization of that which is disclosed in revelation as *Deus absconditus*.

⁓⧆⁓

Karl Barth has been the most spectacularly consistent modern Western defender of Luther's (and, earlier, Saint Paul's) insight. Of course, Barth would not accept the Schleiermacherian or Hartian approach to revelation defended here. But his understanding of Christ as the *divine incognito* is deeply insightful and registers in a brilliantly one-sided way what is presented here in more balanced, less captivating fashion (see Barth 1951–63, especially volume 2:1).

Barth's epistemology of revelation is impeccably consistent. He refuses to explore the possibility of inference from experience of revelation to its metaphysical conditions, deeming this attempt at "natural theology" to be vitiated by the very same delusions that make absolutely essential a revealed orientation to our radically depraved state. Anything other than revelation of the Totally Other as grace-for-us amounts to a kind of bootstrapping from depraved ignorance to allegedly enlightened wisdom, which Barth interprets as vanity and dangerous self-deception. If mystery is present as grace in Karl Rahner's theology, as the inexplicable aporia of real openness in freedom, then mystery is present as necessary ignorance in Barth, as the aporia of separation from that which would break us out of our self-enclosed world of delusion. Grace is mystery for Rahner; for Barth, grace is the condition for the possibility of an impossible way out of our depravity, and mystery the impenetrable other that shows itself as unknown and yet gracious. We escape not through knowledge, for revelation discloses only the unknown and unknowable; nor through effort, which is futile; nor through enlightening experiences, which must necessarily be the stuff of this circle of delusion. We escape through grace alone and revelation discloses this impossible possibility.

Impeccable epistemologies cannot be impeached, by definition. And they can't be ignored, either, at least not when they are as important as Barth's. The way to respond to the shining one-sidedness of Barth's view of revelation is to register in my own way of thinking as much of its genius as possible, while fondly surrendering its perfection, releasing it as a dignified but slightly desperate, and finally futile, protest against the messiness of life. Actual revelation is really messy. But it is associated with repeatable patterns in human experience, and inference from those patterns to their conditions is possible, if carried off with care. Enlightenment does occur as a result, effort does make a difference, transformation is possible, and yet the aporia of grace, however understood in detail, persists.

⁓ℰ⁓

The Barthian critique I imagine against my approach to revelation also rides on another horse: the spectacular role Barth and the Confessing Church played in critiquing National Socialism in Germany in the period between the two world wars. History speaks loudly, I agree, and it is true that the theologies of mediation that tried to keep God and world rationally connected failed to say what needed to be said when and how it was most needed. But does this really count against the version of revelation expounded here?

Barth and the Confessing Church did not achieve the deep read on the Nazi era because of Barth's neo-Reformed and anti-natural-theology view of revelation; they did so because they had a way of being sharply conscious of the aporia of grace, whereby humanity is represented as in infinite need of grace, and thus as depraved, deluded, and dangerous without it. Likewise, much of the Lutheran, Reformed, and Roman Catholic churches did not fail to reach the Confessing Church's view of Nazism and German nationalist sentiment because of any intellectual attempt to draw inferences from intense revelatory experiences to their metaphysical, anthropological, and theological conditions; their failure was due to poor observation, poor memory, and poor interpretation of evidence, all shortcomings facilitated by a sleepy assimilation of religious wisdom into precious cultural forms.

In practice, long memory, careful observation, and sound interpretation are the lifeblood of prophetic critique. They functioned superbly in much of Barth's own intellectual practice, as they did in Tillich's, who also accurately diagnosed the National-Socialist threat while holding a very different theological perspective on revelation. Let it not be said that Barth's shining epistemology of revelation leads inevitably to theological fascism and fundamentalistic withdrawal from engagement and inquiry. The unimpeachable gleam of Barth's culture-resistant retrieval of forgotten spiritual insight was sorely needed at the time, as he himself pointed out even as he imagined another way in his late (1956) essay on "The Humanity of God" (Barth 1996). Neither let it be said that theological reflection on intense revelatory experiences leads inevitably to spiritual flatulence and prophetic lassitude. It is bad natural theology and sloppy theological reflection that do so.

ULTIMACY INFERRED

The question driving the philosophical theologian to describe the character of Intensity as Such is now reformulated. What is revealed, or manifested, in the emotional quality and cognitive content of intense experiences? Whatever it is, it is of ultimate concern to us, as Tillich correctly put it. Moreover, whatever else it may be, it is difficult to interpret, easy to misunderstand, and sometimes productive of implausible extremes in belief and practice—both within religious communities and outside them. I make a complex case for the (heavily conditioned and partial) reliability of the cognitive content of intense experiences elsewhere (Wildman 2011). Here I want to state my conclusions straightforwardly, without argument.

I think revelatory moments in intense experiences do not support the many worldviews holding that supernatural agents convey information from the other-worldly domain of those special beings into our worldly domain. In fact, intense experiences offer no evidential support for the existence of disembodied agents that appear in such experiences, such as ancestors and bodhisattvas, angels and demons, ghosts and gods. This is a measure of the extent to which the reliability of the cognitive content of intense experiences is hedged about with limitations.

But intense experiences are not cognitively inert. They do furnish evidence for the valuational depth structures and dynamic processes of nature. *Intensity as Such is those depth structures and dynamic flows.* We see them appear in the mathematizable structures and dynamics of the physical world, in the blessed meaning of personal relationships, and in the aesthetic luminosity of music or dance, literature or architecture.

At one point in our phylogenetic ancestry, probably within the timeline of our own species, we were superb at sense perception but our ability to sense valuational depth structures and dynamics in and through the perception of our senses was sorely limited. Then something happened and we could *see*. The crucial evolutionary change woke us up to value. It is a capacity that would have spread rapidly through our species because of the fitness advantages it confers. Once established, it distinguished our species from others more clearly than probably any other factor. It spurred the so-called great leap forward in human technology and civilization, first about fifty thousand years before the present, and again in the Neolithic agricultural revolution of about ten thousand years before the present. It gave birth to flexible (i.e., rising above merely instinctive) moral traditions. And it enabled religious forms of engagement with ultimate reality.

Some story of that kind seems necessary to explain our prodigious bodily and cognitive capacity for sensitivity to value and meaning. I regard a fully naturalistic interpretation of whatever story wins the day among evolutionary anthropologists to be a highly plausible way to make sense of our value sensitivity. I freely acknowledge that supernaturalistic interpretations are also possible, though I judge them to be relatively less plausible (see chapter 1 and chapter 2 for the relevant structure of argument necessary for that comparative judgment of relative plausibility, as well as Wildman 2011, 2017). There is one key point in the comparison that is especially relevant here. I find the naturalistic interpretation of our evolutionarily stabilized cognitive tendency to experience liminal situations in person-shaped containers, in relation to aware and intentional agents, more convincing than the supernaturalistic interpretation of that same tendency as productive of accurate perceptions of supernatural agents. There is too much fundamentally unintelligible, unrelentingly pluralistic conflict within the family of supernatural interpretations of intense experiences. Those problems are much less pronounced within the naturalistic family of interpretations. That's the main reason naturalistic interpretations win this particular plausibility battle, but it is not victory by a landslide; the supernatural interpretations of intense experiences in relation to supernatural agents remain logically possible and conceptually coherent.

The valuational depth structures and flows of nature would be manifested to any creature with the right cognitive-emotional equipment. Our species didn't have that equipment and then we did. Life is a lot more interesting, but also a lot more confusing, with that cognitive-emotional equipment in place. It is our phylogenetic birthright and the root of the meaning of our lives. And that's equally true for people deeply invested in religious traditions and for people with no religious involvement at all. We are all finders and makers of meaning. Our ultimate concerns about meaning define our personal identities with a greater degree of intimacy and fidelity than any other part of us.

CONCLUSION

I think the study of religious language surrounding intense experiences is a promising line of work for empirically oriented philosophical theologians. We know a lot about language scientifically and culturally, after all, and language use has been a common topic among the mystics, theologians, and philosophers who write on religious experience, so there is plenty of data available. Existing interpretations of religious language are of limited use for inferring anything about ultimate reality from the character of that language. But this changes when we recognize that powerful experiences evoke or provoke religious speaking, as well as resistance to speaking. If intense experiences are responses to intensity, then language motivated by such experiences can be informative about Intensity as Such.

I began this meditation by focusing on the basic linguistic impulses that intense experiences evoke: the pressure to silence, the pressure speak, and the pressure to move. I furnished an atomic theory of those linguistic and bodily pressures through describing five faces of intensity. I showed how they related to other ways of interpreting intense experiences. And then I finally yielded to the philosophical theologian's temptation to ask about Intensity As Such—about what is manifested of ultimate reality in intense experiences.

Inference from phenomenological descriptions of intense experiences to the character of Intensity as Such is plagued by questions about the credibility of the experiences as information sources. I concluded that the surface cognitive content of intense experiences is not always reliably informative, owing to our evolutionary stabilized tendencies to cognitive error in many domains, including extreme experiences where we are understandably not at our cognitive best.

We need cognitive frameworks to make sense of intense experiences, frameworks that help us figure out reliable from unreliable cognitions. It is possible to adopt supernaturalist cognitive frameworks, after which we are more likely to take the surface cognitive content of intense experiences as directly perceptual and reliable. But then we are awash in an unmitigated intellectual disaster in the form of the specter of pluralism of dramatically conflicting interpretations. A naturalistic cognitive framework mitigates that problem while preserving the cognitive relevance of intense experiences for understanding the valuational depth structures and dynamic flows of the reality we engage through intense experiences. That's why I think the naturalistic interpretation of intense experiences has a significant plausibility edge in the competition with supernaturalistic interpretations.

⤳⤳

The five faces of intensity recur in various combinations for all intense experiences, whether declared to be religious or not, and regardless of whether they are dubbed "abnormal" or "aberrant." Both of those points are worth pondering in closing.

First, I have articulated an evolutionary view of intense experiences and defended a naturalistic interpretation of Intensity as Such, of those experiences' vague logical object, and also of the conditional cognitive reliability of intense experiences for making sense of Intensity as Such. It follows that intense experiences are the birthright of *every human being*, at least for the last fifty thousand years or so in the history of our species. Religious traditions sometimes (often!) attempt to sequester intense experiences, claim preeminence in regard to their interpretation, and regulate their expression for the sake of the good of all—or so religious leaders imagine. It is obvious that a lot of wisdom is needed to interpret intense experiences properly, and religious traditions do offer gyroscopic wisdom for their participants. But religion is just one venue for intense experiences, and in certain respects, a somewhat limited venue. The world is valuationally alive. Unlike other Earth animals, our species has awoken to that profound axiological fact of life. Valuational sensitivity came first, and only then did religion follow.

Second, judgments of abnormality tend to turn less on concern with the cognitive-emotional content of intense experiences and more on how much pain such experiences and their interpretation cause, how much unwanted or socially unacceptable behavior they provoke, and how common the experiences are in the surrounding population. That is very important, in my view, because studies of intense experiences suggest that people across the spectrum of mental function experience intensity in basically similar ways, even though the atomic features of intense experiences can be modulated to create spectacular variation. This is the case whether these studies are unsystematic and large-scale (e.g., James 1902), controlled and focused (such as the literature on the hyper-religiosity occasionally experienced by seizure patients; see Bear 1979; Bear et al. 1982; Fenton 1981; Ramachandran and Blakeslee 1998), or discriminating self-reports of religious experiences, sometimes presented as spiritual autobiographies (such as the confessional writings of religious leaders and mystics; see Augustine 1991; Teresa 1979).

Our capacity for intense experiences works roughly the same across the entire spectrum of mental health. This should make us more empathically connected to the intense experiences of the cognitively disordered psychiatric patient suffering from schizophrenic delusions or bipolar manic psychosis. Intense axiological sensitivity is our species birthright, and we are all in the intensity business together.

CHAPTER 9

BLISS

INTRODUCTION

SUPPOSE I'M CORRECT ABOUT WHAT THE FOREGOING CHAPTERS ASSERT AND imply about ultimate reality—that it is not a being or an agent of any kind, but beyond being and not-being; that it surpasses the cognitive grasp of any possible creature and only appears kaleidoscopically fractured in pseudo-rational glimpses; that personal symbols are far less adequate for expressing its nature and significance than impersonal symbols related to the axiologically laden depth structures and dynamic flows of nature; that it is perfectly consistent with both many kinds of religious naturalism and many kinds of apophatic mystical philosophical theology. On that assumption, I find myself confronting a profoundly personal question. This question absolutely fascinates me.

Given my individual peculiarities and our species-conferred cognitive-emotional biases and limitations, and also acknowledging the limitations of human sociality and corporate inquiry, *what is the state of mind appropriate to apprehending ultimate reality most fully, purely, and truly?* What can my kind of being achieve most purely and perfectly in the way of apprehending and engaging ultimacy, allowing that there is no pure purity and no perfect perfection?

Thomas Aquinas asked this question and his answer was "beatific vision." An entire network of South Asian philosophical-theology traditions also had an answer: *ānanda* or bliss. My answer to this question has a lot in common with Thomas's, but my South-Asian influenced approach to bliss centralizes the cognition-breaking quality and the moral impenetrability of ultimate reality in a way that Thomas mutes and rejects, respectively, in his account of beatific vision.

Bliss seems not to be one thing, judging from the way the word is used. But I sense convergence within diverse usages rather than straightforward equivocation, particularly in spiritually alert language wielders. That convergence

197

invites further reflection on bliss, and on what the qualities of bliss suggest about the ultimate reality to which it is a faithful and spontaneous response. With that goal in place, I begin here with a personal story about encountering bliss. That serves as an entry point into an analysis of the concept of bliss. I then ponder the manifold ways we tame bliss in an attempt to cope both with the overwhelming luminosity of ultimate reality and with our challenging life situations.

Encountering Bliss

I was lying in a hospital emergency room with a drip in my arm to pump fluids and pain medications. I was five hours into a fourteen-hour battle with a kidney stone on my left side. The pain was extreme for long periods of time and driving me into a desperate state of mind. On the standard zero-to-ten pain scale, I was at ten. When medical personnel asked me for my pain level, though, I would only report nine out of ten. I was consciously reserving ten out of ten for torture victims. It was a weird kind of self-protective piety: it was my way of telling myself that things could be worse. It was also a kind of spiritual practice, empathizing with people whose cruelty-abetted agony felt so abstract at other times. My pain unexpectedly opened up a potent imaginative connection with them.

I later checked with a friend who had both suffered through kidney stones and given birth to two children. She said there was no question: a kidney stone was much more painful for her. For me the pain was basically unimaginable, in the sense that I had never previously imagined that such pain was possible. It's imaginable now, though. In fact, I constructed detailed interpretations of the higher numbers on the pain scale. Ten was reserved, as I've explained. Eight and nine were for pain so severe that I would beg relief from supernatural powers I didn't even believe existed—eight when I could force myself to stay silent while begging, nine when I couldn't prevent myself from vocalizing the pointless pleas. Six and seven were for intolerable pain that defeated my reasonably well-developed ability to concentrate—six when I could sense that it was me who was the subject of the pain but I couldn't concentrate well enough even to try meditation-type pain management techniques—and seven when my very sense of self was skittled by the pain and scattered in all directions. Five, the midpoint, was all ambiguity: heaven-like relief when traveling downward and powerful pain with hell-like promise for more on the way up.

Only one of the medications the doctors were giving me seemed to take the edge off the pain. They first gave it to me about one hour into the ordeal after concluding that the other medications they tried weren't doing the job. They told me a lot of people found it effective against this kind of pain. Sure enough, fifteen minutes later, the pain started dropping downwards, moving out of the begging zone of nine and eight, passing through the non-concentration zone of seven and six, pausing at ambiguous five, and then coming to tremulous rest around a blessed four, meandering up or down a bit as my body processed the ongoing assault on its geometry. Such relief! I actually got an hour's sleep, thanks to the pain drop and the sedative effects of some other medication.

Unfortunately, the doctors could only pump me with that magical pain medication every six hours, and it would wear off after about three hours, leaving me on my own meager pain-management resources the rest of the time. The sum total of those resources when the pain was above five consisted either of just lying in bed, writhing, or pacing slowly along one wall of my cubicle, bent over and mumbling pleas for release to non-existent deities, bodhisattvas, ancestor ghosts, mother nature, and nobody in particular.

It was at the five-hour mark that I heard over the emergency room's crackling radio that EMT's were bringing in a young woman in extreme discomfort, ten out of ten on the accursed pain scale. That's where I was, too, at the time, though I was still describing it as nine out of ten. Sure enough, this woman arrived, screaming in agony, and I could hear the medical staff rushing to attend to her. In my little cubicle, lying on my mechanical cot, with the privacy curtain mostly closed, I pulled the meager sheet up over my head, curled into a fetal ball, and felt completely crushed. I was overwhelmed by a potent realization of how much pain there is in our world, of how much the beings of our planet suffer. I began quietly sobbing, utterly immersed in empathic connection to all pain, everywhere. My mother's pain as she patiently died from chilling bone cancer, my father's pain as he slowly drowned while losing a bacterial war in his ravaged lungs, the dental patient from the endlessly harsh era before effective anesthesia, my suicidal friends over the years, the gazelle caught by the rampaging lioness—they were all with me. I was at the top of the pain scale with a fractured sense of self and no ability to concentrate on anything except begging, yet I was flooded with empathy. The begging yielded to dark despair even as the pain cracked me open to empathy. I was laid bare, with no defense. I surrendered to the pain roaring around me, as potent in empathic imagination as in bodily realization.

Perhaps fifteen minutes into this extraordinary state of mind, a nurse came in to check on me. She spoke to me, while I was buried under my sheet. I pulled the sheet down and, with tears in my eyes, not really looking directly at her, asked her how she could bear to witness the pain she sees on a daily basis. She seemed momentarily stumped by my question before replying that "a good sense of humor helps." I was so grateful for that simple, practical answer. Slowly rising from the cot and from the overwhelmingly depressive depths of empathic despair, I resumed micro-pacing to and fro along that oh-so-familiar wall of my little cubicle, vainly trying to keep the unbearable pain at bay.

⸙

This vision of pain has been so seared into my memory that it is has never left me since that miserable experience. A mere passing mental glance in its direction causes the vision to bloom vividly in my mind, empathically connecting me to the depths of nature and its suffering creatures. In this vision, nature is awesome, mostly unscaled to the interests and needs of Earth organisms such as human beings, and yet somehow still supportive of our lives and aspirations, at least at a few special places and in a few precious epochs. Of course, even regimes of stable fecundity mostly friendly to life are suffused with predation, physical pain, emotional suffering, and existential anxiety. Moreover, as many recent novels and movies have reminded us, those wondrous regimes are still vulnerable to extinction-level events, mere side effects of nature just blindly doing its natural, neglectful thing.

The experience giving rise to this vision of pain and suffering is one I would not willingly choose to go through again. After all, extreme pain was the engine that levered me open to that arresting vista with its astonishing gift of empathic connection to endless hordes of suffering organisms. Very few people choose to embrace extreme pain no matter how intense the experiential payoff might be. The experience was affectively ambivalent, centrally horrifying yet festooned with ribbons of wonder. It was not a pleasant experience, therefore, and it is best remembered, not relived. In memory, the miserable accompaniment of raw physiological pain abates while the ribbons of wonder decorating an abysmal horror become more prominent. Especially as remembered, this experience is well worth pondering.

⸙

To begin the reflective process, the reality of human tendencies to cognitive error obliges me to evaluate the cognitive reliability of the various aspects of the experience. The vision of suffering itself passes muster with everything I think I know about the world—a judgment made with reasoning skills unimpaired by pain—so I take it to be cognitively reliable and actually insightful.

The feeling of wide-hearted empathic connection to other suffering creatures is more difficult to validate, and I am sure there was a lot of projection involved (what do I really know about a gazelle's pain when a lioness runs it down, or about the suicidal ideation of a number of friends over the years?). Nevertheless, I trust this feeling of empathic connection for two main reasons. On the one hand, biological continuity across species with central nervous systems means we have a basis for interpreting the experience of non-human species. In many cases that gives us good reason to think that pain systems are operative and important, even though we can never know for certain what the subjective experience of pain might be. On the other hand, there is an inspirational heritage of spiritual practices in many religious, humanistic, and ecological traditions that centralize the cultivation of empathy as a virtue. For example, some Buddhist traditions have specific meditation techniques to induce wide-hearted *karuṇā*, or compassion, and these techniques can involve visualizing the suffering of other people and non-human beings in much the way that I did in this experience. The momentum of this heritage indicates that the cultivation of the virtue of compassion is passing many concrete validation tests in millions of lives more or less constantly.

What about my vocalized begging for relief from supernatural agents? I regard this with more skepticism: it tells me about my inbuilt cognitive tendencies but not about what's real. After all, I indiscriminately implored ancestor ghosts, Mother Nature, bodhisattvas, gods, and even the molecules of the air I was breathing because I would have taken relief from absolutely anywhere. The wild metaphysical pluralism of my casting about for relief seems comical in retrospect. So I don't trust the cognitions tangled up in those helpless pleas for mercy, and I didn't take them seriously even at the time. It's just that I couldn't help myself.

❧

Using the five faces of intensity to parse the phenomenological features of this experience is illuminating (see chapter 8). The experience was strong on depth and horizon simultaneously, and to about the same degree. After all, it involved cognitive-emotional connections both to the profound character of nature as such and to other natural creatures.

The scale face was the most prominent, with fractured self-awareness yielding to wide-hearted empathic merging with the surrounding world in its vastness, in its indifference to suffering organisms, and in its clumsy evolutionary carelessness that produced greater sensitivity to pain than organisms actually need to optimize their inclusive fitness.

But the vastness of scale was not an abstract merging of self and world; the complexity face was also prominent in the details of empathic connection.

Particular people and their stories were present, along with a particular spider consuming its mate, a particular gazelle being run down by a murderous cat, predation's unsettling of the Hardy-Weinberg equilibrium and details of fitness calculations from evolutionary theory, and biochemical visions of cellular pain receptors in overdrive and neural processing of in-flooding pain signals—there was a high order of cognitive complexity.

Meanwhile, the mystery face was less prominent. There was no sanctified perplexity and no deference to ignorance. On the contrary, this was an experience of knowledge hard and clear as perfect diamonds. But the "why is it so?" question was present, with its inevitably mysterious answer: *suchness*. This nature is neither envisaged nor planned; it is what it is. Pain is simply the way of things. The suchness answer is an inquiry-blocker, and thus it seems also to involve a mystery-savoring embrace of the irrational. Yet this answer arrives when inquiry has fully exhausted itself so it is no rational retreat into mystery. Suchness is just what we're left with when all other answers fall away under the pressure of carefully interpreted experience.

CONCEIVING BLISS

Overall, I think the quality of this experience is fairly described as bliss. In fact, I'd go so far as to say that this was an *encounter with bliss*. I've experienced other encounters with bliss, some of them extremely pleasant in contrast with this appalling episode. Surely many people think of bliss in terms of orgasm, particularly when it creates the most intense feeling of togetherness with an intimate companion. That intoxicating feeling is also rightly described as bliss, I think, though we must beware our bias toward the pleasant (chapter 7).

Despite the emotional and other qualitative differences between orgasmic bliss and the bliss of pain-driven empathic despair, I sense profound similarities. To begin with, both are affectively complex. In obviously basically pleasant orgasmic bliss, particularly when two people are mutually infatuated, pleasure is deeply tinged with an intense pain of longing for merger, for completion; while in the obviously basically unpleasant bliss of pain-driven empathic despair, the glorious magnificence of scale fragments self and wondrously merges self with world. Other similarities bear on bodily factors such as the neurochemically extreme nature of these situations and the time course of their waxing and waning. I find myself driven to think of these and other similar experiences all together, as encounters with something having a stable yet only partially assimilable character, something also worthy of the name bliss.

~⊷~

In chapter 8, I supplied an evolutionary framing of our species' bodily capacity for intense sensitivity to the valuational depth structures and dynamics of reality. I acknowledged there that every manner of question about existential validity and cognitive reliability swirls around intense experiences. I showed that a strictly conditioned judgment of reliability can be assigned to certain qualities of intense experiences—qualities that, in a suitable cognitive framework, mitigate rather than exacerbate the problem of plural conflicting interpretations, which haunts the interpretation of intense experiences. I argued that naturalistic frameworks for interpreting the cognitive reliability of intense experiences fare much better against the mitigating-pluralistic-conflict criterion than cognitive frameworks privileging one interpretation over others for reasons that can't win consensus among all qualified inquirers because of the function of kind of special pleading. On that basis, I embraced a critically realistic interpretation of Intensity as Such: our bodily capacity for intense experiences engages us with the actual valuational depth structures and dynamics of our world. Those depth structures and dynamics are complex, but they are also partially rationally penetrable thanks to our exquisite sensitivity to the valuational dimensions of reality.

When we place experiences of bliss within this interpretative framework, a cascade of consequences flows. First, we enjoy a limited rational entitlement to treat those experiences as encounters with Bliss, now (as the capitalization suggests) in the objective sense of an axiologically potent aspect of reality itself. Second, our attention is drawn to the features of our encounters with bliss that recur across the range of such experiences as most likely to prove reliable in manifesting the stable character of Bliss. Third, the features of bliss that don't recur widely across the range of relevant experiences testify to the multi-dimensional superfluity of Bliss and the fractionated character of all encounters with it. Fourth, focusing on diverse encounters with Bliss rather than a favored and spiritually convenient instance serves to disclose the bias to the pleasant that often operates in this area of philosophical theology. Fifth, this drives us to seek a properly balanced account of Bliss, one in which we take its disturbingly chilling aspects as seriously as its mesmerizingly enjoyable aspects. Sixth, thought of as an indicator of the character of ultimate reality, Bliss is strongly resonant with the language-straining, only-partially-rationally-graspable, morally inassimilable apophatic vision of ultimacy presented throughout this book.

I won't re-argue this line of reasoning here. For the purpose of this meditation, it's enough to point back to chapter 8 (as well as to Wildman 2011) and then focus my efforts on explaining and drawing out some consequences of Bliss, so understood.

∽≈∽

The most popular and influential work in the Pāli canon of Indian Buddhism is the *Dhammapada*. It happens to be my favorite Buddhist scripture and the one with which I have spent the most meditative time. The *Dhammapada* contains a famous description of the spiritual goal of enlightenment in terms of bliss (in Buddharakkhita's translation):

> There is no fire like lust and no crime like hatred. There is no ill like the aggregates (of existence) and no bliss higher than the peace (of Nibbana). Hunger is the worst disease, conditioned things the worst suffering. Knowing this as it really is, the wise realize Nibbana, the highest bliss. Health is the most precious gain and contentment the greatest wealth. A trustworthy person is the best kinsman, Nibbana the highest bliss. Having savored the taste of solitude and peace (of Nibbana), pain-free and stainless he becomes, drinking deep the taste of the bliss of the Truth. (Buddharakkhita 1990, 15: 202–5)

The fifteenth chapter of the *Dhammapada* is titled "Sukhavagga" and usually translated "Happiness." Both the title and the chapter's content display the bias toward the pleasant at work, framing as affectively wholly positive, rationally intelligible, and morally good an experience that is in fact affectively complex, cognitively ineffable, and morally inassimilable—as other Buddhist texts, and other parts of the *Dhammapada* itself, testify.

A more realistic encounter with Bliss is depicted in the eleventh chapter of the Bhagavad-Gita, from the classic Indian Mahabharata epic. The charioteer Krishna accedes to the request of his warrior-master, Arjuna, to reveal Krishna's universal form. The manifestation is awesome and profoundly unnerving for Arjuna. In fact, that may be two ways of saying the same thing given typical human physiological responses to vast spaces and encompassing visions that take us beyond the comforting simplifications of conventional reality.

The transfiguration story in the New Testament depicts an encounter with Bliss for subgroup of Jesus's disciples. They are swept away with emotion to the point that they behave slightly irrationally, seeking to build shelters so that they could remain in a state that was necessarily short-lived. I interpret that as a sign of the cognitively overwhelming nature of encountering Bliss.

Toward the end of the Hebrew Bible's famous book of Job, Yahweh silences Job, his arrogant friends, and the reader with a theophany akin to Krishna's self-manifestation in the Bhagavad-Gita. The sheer terror and unlimited wonder of this encounter with Bliss reduces Job to utter humility and submission. His reasonable parsing of evidence concerning the reasons for his suffering is scattered to the winds as he ponders where he was when the foundations of the earth were laid (Job 38:4). The fierceness of Yahweh, mocking and provoking Job, is a fitting expression of the emotionally multivalent, comprehension-defying, morality-transcending character of Bliss when we encounter it unfiltered by buffering social conventions and handy psychological defenses. Those are the three features I want to focus on: emotional multivalence, cognitive ineffability, and moral inassimilability.

～◦◦～

In my research on intense experiences using quantitative measurement strategies, I have seen in the numbers what many interpreters have asserted based on introspection: intense experiences tend to be *both* affectively more positive *and* affectively more negative than ordinary experiences (see Wildman 2011; Wildman and McNamara 2010). The co-occurrence of emotional extremes—one of the markers of intense experiences generally—is especially applicable to encounters with bliss. Just as the ecstatic bliss of orgasm is most intense when accompanied by the deep pain of insatiable longing to merge with another; and just as the pain-driven expansion of empathic awareness into an ecstatic vision of suffering is most intense when laced with wonder; so every experience of bliss involves emotional complexity. That complexity is immediately apparent, often enough, but it certainly becomes apparent as soon as we dig beneath the phenomenological surface of such experiences.

I think the reason for this is the superfluity of meaning that we detect in encounters with bliss. Our axiological sensitivity equipment, as impressive as it is, has limits. In moments of bliss, we are flooded with meanings vectored in all directions, not necessarily mutually consistent yet coherent in an emotionally recognizable way across experiences. That's we human beings hitting our limits in value apprehension. As value-detection devices, emotions seem custom fitted to handle basic social interactions. We need to know what will make us happy or sad, angry or afraid, content or restless, and our emotions speak with a relatively clear voice in those ways. But the same system can detect values for which it wasn't adapted in the long phylogenetic history of hominid species. Such high-order values won't show up as neatly correlated with simple emotions; rather, we will detect them through complex combinations of simple emotions that seem inconsistent, in the presence of rich cognitions that express the significance of the value-infused moment. These are the very markers of intense experiences, generally. The same point applies to encounters with bliss, save that the cognitive content of blissful moments may be even more fractured than in some other intense experiences.

⥈⥇

With that we come to cognitive ineffability. This is perhaps the most famous marker of encounters with bliss given the degree to which mystical writers and the secondary students of mystical authors strive to wrap their extraordinary minds around it. In Michael Sells's *Mystical Languages of Unsaying* (1994), we read a marvelous analysis of linguistic techniques in multiple traditions for managing the cognition-breaking qualities of ineffable experiences. Sells focuses especially on techniques of negation, and Timothy Knepper takes this further with a distinction between proposition-content negation and illocutionary-force negation. This is worth exploring as a way into the understanding of cognitive ineffability.

John Searle's speech-act theory, expanding on John Austin's famous *How to Do Things with Words* (1962), distinguishes between the propositional content of a speech act and its illocutionary force (see Searle 1969, 30). Illocutionary force is the intention of the speaker in making an utterance. This might include asserting a purported fact, exclaiming that I'm in pain, promising to take out the garbage, or officially declaring a marriage. Not all speech acts have propositional content ("Ouch!"), but most do and such propositions can be expressed in the usual subject-predicate way. To declare a marriage, an officially recognized celebrant in a quite specific context utters, "I declare that P" where P is a proposition expressing the fact of the marriage, a fact that is becoming true as the declaration is made. To assert that the marriage is long overdue, the illocutionary force is assertion and the propositional content is that "this marriage is long overdue."

When cognition and thus language are under great stress, we may not know how to ASSERT P for any relevant proposition P. That's an indication of ineffability, and if we are supposed to be an expert language wielder it'd be good evidence of ineffability. Instead of asserting anything, mystics have universally found it more convenient to deny things instead, indirectly hinting at what they feel can't be directly stated. Here's where Knepper's contribution becomes so valuable. In the context of a speech-act analysis of the denials so common in mystical writing, it becomes obvious that there is more than one mode of denial. We can deny either the propositional content (ASSERT NOT-P) or the illocutionary force (NOT-ASSERT P). We can also deny both (NOT-ASSERT NOT-P). All three combinations of denial arise within mystical texts and are indicative of the intricacy of the language games dedicated to fathoming the depths of cognitively ineffable experiences.

The *via negativa* (see chapter 1) employs the first pattern, the denial of propositional content, and does so in a way that involves entire systems of symbols with denials organized in a very particular way. By contrast, the pressure to silence (see chapter 8) is a failure of the *will to express*, and thus is an extreme instance of the combination of the second and third patterns, denying illocutionary force (assertion) both for all relevant propositions and for negations of those propositions. Often enough illocutionary-force negation is simpler and less comprehensive than this, as when a lawyer addressing a panel of judges employs the utterance device, "I don't say that this case is totally without merit, but. . . ." But in relation to mystical experiences, when language is under severe stress, the two kinds of negation and their combination—both in individual utterances and in relation to entire systems of symbols—are pressed into service to wrangle with the cognitive breakdown that seems to accompany all attempts to comprehend the mystical object.

If the intricacy of mystical language games is any indication, intense experiences of many kinds—encounters with bliss included—bear the marks of cognitive ineffability. They resist clear and coherent expression, they possess a superfluity of meanings, their valuational potentials point in manifold directions, they skittle the capacities of ordinary language, and they provoke the creation of specialized linguistic techniques as well as expert communities to use and sustain those techniques.

In addition to this, however, I think that bliss is *especially* cognitively challenging. Our normally quite serviceable value-detection equipment is utterly overwhelmed in encounters with bliss. The complexity face of intensity can be in overdrive, struggling to assimilate all of the cognitive content, while personal identity fragments and the scale face of intensity dominates the experience. And all of that happens to the accompaniment of potent and opposed, yet somehow fitting, emotions, driving home the impossibility of registering everything there is to understand about encounters with bliss.

～∾～

Unlike the moral clarity of Dhammapada 15 and Aquinas's depiction of the beatific vision, moral inassimilability is the norm in encounters with bliss. In the theophanies of Job and the Bhagavad-Gita, the moral qualities of the divine personage are utterly unscaled to human interests and needs, neither rationally comprehensible nor ethically defensible. My favorite symbols for ultimate reality—the ground and abyss of being, the depth structures and dynamics of nature—bespeak a wellspring for *all possibilities and their realization*, not merely the ones we can appreciate. To attribute moral character to ultimate reality so understood is deeply questionable. It is a forcing of the available data to fit a preconceived, spontaneously arising conception of the moral intelligibility of the cosmos, one that ramifies the social orders we prize and confirms the shape of our personal moral striving.

In the personal encounter with bliss I describe at the beginning of this chapter, there is no possibility of exculpation of ultimate reality (for all of the reasons discussed in chapter 2). But there is also no fidelity to theodicy's charge of moral badness. Rather, the charge of moral badness or neglect, along with interest in arguing over acquittal, drop away entirely, as so much socially constructed wistfulness. What is manifested beneath those moral and theological exertions is a comprehensive vision of unlimited fecundity with no intrinsic moral interests, yet ontologically grounding all axiological possibilities whatsoever—including all moral possibilities. The pleasant and the unpleasant, the beautiful and the ugly, the good and the bad—as we see these polarities and as any other possible being might see them—are all equally the creative fruit of this ultimate reality.

What I am describing is very far from a morally groundless reality, at least in one sense. Of course, there is no morally homey deity to define the morally good with the clarity of a just lawgiver, and to some that may seem to be the very definition of a morally groundless reality. But what we actually sense in the moral possibilities around us are definite axiological structures, including a moral logos pointing neither to the Bad nor to the Good but to if-then relationships. If I repeatedly lie, then people will stop trusting me. If I love my enemies and forgive those who persecute me, then I will experience greater peace of mind and happiness while my enemies may eventually find themselves transformed. If I secretly torture and kill many people, then I will realize abysmal axiological possibilities that hardly anyone understands or appreciates.

The moral possibilities of reality are intricately structured with determinate patterns and dynamics. They don't point in a particular moral direction, just as biological evolution in our ecosystem is a constrained but undirected walk through a space of biological possibilities, and just as there is no teleological envisagement guiding cosmic evolution beyond the mathematically traceable outworking of the fundamental regularities of nature. We engage axiological depth structures and dynamics in everything we do and in all that we are. But there is finally nobody beyond ourselves—as individuals and in our morally invested groups— to command that we navigate the moral depth structures and dynamics in any particular way.

To see these depth structures and dynamics more or less comprehensively, in their morally inassimilable glory, in their cognitive complexity, in their emotional multivalence, is to encounter bliss. Indeed, those very axiological depth structures and dynamics may be the closest we ever get to describing rationally the logical object of encounters with bliss, Bliss as Such.

Taming Bliss

Given the emotional complexity, cognitive ineffability, and moral inassimilability of encounters with bliss, what's happening in the moral assurance of Aquinas's depiction of the beatific vision? What's going on in the moral clarity of the uncharacteristically short-circuited description of bliss in Dhammapada 15? Well, Aquinas is simply describing the way ultimate reality must be if his theology is sound, probably on the basis of intense experiences of awareness of what he conceived as the divine presence. And Dhammapada 15 is addressing the practical moral dimensions of life, testifying that seeking nibbāna (in Sanskrit, nirvāṇa; liberation in the sense of the goal of the Buddhist Noble Eight-Fold Path) is incomparably better than all other human activities. These are worthy testimonies. After all, Aquinas does pick up on the cognitive ineffability element of bliss to some degree, reminding us that even the unmediated beatific vision will be a finite image of the infinite God (see Aquinas 1948: Summa Theologica I, question 12). And Dhammapada 15 rightly contrasts the existential fulfillment of seeking nibbāna with the frustration and even the simple happiness of other human life adventures. Nevertheless, part of the net effect of such descriptions of bliss is one-sidedness, a yielding to the ever-present temptation that is the bias to the pleasant (again, see chapter 7).

I think of this as taming Bliss. The emotional complexity, cognitive ineffability, and moral inassimilability of encounters with bliss individually and jointly imply that the logical object of those encounters, Bliss as Such, should be a wild thing. Its mercurial logos, its axiological structures and dynamics, its givenness in suchness, its grounding of all value possibilities, its lack of morally or aesthetically vectored preferences, and its spontaneous (non-envisaged and non-purposeful) exploration of a vastly complex space of axiological possibilities—all of these qualities lead me to think of it as wild, and therefore also as untamed relative to the manifold ways we human beings have an interest in taming it.

In fact, I think there are both disadvantages and advantages for individual and social wellbeing associated with taming Bliss. I made this case in a preliminary way earlier (see chapter 6 on the "Eclipsing" of ultimate reality's wildness at the level of an entire symbol system). Here I approach this theme from a more existential angle.

~≈~

Nietzsche's Madman from *The Gay Science* absolutely refuses to tame bliss (see Nietzsche 1974). Nobody understands him, locked as each one is into the socially constructed world where taming bliss is actually a survival skill. The Buddha absolutely refused to tame bliss, devoting his life to helping people see ultimate reality beneath the robust delusions of bliss-taming conventional reality. In both cases enlightenment is presented as monumentally difficult. To see reality as it most truly is—as grounded, pervaded, relativized, deconstructed, and negated by bliss—is emotionally uncomfortable, psychically destabilizing, and socially disruptive. This is why it is advantageous for individuals and societies to tame bliss.

As implied earlier (see chapter 6), completely denying bliss is an empirical dead end. Encounters with bliss keep popping up in our experience so outright denials run aground on the shoals of implausibility. What's required is eclipsing, reducing bliss to a mere aura of light; or taming, confining bliss to a safe and sturdy cage; or distraction, being too busy with material acquisition and social duties to notice the bliss-perfused spiritual depths of reality.

This point can be elaborated by extending the conception of "sacred canopy" as Peter Berger developed it in his book of that name (see Berger 1967). Sacred canopies are cosmically ramified legitimations of the social construction of reality that generate social commitment and warrant the exercise of social control. But they are more than that, too. Like our planetary ozone layer, which shields us from harsh ultraviolet light, a sacred canopy also protects us from the searing light of ultimate reality. This isn't Moses beholding Yahweh from the cleft of a rock; after all, Moses was placed there for his own protection and he would have taken more in if he could have tolerated it. Rather, this is the taming of bliss as an essential part of maintaining social stability. Bliss untamed is the power source for the deconstruction of our social worlds, and sacred canopies work much better when we don't understand the magic behind the scenes. Therefore, social stability requires both the taming of bliss and the control of individuals who encounter bliss so forcefully that the social construction of reality becomes transparent for them—think of the death of Socrates or the crucifixion of Jesus, as extreme cases, and the marginalization of disruptive individuals, more generally.

René Girard's scapegoating theory describes a form of social control that periodically releases pent-up anxiety, a pressure that can be understood as the accumulating awareness of bliss. Bliss can't be denied outright because encounters with bliss can't be prevented, so it must be regulated, like pressure in a steam engine. The key to effective regulation is release valves that allow pressure buildup to escape when it passes some critical threshold. The scapegoating mechanism is one such release valve. Another is the eclipsed glow of bliss in heart-rending art and architecture, music and literature. By seeing this aura of glory—a tantalizing hint of bliss—people make limited sense of their encounters with bliss, and actually effectively engage ultimate reality. But bliss is tamed at the same time. Its winking disruption of the social construction of reality becomes barely noticeable. Its spontaneous and unruly underwriting of all axiological possibilities is pared back to a useful set of pro-social moral laws, typically marked by in-group obliviousness to the Other. Its prophetic testimony to the emotional complexity, cognitive ineffability, and moral inassimilability of ultimate reality is almost inaudible.

⁓≈⁓

Individual emotional health is also a non-trivial consideration when weighing the advantages of taming bliss. Bliss untamed can skittle psychic stability. Bipolar disorder has something to teach us here. A manic state is emotionally and cognitively overwhelming because of the sheer extent of the vision of reality that is involved. Akin to the prismic unpacking of white light into a rainbow of colors, manic awareness sees much that ordinarily lies hidden—indeed, sees too much too fast for any degree of mental clarity. Tragically, manic awareness is often delusionally self-aggrandizing, biasing and distorting a vision of reality that might be illuminating if there were psychic space to evaluate it and refine it. The manic state can also yield to dangerous full-blown psychosis in those with the Type-I version of bipolar disorder. Yet some people living with bipolar disorder sometimes learn how to regulate the inner experience of mania through deep familiarity with the world that arises in that spectacular and dangerous state of awareness, aided by discipline born from painful experience.

At the very least, this is a good analogy for the psychic dangers of bliss untamed. But I think the point can be taken further. Consider the likely prominent role of bipolar disorder and schizophrenia in shamanism, probably the original religion of our species. This way of socially accommodating people burdened with what we now call psychiatric illness conferred upon them an honorable role at the periphery of the social order. There they proved to be efficacious problem solvers and healers, through expertise in the unleashing of dissociative states both in themselves and in psychologically healthy people suffering from failures of emotional and physical wellbeing. In fact, I suspect that the shamanic function was another of the pressure-release valves helpful for maintaining social stability, simultaneously marginalizing and employing disruptive individuals. Without saying that the cognitive content of manic and schizophrenic states of awareness is reliable, I do see powerful resonances between mania and the encounter with bliss untamed, especially as interpreted against the background of shamanism. More than that, I think the truth of manic cognitions lies in their awareness of bliss. By the same token, the danger of bliss untamed is manifested in the psychically destabilizing quality of manic awareness. I have considerable respect for the value of manic awareness for shedding light on the profundity of the blissful state of awareness.

Many people are utterly incapable of falling prey to manic or schizophrenic psychosis, for want of brains peculiar in the requisite ways. No matter what kind of stress they experience, or how intense their encounters with bliss, most people don't experience manic states of awareness, with all of the ambiguous advantages of such states for grasping the quality of bliss untamed. Yet some of them can still cultivate awareness of bliss through meditation, and especially intellective types of contemplative practice. Such practices lie at the origins of ancient warnings about the psychologically destabilizing effects of some meditative states of awareness.

Nietzsche wasn't thinking of contemplative adepts when he pondered the utter failure of people to grasp the Madman's testimony to bliss untamed. The problem ordinary people have in encounters with bliss is the cognitive dissonance it provokes. Manifestations of bliss comport with no extensively socially embedded portrayal of ultimate reality. Yet the perceptive among the non-ill, non-adept ordinary will discern hints of bliss untamed in their own sacred scriptures and other cultural products. Consequently, they are left wondering about the emotional complexity, cognitive ineffability, and moral inassimilability of their encounters with bliss and what those features of their experience portend for the character of ultimate reality, as their ultimate concern. Most will not choose to conceive of their ultimate concern as emotionally, cognitively, and moral unscaled to their interests, no matter what their encounters with bliss and their sacred theophanies suggest. Fortunately for them, anthropomorphic cognitive-emotional machinery, long stabilized in the phylogenetic history of our species, lies ready and waiting to deliver them from the dark and stormy ocean surge into the relatively calmer waters of more personal portrayals of their ultimate concern. Psychological threat resolved, bliss tamed, all is well.

⮜⮞

What, then, are the advantages of bliss untamed? What virtues properly belong to beholding one's ultimate concern as emotionally complex, cognitively ineffable, and morally inassimilable? In a nutshell, the virtue is enlightenment. There can be authentic engagement with ultimate reality under misleading symbolic descriptions of its character. But enlightenment arises only where reality is taken for what it is.

The one seeking enlightenment strains to rise above the convenient and pleasant distortions of ultimate reality, as well as the suffering endemic to it, stretching every muscle to reach the next toehold, the next fingerhold, ascending an impossibly sheer rock face. At the top of the climb, nothing short of bliss untamed will satisfy, despite the fact that lower down such an insight was unthinkable. In the enlightened state, the bodhisattvas assure us, we experience the cessation of suffering through the elimination of attachment. This is not only the bliss of nirvāṇa; the encounter with bliss is the very condition for the loosening of the grasping of attachment in the first place. We have no interest in non-attachment at the foot of the sheer rock face. But that desire blossoms in us as we rise. And our yearning for bliss untamed blooms right along with it.

CONCLUSION

I have nothing more to say about the virtues of bliss untamed except this: enlightenment is not for everyone. Indeed, for some it is appalling. For others it is the only truth, the only comfort.

This sparkling vision of dazzling darkness and blinding light inspires me to testify to unruly ultimacy, to bliss untamed, and I'll play my part in keeping alive that memory in the larger story of human religion. But I won't turn my back on the institutional conditions for the very possibility of my own awareness of ultimacy, nor on the religious symbols systems that enable speech about the theological depths of reality, nor on the religious venues in which people encounter the aura-like presence of bliss eclipsed, nor on the spiritual pathways by which people migrate in my direction away from the anthropomorphically reassuring delusions of conventional reality and toward bliss untamed. Even when not welcome in the assemblies of the religious, I'll still speak up for them. And when welcome, I'll sink into my favorite variety of bliss: undimmed perception of ultimacy joined with the hearts of fellow spiritual travelers who know, like I do, that nothing less searing than ultimacy undimmed, nothing less disturbing than bliss untamed, and nothing less wondrous than abysmal suchness, will be worthy of our peculiar worship.

THE TREACHERY OF WORDS
(THIS IS NOT A CONCLUSION)

THIS BOOK'S JOURNEY THROUGH THE WILD LANDSCAPE OF RELIGIOUS LAN-
guage began with comparative metaphysics (part 1). I showed how the prodigious linguistic achievements of specialized discourse communities permit the
articulation and clarification of competing models of ultimate reality, and their
subsequent comparative evaluation. The aim of such comparative evaluation is
not knockdown dismissals of some ultimacy models in favor of others, but the
identification of respects in which one ultimacy model is more plausible than
competitors. Such modest ventures in speculative philosophy take their rise in
the ambit of the post-foundationalist and fallibilist epistemology of pragmatist
philosophy, particularly in the American philosophical tradition.

I then moved on to consider the linguistic genius of symbol systems (part 2).
Employing an approach more akin to Anglo-American analytical philosophy than
to American pragmatism, I unearthed system-level linguistic techniques that
perform essential functions in stabilizing religious symbol systems, the social
environments that depend on them, and the individuals that employ them to
engage their ultimate concerns.

Finally, I activated a distinctive style of phenomenological inquiry (part 3)
to see how language fares when pressed into service to describe the most challenging existential and ontological realities we engage. This is an intellectual
activity having most in common with Continental traditions of philosophical
theology. What we see when we are properly attentive to the phenomenological
features of our most profound experiences is an ultimate reality that is unscaled
to human emotion, cognition, and morality. Or so I claim at any rate.

The condition for the possibility of such a vision, however interpreted, is
a bodily one: an evolutionarily stabilized capacity for value detection. This is
an axiological awareness that probably neurologically extends ordinary sense
awareness, and it is the feature that probably most clearly distinguishes human
beings from ancestral hominid and primate species. While skepticism about the

215

cultural containers we employ to make sense of the deliverances of this axio-logical sensitivity is appropriate, I argued that there is good reason to trust the generalized phenomenological features (not the specific conceptual content) of its deliverances as cognitively reliable.

The upshot of all this is the manifestation in and through our most intense experiences of ultimate reality—as emotionally complex, cognitively ineffable, and morally inassimilable. This is a claim belonging to philosophical theology, and I have asserted it from the first chapter to the last, supporting it by means of a variety of insights about how language stretches to make sense of such experiences.

Without religious language, without its technical tricks and its specialized discourse communities, without its poetic indirection and its glorious aspira-tions, we'd be mute in the face of ultimate reality. Even if the ultimate reality I see through language and experience—my personal ultimate concern—flies in the face of the anthropomorphic and semi-anthropomorphic depictions of ultimate reality that capture the hearts and minds of so many, I can say nothing at all about it, and it remains unthinkable, without the linguistic exertions of vast religious traditions with their memorial encodings of insight. This fact morally obliges me to take religion seriously even when its doctrines are fantastic and its fanatics are dangerous. And the same fact makes religious language utterly fascinating.

∽≈∾

In 1983, Michel Foucault's *This Is Not a Pipe* was published in English, with illustrations and letters by renowned artist René Magritte. Foucault's book is a meditation on the perverse gap between language and that to which language refers, inspired by Magritte's famous 1929 surrealist painting entitled *Le Trahison des images* (*Ceci n'est pas une pipe*) or *The treachery of images* (*This is not a pipe*)." Magritte's painting, produced when he was thirty years of age, depicts a pipe accompanied by the words "Ceci n'est pas une pipe." Obviously it's a picture of a pipe, but you can't hold it or smoke it. So obviously it's not a pipe. The words "Ceci n'est pas une pipe" successfully refer to the image, while drawing our attention to the way linguistic reference never fully captures the logical objects of sentences— thus the treachery of images (the name of the painting) and the treachery of words (the name of these paragraphs, which are obviously a conclusion and obviously not a conclusion).

This book has been an examination of the peculiar treachery of words at play when the logical object is the ultimate concerns of human beings and the ultimate realities they seek to engage in action and comprehend in speech. The essays presented here collectively deploy all seven styles of religious philosophy—

the phenomenological, the comparative, the historical, the analytical, the the-oretical, the literary, and the evaluative. They also exhibit three major Western philosophical traditions: the American Pragmatist Tradition (part 1), the Anglo-American Analytic Tradition (part 2), and the Continental Tradition (part 3). All three traditions and all seven styles register the treachery of ultimacy talk.

We should see this with appropriate apophatic wholeheartedness. Doing so liberates us to play, and play hard, celebrating our species's linguistic genius and taking delight in mocking our linguistic pretensions. In the process we see our words anew, along with the furiously busy structures of language that stabilize the meanings of our words like hummingbirds hovering seemingly motionless while tiny hearts ticker and fine wings flutter. Complete failure of reference to ultimate matters would make reference impossible and ultimacy talk pointless. Complete success of reference to ultimate matters is utterly delusional. We live in the in-between, where words both empower and mislead, both refer and distort—and nowhere more than in our outrageous attempts to speak of ultimacy. Effing the ineffable is our inescapable fate. The treachery of such words, above all other words, is power—power to control and also power to liberate. So let us eff the ineffable, but with eyes wide open and a wry smile.

WORKS CITED

Alston, William P. 1991. *Perceiving God: The Epistemology of Religious Experience.* Ithaca, NY: Cornell University Press.

Andresen, Jensine, ed. 2001. *Religion in Mind: Cognitive Perspectives on Religious Belief, Ritual, and Experience.* Cambridge: Cambridge University Press.

Andresen, Jensine, and Robert K. C. Forman, eds. 2000. *Cognitive Models and Spiritual Maps.* Special issue of *Journal of Consciousness Studies* 7: 10–11.

Aquinas, Thomas. (1911) 1948. *The Summa Theologica of St. Thomas Aquinas.* Reprint of 1920 edition. Translated by Fathers of the English Dominican Province. Notre Dame, IN: Christian Classics.

———. 1955. *Summa Contra Gentiles.* Notre Dame, IN: University of Notre Dame Press.

Aristotle. 1966. *Metaphysics.* Bloomington: Indiana University Press.

Atran, Scott. 1998. "Folk Biology and the Anthropology of Science: Cognitive Universals and Cultural Particulars." *The Behavioral and Brain Sciences* 21 (4): 547–69.

———. 2002. *In Gods We Trust: The Evolutionary Landscape of Religion.* Oxford: Oxford University Press.

———. 2004. "Religion's Evolutionary Landscape: Counterintuition, Commitment, Compassion, Communion." *The Behavioral and Brain Sciences* 27 (6): 713–30.

Augustine. 1991. *Saint Augustine: Confessions.* Translated with an introduction by Henry Chadwick. Oxford World Classics. Oxford: Oxford University Press.

Austin, John L. 1962. *How to Do Things with Words.* Oxford: Oxford University Press.

Bagger, Matthew C. 1999. *Religious Experience, Justification, and History.* Cambridge: Cambridge University Press.

Barkow, Jerome, Leda Cosmides, and John Tooby, eds. 1992. *The Adapted Mind: Evolutionary Psychology and the Generation of Culture.* New York: Oxford University Press.

Barrett, Justin L. 2011. *Cognitive Science, Religion, and Theology: From Human Minds to Divine Minds.* West Conshohocken, PA: Templeton Press.

———. 2012. *Born Believers: The Science of Children's Religious Belief*. New York: Free Press.

Barnett, Justin L., and M. A. Nyhof. 2001. "Spreading Non-natural Concepts: The Role of Intuitive Conceptual Structures in Memory and Transmission of Cultural Materials." *Journal of Cognition and Culture* 1: 69–100.

Barth, Karl. 1951–63. *Church Dogmatics*. Edited by Thomas F. Torrance and Geoffrey W. Bromiley. Edinburgh: T. and T. Clark.

———. 1996. *The Humanity of God*. Philadelphia, PA: Westminster John Knox Press.

Bear, David M. 1979. "Temporal Lobe Epilepsy—A Syndrome of Sensory-limbic Hyperconnection." *Cortex* 15: 357–84.

Bear, David M., Kenneth Levin, Dietrich Blumer, Diedre Chetham, and John Ryder. 1982. "Interictal Behaviour in Hospitalised Temporal Lobe Epileptics: Relationship to Idiopathic Psychiatric Syndromes." *Journal of Neurology, Neurosurgery, and Psychiatry* 45: 481–88.

Berger, Peter L. 1967. *The Sacred Canopy: Elements of a Sociological Theory of Religion*. Garden City, NY: Doubleday.

Boyer, Pascal. 2001. *Religion Explained: The Evolutionary Origins of Religious Thought*. New York: Basic Books.

Boyer, Pascal, and C. Ramble. 2001. "Cognitive Templates for Religious Concepts." *Cognitive Science* 25: 535–64.

Buddharakkhita, Thera. 1990. *The Dhammpada: The Buddha's Path of Wisdom*. Translated by Buddharakkhita Thera with an introduction by Bhikkhu Bodhi. Kandy, Sri Lanka: Buddhist Publication Society.

Bulbulia, Joseph. 2006. "Nature's Medicine: Religiosity as an Adaptation for Health and Cooperation." In *Where God and Science Meet*. Vol. 1, edited by McNamara, 87–121.

Cardeña, Etzel, Steven Jay Lynn, and Stanley Krippner, eds. 2000. *Varieties of Anomalous Experience: Examining the Scientific Evidence*. Washington, DC: American Psychological Association.

Cooper, John, Ronald Nettler, and Mohamad Mahmoud. 1998. *Islam and Modernity: Muslim Intellectuals Respond*. New York: I. B. Tauris. Distributed by St. Martin's Press.

Cowell, E. B., trans. 1884. "Buddha-carita of Ašvaghosha." In *Buddhist Mahayana Texts*. Vol. 49 of *Sacred Books of the East*, edited by Max Müller. New Delhi: Atlantic Publishers. Reprint edition, 1990.

d'Aquili, Eugene, and Andrew B. Newberg. 1999. *The Mystical Mind: Probing the Biology of Religious Experience*. Minneapolis, MN: Fortress Press.

Darwin, Charles. 1859. *On The Origin of Species*. London: John Murray.

Dawkins, Richard. 1996. *Climbing Mount Improbable*. New York: W. W. Norton.

———. 1998. *Unweaving the Rainbow*. Boston: Houghton Mifflin.

———. 2006. *The God Delusion*. London: Houghton Mifflin.

Dennett, Daniel C. 2006. *Breaking the Spell: Religion as a Natural Phenomenon*. New York: Viking.

Dorrien, Gary. 2001, 2003, 2006. *The Making of American Liberal Theology*. 3 vols. Louisville, KY: Westminster John Knox Press.

Durkheim, Emile. 1954. *The Elementary Forms of the Religious Life*. Glencoe, IL: Free Press.

Eckhart, Meister. 1986. *Meister Eckhart: Teacher and Preacher*. Edited by Bernard McGinn. The Classics of Western Spirituality. New York: Paulist Press.

Fenton, G. W. 1981. "Psychiatric Disorders of Epilepsy: Classification and Phenomenology." In *Epilepsy and Psychiatry*, edited by E. Reynolds and M. Trimble, 12–26. New York: Churchill Livingstone.

Feuerbach, Ludwig. 1854. *The Essence of Christianity*. London: John Chapman.

———. 1873. *The Essence of Religion: God the Image of Man; Man's Dependence on Nature the Last and Only Source of Religion*. New York: A. K. Butts.

Forman, Robert K. C., ed. 1990. *The Problem of Pure Consciousness: Mysticism and Philosophy*. New York: Oxford University Press.

———. 1999. *Mysticism, Mind, Consciousness*. Albany: State University of New York Press.

Foucault, Michel. 1983. *This Is Not a Pipe*. Edited and translated from *Ceci n'est pas une pipe* by James Harkness. Berkeley: University of California Press.

Frazer, James George. 1900. *The Golden Bough: A Study in Magic and Religion*. 2nd ed. London: Macmillan.

Freud, Sigmund. 1928. *The Future of an Illusion*. New York: Institute of Psycho-Analysis.

———. 1930. *Civilization and Its Discontents*. New York: J. Cape and H. Smith.

———. 1939. *Moses and Monotheism*. New York: Alfred A. Knopf.

Gilovich, Thomas. 1991. *How We Know What Isn't So: The Fallibility of Human Reason in Everyday Life*. New York: Free Press.

Girard, Rene. 1977. *Violence and the Sacred*. Baltimore: Johns Hopkins University Press.

Graham, Jesse, Jonathan Haidt, and Brian Nosek. 2009. "Liberals and Conservatives Use Different Sets of Moral Foundations." *Journal of Personality and Social Psychology* 96: 1029–46.

Haidt, Jonathan. 2001. "The Emotional Dog and its Rational Tail: A Social Intuitionist Approach to Moral Judgment." *Psychological Review* 108: 814–34.

————. 2007. "The New Synthesis in Moral Psychology." *Science* 316: 998–1002.

Hardy, Alistair C. 1979. *The Spiritual Nature of Man: A Study of Contemporary Religious Experience.* New York: Oxford University Press.

Hart, Ray L. 1968. *Unfinished Man and the Imagination: Toward an Ontology and a Rhetoric of Revelation.* Freiberg: Herder and Herder.

————. 2016. *God Being Nothing.* Chicago: University of Chicago Press.

Hartshorne, Charles. 1948. *The Divine Relativity: A Social Conception of God.* New Haven, CT: Yale University Press.

Haselton, Martie G., and D. Nettle. 2006. "The Paranoid Optimist: An Evolutionary Model of Cognitive Biases." *Personality and Social Psychology Review* 10 (1): 47–66.

Hegel, Georg Wilhelm Friedrich. 1984. *Lectures on the Philosophy of Religion.* Berkeley: University of California Press.

Hick, John. 2004. *An Interpretation of Religion: Human Responses to the Transcendent.* 2nd ed. Basingstoke: Palgrave Macmillan.

Huntington, Samuel P. 1996. *The Clash of Civilizations and the Remaking of World Order.* New York: Simon and Schuster.

James, William. 1902. *The Varieties of Religious Experience: A Study in Human Nature.* New York: Longmans Green.

Katz, Steven T., ed. 1978. *Mysticism and Philosophical Analysis.* New York: Oxford University Press.

————, ed. 1984. *Mysticism and Religious Traditions.* New York: Oxford University Press.

————, ed. 1992. *Mysticism and Language.* New York: Oxford University Press.

————, ed. 2000. *Mysticism and Sacred Scripture.* New York: Oxford University Press.

Kaufman, Gordon D. 1993. *In Face of Mystery: A Constructive Theology.* Cambridge, MA: Harvard University Press.

Kirkpatrick, Lee A. 2006. "Religion Is Not an Adaptation." In *Where God and Science Meet.* Vol. 1, edited by Patrick McNamara, 159–79.

Knepper, Timothy D. 2005. "How to Say What Can't Be Said: Techniques and Rules of Ineffability in the Dionysian Corpus." Ph.D. diss., Boston: Boston University.

Kurzman, Charles, ed. 1998. *Liberal Islam: A Source Book.* New York: Oxford University Press.

Lévi-Strauss, Claude. 1963. *Totemism.* Translated from the French by Rodney Needham. Boston: Beacon Press.

Livingston, James C. 1997, 2000. *Modern Christian Thought.* 2 vols. Upper Saddle River, NJ: Prentice Hall.

Marx, Karl. 2002. *Marx on Religion*. Edited by John Raines. Philadelphia, PA: Temple University Press.

McClenon, James. 2002. *Wondrous Healing: Shamanism, Human Evolution, and the Origin of Religion*. De Kalb: Northern Illinois University Press.

McNamara, Patrick, ed. 2006. *Where God and Science Meet: How Brain and Evolutionary Studies Alter Our Understanding of Religion*. Vol. 1, *Evolution, Genes, and the Religious Brain*. Vol. 2, *The Neurology of Religious Experience*. Vol. 3, *The Psychology of Religious Experience*. Westport, CT: Praeger.

Meyer, Michal A. 1988. *Response to Modernity: A History of the Reform Movement in Judaism*. New York: Oxford University Press.

Miller, Barbara Stoler, ed. and trans. 1986. *The Bhagavad-Gita: Krishna's Counsel in Time of War*. New York: Bantam Books.

Mujiskovic, Ben Lazare. 1974. *The Achilles of Rationalist Arguments*. Leiden, The Netherlands: Martinus Nijhoff Publishers.

———. 1979. *Loneliness in Philosophy, Psychology and Literature*. Assen, The Netherlands: Van Gorcum.

Nagarjuna. 1955. *The Fundamental Wisdom of the Middle Way: Nagarjuna's Mulamadhyamakakarika*. Translated by Jay Garfield. New York: Oxford University Press.

Neville, Robert Cummings. 1968. *God the Creator. On the Transcendence and Presence of God*. Chicago: University of Chicago Press.

———. 1991. *Behind the Masks of God: An Essay Toward Comparative Theology*. Albany: State University of New York Press.

———. 1996. *The Truth of Broken Symbols*. Albany: State University of New York Press.

———, ed. 2000a. *The Human Condition: A Volume in the Comparative Religious Ideas Project*. Albany: State University of New York Press.

———, ed. 2000b. *Ultimate Realities: A Volume in the Comparative Religious Ideas Project*. Albany: State University of New York Press.

———, ed. 2000c. *Religious Truth: A Volume in the Comparative Religious Ideas Project*. Albany: State University of New York Press.

———. 2001. *Symbols of Jesus: A Christology of Symbolic Engagement*. Cambridge, UK: Cambridge University Press.

———. 2013–2015. *Philosophical Theology*. Vol. 1, *Ultimates*. Vol. 2, *Existence*. Vol. 3, *Religion*. Albany: State University of New York Press.

Newberg, Andrew, Eugene d'Aquili, and Vince Rause. 2001. *Why God Won't Go Away: Brain Science and the Biology of Belief*. New York: Ballantine Books.

Nicosia, Frank. 1966. *Consumer Decision Processes*. Englewood Cliffs, NJ: Prentice Hall.

Nietzsche, Friedrich. 1933. *The Genealogy of Morals: A Polemic*. London: Allen and Unwin.

———. 1974. *The Gay Science: With a Prelude in Rhymes and an Appendix of Songs*. Translated with commentary by Walter Kaufmann. New York: Vintage Books.

Nisbett, R. E., K. Peng, I. Choi, and Ara Norenzayan. 2001. "Culture and Systems of Thought: Holistic versus Analytic Cognition." *Psychological Review* 108 (2): 291–310.

Nishida, Kitaro. 1960. *A Study of Good*. Tokyo: Print Bureau of the Japanese Government.

Nishitani, Keiji. 1982. *Religion and Nothingness*. Berkeley: University of California Press.

Otto, Rudolf. 1917. *The Idea of the Holy: An Inquiry into the Non-Rational Factor in the Idea of the Divine and its Relation to the Rational*. 3rd English ed., 1925. Translated by John W. Harvey from the 9th German edition. London: Oxford University Press.

Paley, William, 1802. *Natural Theology; or, Evidences of the Existence and Attributes of the Deity, Collected from the Appearances of Nature*. London: R. Faulder.

Pelikan, Jaroslav. 1996. *Mary through the Centuries: Her Place in the History of Culture*. New Haven, CT: Yale University Press.

———. 1999. *Jesus through the Centuries: His Place in the History of Culture*. New Haven, CT: Yale University Press.

Pickthall, Marmaduke, trans. 1930. *The Meaning of the Glorious Koran*. New York: Dorset Press.

Plantinga, Alvin. 2000. *Warranted Christian Belief*. Oxford: Oxford University Press.

———. 2007. "The Dawkins Confusion: Naturalism ad absurdum." *Books and Culture: A Christian Review* 13 (2).

Plotinus. 2004. *Plotinus: The Enneads*. LP Classic Reprint Series. Edited by Stephen MacKenna. Larson Publications.

Plous, Scott. 1993. *The Psychology of Judgment and Decision Making*. New York: McGraw-Hill.

Pseudo-Dionysius. 1987. *Pseudo-Dionysius: The Complete Works*. Translated by Colm Luibheid. The Classics of Western Spirituality. New York: Paulist Press.

Rachlinksi, Jeffrey J. 2006. "Cogntive Errors, Individual Differences, and Paternalism." Symposium on "Homo Economicus, Homo Myopicus, and the Law and Economics of Consumer Choice." *The University of Chicago Law Review* 73 (1): 207–29.

Radhakrishnan, Sarvepalli, ed. and trans. 1948. *The Bhagavadgita*. New York: Harper.

Radhakrishnan, Sarvepalli, and Charles A. Moore, eds. 1957. *A Sourcebook in Indian Philosophy*. Princeton, NJ: Princeton University Press.

Rahner, Karl. 1978. *Foundations of Christian Faith: An Introduction to the Idea of Christianity*. New York: Seabury Press.

Ramachandran, Vilayanur S., and Sandra Blakeslee. 1998. *Phantoms in the Brain: Probing the Mysteries of the Human Mind*. New York: William Morrow.

Ramsey, William. 2002. "Naturalism Defended." In *Naturalism Defeated? Essays on Plantinga's Evolutionary Argument Against Naturalism*, edited by James Beilby, 15–29. Ithaca: Cornell University Press.

Randi, James. 1982. *Flim-Flam: Psychics, ESP, Unicorns, and other Delusions*. Amherst, NY: Prometheus Books.

Reardon, Bernard M. G. 1970. *Roman Catholic Modernism*. Stanford, CA: Stanford University Press.

Roberts, Alexander, and James Donaldson, eds. 1951. *The Ante-Nicene Fathers*. Vol. 3, "Latin Christianity: Its Founder, Tertullian." Edinburgh: T. and T. Clark.

Schilbrack, Kevin. 2014. *Philosophy and the Study of Religions: A Manifesto*. Malden, MA: Oxford University Press.

Schleiermacher, Friedrich D. E. 1928. *The Christian Faith*. English translation of the 2nd German edition of 1830–31 by H. R. Mackintosh and J. S. Stewart. 1st German edition published in 1820–21. Edinburgh: T. and T. Clark.

Searle, John. 1969. *Speech Acts: An Essay in the Philosophy of Language*. Cambridge, UK: Cambridge University Press.

Sells, Michael A. 1994. *Mystical Languages of Unsaying*. Chicago: University of Chicago Press.

Smith, Huston. (1976) 1992. *Forgotten Truth: The Common Vision of the World's Religions*. 2nd ed. San Francisco: HarperSanFrancisco.

———. 2000. *Why Religion Matters: The Fate of the Human Spirit in an Age of Disbelief*. San Francisco: HarperOne.

Speiser, E. A., trans. 1969. "The Epic of Gilgamesh." In *Ancient Near Eastern Texts*. 3rd ed. with supplement, edited by James B. Pritchard, 72–99. Princeton, NJ: Princeton University Press.

Strenski, Ivan. 2006. "The Only Kind of Comparison Worth Doing: History, Epistemology, and the 'Strong Program' of Comparative Study." In *Comparing Religions: Possibilities and Perils?* edited by Thomas Athanasius Indinopulos, Brian C. Wilson, and James Constantine Hanges, 271–92. Numen History of Religion Series. Leiden: Brill Academic Publishers.

Swinburne, Richard. 1979. *The Existence of God*. New York: Oxford University Press.

Tambiah, Stanley Jeyaraja. 1990. *Magic, Science, Religion, and the Scope of Rationality*. Cambridge: Cambridge University Press.

Tanabe, Hajime. 1986. *Philosophy of Metamoetics*. Berkeley: University of California Press.

Teresa of Avila. 1979. *The Interior Castle*. The Classics of Western Spirituality. Mahwah, NJ: Paulist Press.

Tillich, Paul. 1951. *Systematic Theology*. Vol. I. Chicago: University of Chicago Press.

———. 1963. *Systematic Theology*. Vol. 2. Chicago: University of Chicago Press.

Tobena, A., I. Marks, and R. Dar. 1999. "Advantages of Adaptive Bias and Prejudice: An Exploration of their Neurocognitive Templates." *Neuroscience and Biobehavioral Reviews* 23 (7): 1047–58.

Tyler, Edward Burnett. 1873–74. *Primitive Cultures: Researches into the Development of Mythology, Philosophy, Religion, Art, and Custom*. 2 vols. London: Murray.

Vyse, Stuart A. 1997. *Believing in Magic: The Psychology of Superstition*. New York: Oxford University Press.

Weber, Max. 1930. *The Protestant Ethic and the Spirit of Capitalism*. London: Allen and Unwin.

Welch, Claude. 1972, 1985. *Protestant Thought in the Nineteenth Century*. 2 vols. New Haven, CT: Yale University Press.

Whitehead, Alfred North. 1978. *Process and Reality: An Essay in Cosmology*, corrected edition. Edited by David Ray Griffin and Donald W. Sherburne. New York: Free Press.

Wierzbicka, Anna. 1992. *Semantics, Culture, and Cognition: Universal Human Concepts in Culture-Specific Configurations*. New York: Oxford University Press.

Wildman, Wesley J. 2006a. "Comparative Natural Theology." *American Journal of Theology and Philosophy* 27 (2 and 3): 173–90.

———. 2006b. "Ground-of-Being Theologies." In *The Oxford Handbook of Religion and Science*, edited by Philip Clayton. Oxford: Oxford University Press.

———. 2006c. "Comparing Religious Ideas: There's Method in the Mob's Madness." In *Comparing Religions: Possibilities and Perils?* edited by Thomas Athanasius Indinopulos, Brian C. Wilson, and James Constantine Hanges. Numen History of Religion Series. Leiden, The Netherlands: Brill Academic Publishers.

———. 2007. "From Law and Chance in Nature to Ultimate Reality." In *Creation, Law, and Probability*, edited by Fraser Watts. Aldershot, UK: Ashgate Publishing.

———. 2009. *Science and Religious Anthropology: A Religious Naturalist Interpretation of the Human Condition*. Farnham, UK: Ashgate Publishers.

———. 2010. *Religious Philosophy as Multidisciplinary Comparative Inquiry: Envisioning a Future for the Philosophy of Religion*. Albany: State University of New York Press.

———. 2011. *Religious and Spiritual Experiences*. Cambridge, UK: Cambridge University Press.

———. 2017. *In Our Own Image: Anthropomorphism, Apophaticism, and Ultimacy*. Oxford, UK: Oxford University Press.

Wildman, Wesley J., and Leslie A. Brothers. 1999. "A Neuropsychological-Semiotic Model of Religious Experiences." In *Neuroscience and the Person: Scientific Perspectives on Divine Action*, edited by Robert J. Russell, Nancey Murphy, Theo C. Meyering, and Michael A. Arbib, 347–416. Vatican City State, Vatican Observatory: Center for Theology and the Natural Sciences.

Wildman, Wesley J., and Stephen Chapin Garner. 2009. *Lost in the Middle? Claiming an Inclusive Faith for Christians Who Are Both Liberal and Evangelical*. Herndon, VA: Alban Institute.

Wildman, Wesley J., and Patrick McNamara. 2010. "Evaluating Reliance on Narratives in the Psychological Study of Religious Experiences." *International Journal for the Psychology of Religion* 20 (4): 223–54.

INDEX

Adam, 8, 84–87
Agential-being theism, 30–31, 47–48, 54
  critique of, 37–38, 42–44, 59–61
  definition, 31–35
  responses to suffering, 34–35,
    40–42, 50–52, 56–58, 61
  see also anthropomorphism;
    argument from neglect; bal-
    ancing; conservative theology;
    creation, *emanatio ex deo*;
    Great Models; liberal the-
    ology; kenosis; Neoplatonism;
    ontology; philosophical the-
    ology; religious symbol systems,
    personal vs. impersonal; reve-
    lation; suffering; symbols, reli-
    gious; theism, personal; ultimate
    reality, models of
Alston, William, 184–86
  see also Bagger, Matthew; intense
    experiences; philosophical
    theology
anthropomorphism, xiv, 3, 7–8, 13, 15,
    21–25, 27, 32–33, 37–39, 42–43,
    61, 127, 129, 212–13
  in agential-being theism, 33–34
  see also agential-being theism; bal-
    ancing, strategies; cognitive
    defaults; cognitive psychology;
    evolutionary psychology; liberal
    theology; phenomenology; reli-
    gious symbol systems, personal
    vs. impersonal; sociopolitical

organization, low–energy; suf-
    fering, and supernatural agents;
    symbols, religious; theism,
    personal
apophaticism, xiv, 25–27, 39, 48,
    137–38, 170–71, 206–7
  techniques of, 69–70
  via positive, 26, 103–6, 171
  via negative, 26, 103–4, 158, 171,
    207
  see also ground-of-being theism;
    bliss; intense experiences;
    mysticism; Pseudo-Dionysus;
    religious and spiritual experi-
    ences; religious symbol systems;
    silence, pressure to
Aquinas, Thomas, 16, 103, 193, 207, 209
Aristotle, 20, 143
Atran, Scott, 10, 12, 13, 133, 163
  see also cognitive defaults; evolu-
    tionary psychology
Augustine, 9, 20, 54–55, 71, 72, 79, 143

Bagger, Matthew, 184–186
  see also Alston, William; intense
    experiences; philosophical
    theology
balancing, 32, 69–70, 97–98, 170
  strategies, 98–99, 110–18
  see also Bhagavad Gita, the; Pseudo-
    Dionysus; religious symbol
    systems; Smith, Huston; Tillich,
    Paul; ultimacy

Printed in Great Britain
by Amazon

83194159R00147